D0942949

BOOK LOVERS'
LONDON

Dedicated to Joy Wright
1931-2007

Book Lovers' London

Written by Andrew Kershman
Photography by Metro
Edited by Abigail Willis
Book design by Lesley Gilmour & Susi Koch

All rights reserved. No part of this publication may be reproduced, stored in a retrieval system or transmitted in any form or by any means electronic, mechanical, photocopying, recording or otherwise without the prior consent of the publishers and copyright owners. Every effort has been made to ensure the accuracy of this book; however, due to the nature of the subject the publishers cannot accept responsibility for any errors which occur, or their consequences.

Published in 2015 by
Metro Publications Ltd, PO Box 6336, London, N1 6PY

Metro® is a registered trade mark of Associated Newspapers Limited. The METRO mark is under licence from Associated Newspapers Limited.

Printed and bound in China

British Library Cataloguing in Publication Data. A catalogue record for this book is available from the British Library.

ISBN 978-1-902910-49-9

BOOK LOVERS'
LONDON

Contents

Introduction

If you are a book lover who values bookshops and who fears for their future in the digital age you will be reassured to know that London is still home to some incredible bookshops, run by dedicated booksellers who will provide a place where you can browse in comfort, and who offer advice, make book buying a pleasure and generally add to the sum of human happiness.

In the course of researching this new edition I have met some fascinating booksellers and enjoyed browsing in over 300 bookshops across the capital. Among the second-hand and antiquarian bookshops, my visit to Henry Pordes on Charing Cross Road stands out. It was there I witnessed an American tourist finally track down a Smith Elder edition of 'Jane Eyre' for her father and joyfully clasp the book to her heart while she recounted her struggles to find her prize. Further out in distant Wandsworth, I spent a wonderful afternoon with Doug Jeffers, a bookseller who has been in the book trade for over thirty years and who briefly retired before setting up Turn the Page Bookshop because he missed the business and its customers so much.

Along the way there have been some sad closures but it's great to be able to report that some bookshops are not only surviving but thriving. It has been a few years since the Borders chain of bookshops closed but there are still some vast book emporiums in the capital, such as the new Foyles flagship shop on Charing Cross Road. The store is the largest new bookshop to be built in London in living memory and it's a striking addition to the capital's book scene, with its grand entrance leading to a huge central atrium from where visitors can explore four floors and over 200 thousand titles. Waterstones on Piccadilly remains one of Europe's largest bookstores and just a few doors down the grand edifice of Hatchards has been selling books since 1797 and is still going from strength to strength, having just opened a new branch in St Pancras International station.

London's book scene is not just about the mammoth bookshops of central London, it is also home to independent stores that provide great service and usually have some unique aspect that makes them stand out from the crowd. Relative newcomer Book & Kitchen in Notting Hill, has a great café in the basement and stages all kinds of book events to engage the book (and cake) loving public. Lutyens & Rubinstein offer a special 'Year in Books' gift scheme, sending a chosen recipient a different book each month based upon their past reading, which has proved hugely popular; the shop also benefits from being part of the eponymous literary agency that shares the premises. Moving further east, Brick Lane Bookshop has a history that stretches back to their days as radical traders in the 70s, but now flourishes as a going concern on one of London's busiest market streets with hordes of passing trade and a loyal local following. Against a background of rising rents and unfair internet competition these independent bookshops are making a stand and they deserve your support.

There is a lot more to London's literary scene than just its bookshops and this new edition of Book Lovers' London contains a section devoted to alternative book outlets such as markets, charity shops, book fairs and book dealers. Bookbinders and letterpress printers are new to this edition and the libraries section has been greatly increased in scope and detail to reflect the diversity of private and public libraries now found in the capital. There are also chapters covering places of literary interest, book festivals and literary walking tours, for those who want to experience London's literary heritage rather than just read about it.

Whatever aspect of London's book world you explore with the aid of this book, I hope you enjoy the experience and look forward to your comments and suggestions for future editions.

Andrew Kershman
andrew@metropublications.com

bookshop
entrance

THE LONDON BOOKBARGE

BOOKS NEEDED

word
on the
water

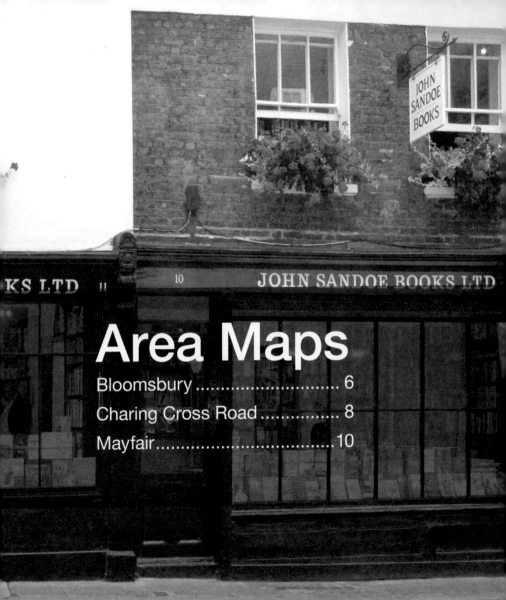

Area Maps

① Bloomsbury Map

Bloomsbury

Charing Cross Road Map

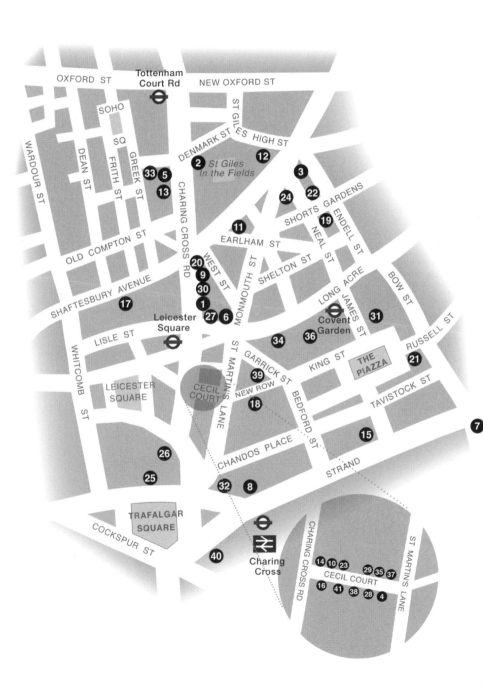

③ Mayfair Map

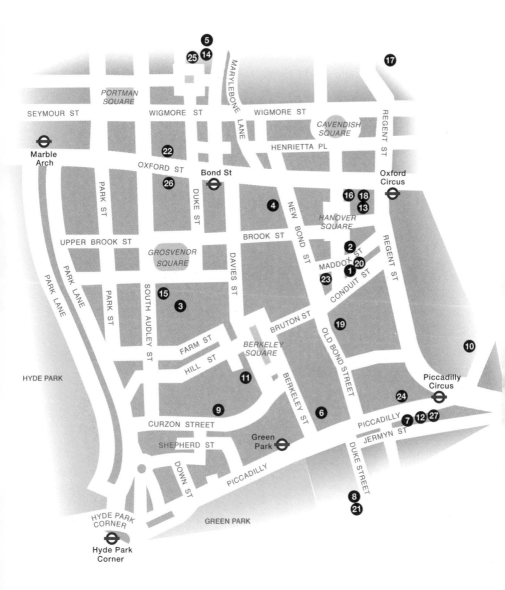

Bookshops
New Books

A

AA Bookshop

⌗ Architectural Association,
32 Bedford Square, WC1B 3ES
☎ 020 7887 4041
✎ www.aabookshop.net
🚇 Goodge Street LU, Holborn LU
🕒 Mon-Fri 10am-6.30pm, Sat 10am-6.30pm

A specialist bookseller and publisher situated in a grand ground floor room overlooking Bedford Square. The shop has a fabulous choice of books, magazines and journals on architecture, design, landscape and urban development and (for those with interests beyond architecture) an impressive selection of philosophy and critical theory books. The stock includes AA publications but most of the titles come from other publishers and from small presses. There is also a selection of antiquarian and out-of-print material and DVDs on architecture-related subjects. The helpful staff produce an online newsletter with regular updates of recently published architecture titles and the shop hosts regular book launches and a book club.

Agape Arabic Christian Centre

⌗ 11 Porchester Road, W2 5DP
☎ 020 7221 4355
✎ www.agapearabic.co.uk
🚇 Bayswater LU, Royal Oak LU
🕒 Mon-Sat 10am-8pm

This store specialises in Christian books in Arabic and English plus DVDs and CDs. The bookshop incorporates a coffee shop for thirsty browsers and the centre hosts numerous events, including English and Arabic language classes.

Aisenthal Judaica

⌗ 11 Ashbourne Parade,
Finchley Road, NW11 0AD
☎ 020 8455 0501
✎ www.aisenthaljudaica.com
🚇 Golders Green LU
🕒 Mon-Thurs 9am-6pm, Fri 9am-
(varies – ring to check), Sun 9.30am-4pm

A Jewish religious goods store with books in Hebrew and English on Jewish scripture, philosophy and life, plus a selection of Jewish fiction.

FOR **SHEET MUSIC** & **MUSIC BOOKS**
IT HAS TO BE **musicroom**

The capital's largest retailer of Sheet Music & Music Books

Argents (Musicroom)
19 Denmark St
London
WC2H 8NA
E - argents@musicroom.com
T - 020 7379 3384

Musicroom
11 Denmark St
London
WC2H 8TD
E - london@musicroom.com
T - 020 7632 3950

Ian Allan

🏠 *45-46 Lower Marsh, SE1 7RG*
☎ *020 7401 2100*
✎ *www.ianallanpublishing.com*
🚌 *Waterloo LU/Rail*
🕐 *Mon-Fri 9am-5.30pm, Sat 9am-5pm*

Located just behind Waterloo Station, this is a specialist shop for books on transport worldwide. As well as its own range of transport titles, Ian Allan also stocks a huge selection of books from other specialist and general publishers with comprehensive sections on road, rail, air and sea transport, as well as military history, transport, equipment and uniforms. In addition, the shop sells magazines, DVDs and models and offers an efficient mail order service.

All Flutes Plus

🏠 *60-61 Warren Street,*
  W1T 5NZ
☎ *020 7388 8438*
✎ *www.allflutesplus.com*
🚌 *Warren St LU, Great Portland St LU*
🕐 *Mon-Fri 10am-6pm, Sat 10am-4.30pm*

A shop devoted to flutes with an impressive selection of sheet music, tutorials and reference books about the instrument. There's also a good range of accessories such as music stands, carrying cases, metronomes and gift items as well as new and used flutes.

Al Saqi Books

🏠 *26 Westbourne Grove, W2 5RH*
☎ *020 7229 8543*
✎ *www.alsaqibookshop.com*
🚌 *Bayswater LU*
🕐 *Mon-Sat 10am-6pm*

Al Saqi Books is a publisher and bookseller offering Arabic and English books on all aspects of the Middle East and Central Asia – they are the UK's largest Middle Eastern specialist bookseller. Children's books are well represented, as are Arabic language-learning materials. Readers can join a mailing list for regular updates on new books. The store also carries a small selection of rare and antiquarian titles.

Musicroom/Argents Printed Music

🏠 *19 Denmark Street, WC2H 8NA*
☎ *020 7379 3384*
✎ *www.musicroom.com*
🚌 *Tottenham Court Road LU*
🕐 *Mon-Fri 9am-6pm, Sat 10am-6pm,*
  Sun 11am-5pm

Located on 'Tin Pan Alley', this specialist shop for musicians is packed with a huge range of printed music of all types: classical, popular, jazz, blues and folk, for all levels of ability. There are books and DVDs about music and a noticeboard full of music related news and events.

Artwords

☐ 20-22 Broadway Market, E8 4QJ
☎ 020 7923 7507
✎ www.artwords.co.uk
🚌 London Fields Rail
🕐 Mon-Fri 10.30am-8pm,
   Sat-Sun 10am-6pm

Artwords has been selling art books in London for over 10 years and despite the problems facing the book trade generally, the business is going from strength to strength. The company now has two shops in the east end of London having moved into this corner location on Broadway Market in 2009. The owner, Ben Hillwood-Harris, spent some time and effort getting the shop design right and commissioned bespoke shelving to display the range of books covering art, photography, fashion, graphic design, architecture, food culture and to a lesser extent, philosophy and art history.

One of the reasons for the new shop's success is its location on one of east London's busiest and most transformed shopping streets, whose popular Saturday market has taken off in the last ten years. Artwords store arrived just as this street began to boom, as Ben puts it:

"Hackney is the only area in the country in which more bookshops have opened than closed. On Saturdays there is a bookseller trading from the market and three bookshops including our store - it's like Charing Cross Road East."

Another big factor in the success of Artwords has been the growing interest in modern art and design in recent years with institutions like Tate and the Saatchi Gallery leading the way. Ben explains that the real skill in this market is to anticipate trends and constantly source cutting-edge books to keep things fresh:

"We're hoping to show our customers new things and to surprise them, we're showing them books and magazines that have just come out... So they visit us to get one book and find other titles they hadn't expected. Local artists and designers often come here just to get inspiration."

Artwords is selective in its stock and uses large table top displays to attract customers to interesting or unusual titles, many of which are not available in high street stores. The Hoxton Mini Press can't be found on the shelves of your local WH Smith, but here their wares are handsomely displayed and selling well.

Artwords is also an important outlet for art and culture magazines that are beautifully produced in relatively small quantities. A large area of shelving is given over to these publications whose names, such as Kinfolk and Like the Wind, will not be familiar to many, but which are a strong draw for the art community of east London, despite the often hefty price tag.

Ben and his team of eight booksellers are chuffed with the way things are going, but don't intend to rest on their laurels with plans to expand the number of book signings and events and develop further their online presence. If you want to enjoy the complete Broadway experience, this shop is best visited on a Saturday when the market is in full swing. Broadway Bookshop (see page 40) and Donlon Books (see page 50) are just a few doors away.

Branch at:
☐ 69 Rivington Street, EC2A 3AY
☎ 020 7729 2000
✎ www.artwords.co.uk
🚌 Liverpool Street or Old Street LU/Rail
🕐 Mon-Fri 10.30am-7pm,
   Sat 11am-7pm, Sun 12noon-6pm

"Hackney is the only area in the country in which more bookshops have opened than closed."

Artwords, Broadway Market

Astrology Shop

- ▣ 78 Neal Street, WC2H 9PA
- ☏ 020 7813 3051
- ✑ www.londonastrology.com
- 🚇 Covent Garden LU
- 🕓 Mon-Sat 11am-7pm, Sun 12noon-6pm

A specialist shop dealing with all aspects of astrology. There's a wide selection of books, periodicals and magazines covering many astrological traditions including Indian and Chinese. Subjects covered include medical astrology, psychology, dreams, numerology, palmistry and Tarot and they also offer a horoscope and Tarot reading service.

Atlantis Bookshop

- ▣ 49A Museum Street
  WC1A 1LY
- ☏ 020 7405 2120
- ✑ www.theatlantisbookshop.com
- 🚇 Holborn LU, Tottenham Court Road LU
- 🕓 Mon-Sat 10.30am-6pm

Situated in the heart of literary Bloomsbury, this shop carries an extensive collection of new and second-hand titles on astrology, witchcraft, magic and myth, healing and associated subjects as well as Tarot cards, candles and even cauldrons. Established in 1922, Atlantis prides itself on being the oldest independent occult bookshop in London. Browsing here is fascinating, with plenty to interest readers new to the field. Past customers include Aleister Crowley, Austin Osman Spare and the founder of modern witchcraft, Gerald Gardner. The Atlantis Bookshop regularly hosts book launches, talks and workshops.

B

Barbican Chimes Music

- ▣ Cromwell Tower, Silk Street
  Barbican, EC2Y 8DD
- ☏ 020 7588 9242
- ✑ www.chimesmusic.com
- 🚇 Barbican LU
- 🕓 Mon-Fri 9am-5.30pm, Sat 9am-4pm

This is the sister shop to Kensington Chimes (see p.70) and is situated close to The Guildhall School of Music and Drama and the Barbican arts complex. The shop stocks sheet music, scores and courses for all instruments and levels as well as books about every aspect of music including its history, personalities and music theory. Music magazines, classical and modern music on CD and attractive gift items complete the ensemble.

The Bookshop North Chingford

- ▣ 135 Station Road,
  North Chingford, E4 6AG
- ☏ 020 8524 9002
- ✑ @ChingfordBooks
- 🚇 Chingford Rail
- 🕓 Mon & Thurs 9.30am-4.30pm,
  Tues-Wed, Fri-Sat 9.30am-5.30pm

Just a few minutes' walk from Chingford Station, this shop offers a beguiling mix of discounted and full price new books covering most subject areas with a particularly strong children's section and a recently expanded Mind Body and Spirit section. The helpful staff will also order books, CDs and DVDs if they don't have what you want in stock. A few doors down Café Delice is a relaxing spot to peruse your purchases over a coffee.

ARTWORDSBO
OKSHOPQRST
UVWXYZ
abcontemporar
yvisualculture
1234567890
&£--/.,:;"!?*""
–(){}@%+=

Based in Shoreditch and Hackney,
'Artwords has its finger firmly on the
pulse when it comes to visual arts
publications'. (Time Out)

69 Rivington Street
SHOREDITCH EC2A 3AY
020 7729 2000
rivingtonstreet@artwords.co.uk

20-22 Broadway Market
HACKNEY E8 4QJ
020 7923 7507
broadwaymarket@artwords.co.uk

We've supplied the local and London-
wide Arts & Media community since
2001 with an excellent, specialist
selection on the Visual Arts and Visual
Culture - Books and Magazines.

Independent since 2001
Open every day

www.artwords.co.uk

ATLANTIS BOOKSHOP

New and secondhand books on all aspects of
the Occult, Witchcraft and Magical Sciences.

49a Museum Street London WC1A 1LY
020 7405 2120
www.theatlantisbookshop.com
atlantis@theatlantisbookshop.com
Mon-Sat 10.30am-6pm

BOOKS™
ARE MY
BAG
#BAMB
LOVE BOOKS
LOVE BOOKSHOPS

Barnes Bookshop

Mini Notebooks

Barnes Bookshop

60 Church Road, SW13 0DQ
020 8741 0786
www.barnesbookshop.co.uk
Barnes Common Rail
Mon-Sat 9.30am-5.30pm,
Sun 11am-5pm

Barnes Bookshop is just what a local bookshop should be, with a smart blue frontage and great window displays to entice passers-by and a friendly welcome assured for those who cross the threshold. The stock is concise but well chosen with particular strengths being paperback fiction and children's books, but there are also sections dedicated to travel, history, biography, cookery and art – all well displayed over two floors. If they don't have the title you're after, Isla and her team offer a remarkably efficient ordering system and can usually source the book for next day delivery. Stationery is also an important part of the mix here and there is an extensive selection of cards, notebooks and other gifts in the basement.

Isla Dawes is the owner of the store, and a regular presence, dispensing advice, dealing with enquiries and taking an active role in the concerns of the local area – the door of the store is awash with posters and cards for various Barnes events and organisations. It's this personal touch, with plenty of staff on hand to help, that has made this store so popular among the denizens of SW13. As Isla puts it:

"I think we are good at engaging with customers and having a more interesting selection of books … People know that they can find something different here and they can trust our advice – we're really a safe pair of hands."

As if to illustrate the point several regular customers enter the store with enquires based on previous recommendations: grandparents wanting a further book – 'The London Eye Mystery' having been a great success with their granddaughter, and another regular wanting advice about the latest Donna Tart novel. It's clear people enjoy visiting the store and value the opinions of the staff.

> " *People know that they can find something different here and they can trust our advice – we're really a safe pair of hands.*"

Another reason for the company's success has been its ability to adapt to circumstances. With the closure of several toy shops in the area, the bookshop has stepped in to fill the breach with a well-chosen selection of children's toys, supplementing the already popular children's books section. The addition has helped boost sales but care has been taken to keep this primarily as a bookshop.

The Barnes store has two sister shops, Kew Bookshop (see p.72) and Sheen Bookshop (see p.107) was acquired in June 2011, but Isla makes clear there are no plans for further expansion. The website for the bookshop has just been relaunched and is a great first point of reference.

THE **BOOK WAREHOUSE**

LONDON'S BEST DISCOUNT BOOK STORES

120 Southampton Row, WC1B 5AB • Tel: 020 7242 1119

72-74 Notting Hill Gate, W11 3HT • Tel: 020 7727 4149

38 Golder's Green Rd, NW11 8LL • Tel: 020 8458 0032

28 Upper Street, N1 0PN • 020 7226 8779

155 Camden High Street, NW1 7JY • 020 7482 4375

104 Lower Marsh Street, SE1 7AB • 020 7620 2318

BOOKS, CARDS & GIFTS

Head office: 020 7242 1119
www.thebookwarehouse.co.uk

SPREAD YOUR WINGS

THE TALK OF THE TOWN FOR 18 YEARS

BOOKSELLERCROW.CO.UK

THE BOOKSELLER CROW on the hill 020 87718831

BOOK & KITCHEN

Combining the literary and culinary in a fresh and modern setting

**31 ALL SAINTS ROAD
NOTTING HILL
LONDON W11 1HE
www.bookandkitchen.com**

Beautiful Books

⊡ 24 Brixton Station Road, SW9 8PD
☎ 020 7738 3302
✐ www.lefi.org
🚎 Brixton LU/Rail
🕓 Mon-Sat 10am-5pm, (Wed closes at 2pm)

This shop offers an extensive array of books and audio-visual material on all aspects of Christianity including a good selection for children. It's located underneath the railway arches in the heart of the Brixton Market area and is a ministry of the Laymen's Evangelical Fellowship UK.

Chris Beetles

⊡ 8 & 10 Ryder Street, St James's
   SW1Y 6QB
☎ 020 7839 7551
✐ www.chrisbeetles.com
🚎 Piccadilly Circus LU
🕓 Mon-Sat 10am-5.30pm

Modern security concerns mean you have to ring the bell to get in but don't let that worry you, once through the door, you are assured a warm welcome. The gallery specialises in illustrations, photographs, cartoons and watercolours and stages an annual 'Illustrators' show from early November through to the New Year, as well as other exhibitions through the year. They publish and sell their exhibition catalogues – fascinating and almost works of art in their own right – and now have more than fifty on the back list at prices from £3 for small pamphlets to £200 for superbly produced limited editions. Featured artists include Thelwell, Mervyn Peake, Mabel Lucie Attwell, Michael Foreman and Quentin Blake among many others. While you can wander in just to browse the catalogues it is also worth having a peek at the art, which includes the largest stock of British watercolours and drawings in the country. Prices start from £100, making this an affordable place to add to your collection

BFI Filmstore

⊡ BFI Southbank, SE1 8XT
☎ 020 7815 1350
✐ www.bfi.org.uk
🚎 Waterloo LU/Rail
🕓 Daily 11am-8.30pm

Located in the British Film Institute complex in the Southbank, this shop is a Mecca for all film buffs. It includes a wonderfully varied selection of books and magazines on all practical and theoretical aspects of film and film-making plus a section on television and other media. While many of the books feature mainstream Hollywood output, there's a great deal on more independent, global work and this includes the selection of Blu-rays and DVDs, plus a significant world cinema section.

Bibliophile

⊡ Unit 5, Datapoint Business Centre
   South Crescent, E16 4TL
☎ 020 7474 2474
✐ www.bibliophilebooks.com
🚎 Canning Town LU/DLR, West Ham LU
🕓 Mon-Fri 9am-4pm

Bibliophile is predominantly an internet and postal business dealing in remainder books. However, customers are welcome (no appointment necessary) to visit the warehouse either to collect orders or to browse the vast stock which covers all subject areas, with about 20,000 titles in stock at any time. The books on the shelves are sometimes awaiting despatch having been ordered and paid for so visitors can't always buy everything they see. This is a working warehouse with potential hazards such as forklifts moving around, so visitor numbers are limited and it is not a safe environment for children.

The Big Green Bookshop

⌖ *Unit 1, Brampton Park Road, N22 6BG*
☎ *020 8881 6767*
✍ *www.biggreenbookshop.com*
🚌 *Wood Green LU, Turnpike Lane LU*
🕓 *Mon-Sat 9am-6pm, Sun 11am-5pm*

Their blog might be subtitled "Two blokes, one bookshop, no idea" but Tim West and Simon Key are doing a great deal right in this fabulous local shop. The stock is carefully selected with particular strengths being literary fiction, local interest, multi-cultural issues and children's titles. The shop has a welcoming atmosphere and involves the community with reading groups, regular events, free coffee, and a lovely sofa for lounging. Every March the shop transforms into a miniscule cinema as part of the Wood Green Film Festival. The shop's blog provides a fascinating insight into life and thought on the other side of the counter.

Blackwell's

✍ www.blackwell.co.uk

Founded in Oxford in 1879, the Blackwell's chain now has more than 40 general, academic, professional and specialist shops in the UK. Their branches retain a serious academic emphasis and a Blackwell Loyalty Card rewards regular shoppers.
Branches at:

Blackwell's Holborn

⌖ *50-51 High Holborn, WC1V 6EP*
☎ *020 7292 5100*
✍ *www.blackwell.co.uk*
🚌 *Holborn LU*
🕓 *Mon-Fri 8am-6.30pm, Sat 10am-4pm*

This plush new Blackwell's store opened in 2015. On the ground floor there is a good stock of fiction and popular reference books, while the basement is dedicated to accountancy, business, law and economics. There are usually a few multi-buy deals and there is an in-house café, for those who want to relax with a cappuccino.

Blackwell's at the Institute of Education

⌖ *Level 3, 20 Bedford Way, WC1H 0AL*
☎ *020 7636 9462 or 020 7612 6556*
✍ *www.blackwell.co.uk/ioe*
🚌 *Russell Sq LU, Goodge St LU, Euston LU*
🕓 *Mon-Fri 9am-5pm*

This campus branch is located within one of the leading establishments for teacher training and the study of education. It strengths are IOE course textbooks and its selection of philosophy, fiction and new releases as well as classic and contemporary children's books. Even teachers have their frivolous side and so you can also find gifts, cards, stationery, posters and toys. The staff host regular in-store events and launches, and provide bookstalls for conferences as part of the Institute's busy events schedule.

Blackwell's at Goldsmiths

⌖ *Goldsmiths, University of London, Lewisham Way, New Cross, SE14 6NW*
☎ *020 8469 0829*
✍ *www.blackwell.co.uk/goldsmiths*
🚌 *New Cross Rail/LU, New Cross Gate Overground, Deptford Bridge DLR*
🕓 *Mon-Fri 9am-5pm (during term time)*

Goldsmiths is one of the leading art colleges in the country. This compact campus branch of Blackwell's caters for the interests of the students with a focus on the arts and humanities as well as a concise range of gifts, stationery and technology products.

Blackwell's – Wellcome Collection

Reviewed as Wellcome Shop
see p.130.

bookartbookshop

⊡ *17 Pitfield Street, N1 6HB*
☎ *020 7608 1333*
⬥ *www.bookartbookshop.com*
🚌 *Old Street LU/Rail*
🕓 *Thurs & Fri 1pm-7pm, Sat 12noon-6pm*
This small shop is situated in the art hub that is Hoxton and specialises in artists' books and small press publications. The store's unusual opening hours cater to its artistic clientele, but the place is still worth searching out for its unique stock and imaginative displays. As well as books there are greetings cards, postcards and badges. Be sure to pay a visit to Artwords (see p.16), which is just around the corner.

Bookcase London

⊡ *268 Chiswick High Road, W4 1PD*
☎ *020 8742 3919*
⬥ *www.bookcaselondon.co.uk*
🚌 *Turnham Green LU*
🕓 *Mon-Sat 9.30am-7pm, Sun 11am-6pm*
This long-established discount shop has a great selection of books. It is particularly strong on art (there's a big selection of Thames and Hudson titles), but design, photography, history, cookery, fiction and children's books also feature prominently.

Book & Kitchens

Book & Kitchen

31 All Saints Road, W11 1HE
020 3417 8266
www.bookandkitchen.com
Westbourne Park LU
Ladbroke Grove LU
Tues-Sat 10am-6pm,
Sun 12noon-6pm

Opened in March 2013, Book & Kitchen is an unusual blend of a bookshop, café and live music and supper club venue. Muna Khogali worked in publishing for many years before getting the idea for this fabulous venture.

"I found many bookshops dark, rather dull places and wanted to do something new and make a place that was light and airy with helpful and knowledgeable staff"

The result is a shop that is both comfortable and stylish with scaffolding used to create chunky, attractive shelves and an eclectic mix of second-hand furniture. On the ground floor there is space for a well-chosen selection of new books with a large table where customers can use the wi-fi facility while enjoying a drink or just browse the stock.

Downstairs is more cosy with a small café, shelves of second-hand books and a snug kid's area with lots of children's fiction and space for youngsters to play while the adults enjoy a browse and a coffee. The café is as generous and thoughtful as the rest of the shop with a long list of different blends of tea and coffee and an appetising selection of cakes and more substantial dishes which are made daily in the small kitchen at the back. The regular supper clubs hosted here are an important part of the business and Muna is proud that she has managed to cook for one hundred people from the small kitchen. The shop hosts regular Supper Clubs for Peirene Press, during which an author and editor get a chance to meet diners while eating food inspired by the book in question. The venture is still new and the energy levels and enthusiasm high, but Muna does realise the difficulty of keeping an independent bookshop as part of a local community:

> **I've got nothing against competition, but many internet companies don't pay their taxes and treat their staff badly, so this is unfair, protected competition... We need to think about the Net Book Agreement again... because price cutting is destroying the book trade ..."**

Despite her justified anger at the state of the book trade, Muna is positive in her approach with lots of plans for the shop which include more live music, ambitious dining experiences and events hosted by the philosopher Nigel Warburton. For all the latest events check their website.

All Saints Road is a few minutes' walk from Portobello Road, but Book & Kitchen is a real find that is well worth seeking out.We left with a bag of books, a poster from their small selection of original art and prints and a determination to visit again, not least to try another of Muna's delicious cakes.

Book Ends Papercrafts

- 🏠 *66 Exmouth Market, EC1R 4QP*
- ☎ *020 7713 8555*
- 🖱 *www.bookendslondon.co.uk*
- 🚌 *Farringdon LU/Rail*
- 🕒 *Mon-Fri 10am-6pm, Sat 10am-5pm*

An unusual shop with a good range of children's books upstairs and a basement that is an Aladdin's cave of craft books and materials.

bookHaus

- 🏠 *70 Cadogan Place, SW1X 9AH*
- ☎ *020 7838 9055*
- 🖱 *www.bookhaus.co.uk*
- 🚌 *Sloane Square LU*
- 🕒 *Mon-Sat 10am-5.30pm*

A small bookshop five minutes' walk from Sloane Square. The shop is a showcase for Haus Publications, who publish quality travel, history and fiction. Other publishers are also stocked and there are plenty of readings and events. John Sandoe (see p.104 and the Saatchi Gallery (see p.103) are within walking distance.

BookMarc

- 🏠 *24-25 Mount Street, W1K 2RR*
- ☎ *020 7399 1690*
- 🖱 *www.marcjacobs.com/bookmarc*
- 🚌 *Piccadilly Circus LU*
- 🕒 *Mon-Sat 11am-7pm, Sun 12noon-6pm*

The Mayfair fashion store Marc Jacobs also contains a small outlet called BookMarc dedicated to art and fashion books. The shelves are home to all kinds of interesting books with particular strengths being contemporary photography and fashion but with a more limited offering of fiction and books on modern culture. If Derrida and Foucault aren't your bag, there are notebooks and other stationery items to peruse and of course the books are surrounded by Marc Jacobs fashion. Book worms are notoriously unkempt, but smarter literary folk will love this chic new London store.

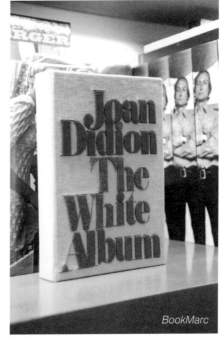

BookMarc

Bookmarks the Socialist Bookshop ❶

- 📖 *1 Bloomsbury Street, WC1B 3QE*
- ☎ *020 7637 1848*
- ✎ *www.bookmarksbookshop.co.uk*
- 🚇 *Tottenham Court Road LU*
- 🕐 *Mon 12noon-7pm,*
  Tues-Sat 10am-7pm

This socialist bookshop began life in Finsbury Park over forty years ago before moving to this prime Bloomsbury location at the start of the new millennium. It has established itself as a key meeting place and source of information for many on the left and the late Tony Benn described it as "The university for activists".

Andrea Butcher is the manager and is as committed to the political cause as she is to the running of this well organised shop which she and her team see as part of a wider struggle against big business and ruthless price cutting.

"He biggest competition to independent bookshops is the internet, because we simply can't compete on price ... We pay our team well and pay our taxes and so we can't compete with the global book retailers, but there's an increasingly large niche market of people who don't want to use the large online book retailers because of their treatment of staff and tax avoidance practices ..."

This loyalty from political sympathisers has kept Bookmarks as a thriving independent bookshop when so many others have fallen by the wayside.

"Because we are a socialist bookshop we have a natural and supportive constituency amongst activists and trade unionists and our business is doing really well ... "

Obvious strengths here are politics, history and gender studies, but the stock also includes a surprising array of left-wing fiction, books about music and a kids' section with plenty of great books that avoid gender stereotypes but still manage to be fun and imaginative. The poet and children's author Michael Rosen is a strong supporter of the shop and does regular readings here. They also have a good selection of second-hand books donated by regular customers.

Like many bookshops that are managing to survive in the internet age, Bookmarks has several strings to its bow. One string is the willingness of Andrea and her team to up sticks and go on the road, setting up pop-up shops at all the major trade union conferences, as well as the Tolpuddle Martyrs Festival in Dorset and the Marxism Festival both of which take place in July and necessitate the shop's closure for a week. This is a lot of work, but Andrea says it is worth the effort:

"We make lots of contacts at these events and build long-term relationships with customers. The Tolpuddle and Marxism festivals are our busiest events, so July is like Christmas for us!"

Another strength of Bookmarks is its publishing business, which produces all kinds of titles including a great pocket series of 'Rebel's Guides' which offer introductions to key left-wing figures for just £3 a copy.

The book displays are always topical and the staff are good at offering suggested reading for any issue. For example, on the centenary of the start of World War One the staff produced a large display with suggested reading on the conflict from a socialist perspective.

On a lighter note, Bookmarks are always on the search for left wing gift ideas from plaster busts of Lenin and Marx to 'I Still Hate Thatcher' mugs.

For a small independent, Bookmarks is active on social media and their newly revamped website is a useful resource, keeping readers informed of future events and publications.

Probably the most unique feature of Bookmarks is the 2-metre high steel model of the Tatlin Tower which was envisaged as a vast testament to the Soviet future at the Third International of 1919. The tower remains an unrealised dream, but in this bookshop – where the staff call each other 'comrade' – the Socialist dream is still alive.

"Because we are a socialist bookshop we have a natural and supportive constituency amongst activists and trade unionists and our business is doing really well ..."

Bookmarks the Socialist Bookshop

Bookseller Crow on the Hill

⌨ *50 Westow Street, Crystal Palace SE19 3AF*

☎ *020 8771 8831*

✍ *www.booksellercrow.co.uk*

🚌 *Crystal Palace Rail*

🕐 *Mon-Fri 10am-7pm, Sat 9.30am-6.30pm, Sun 11am-5pm*

Just up the road from the large Sainsbury's supermarket, this is a cracking local bookstore. Although small, it has room for a quality, well-selected stock, which is always thoughtfully displayed. They have a garden bench, small table and chairs for children and especially good displays of fiction, children's books, travel, art titles and American imports. The shop hosts weekly author events and has a popular monthly book group. Crystal Palace has an abundance of excellent cafés and restaurants to suit every taste – alternatively a picnic in Crystal Palace Park is no bad way to round off a book-buying spree. Combine a trip here with a visit to Haynes Lane Collectors Market (see p.210).

Books For Cooks

⌨ *4 Blenheim Crescent, W11 1NN*

☎ *020 7221 1992*

✍ *www.booksforcooks.com*

🚌 *Ladbroke Grove LU*

🕐 *Tues-Sat 10am-6pm*

(Closed three weeks in August and 10 days at Christmas, ring to check)

Opened in 1983, this shop just off Portobello Road is possibly the most famous dedicated cookery bookshop in the world. It has more than eight thousand titles (including a few rare and out of print volumes), has won numerous awards, is reviewed regularly in the press and is a place of pilgrimage for foodies from all over the world. The shop sells books on all aspects of food, from specialist professional manuals to family cookbooks. There is a delightful café/restaurant at the back of the shop where a rota of chefs prepare meals based on recipes from the books on the shelves. The demonstration kitchen upstairs holds regular workshops and the shop also hosts literary lunches featuring authors and dishes from particular books. A remarkable bookshop and one all London foodies should visit for inspiration.

THE COOKBOOK SHOP

BOOKS *for* COOKS

4 Blenheim Crescent
Notting Hill London W11 1NN
020 7221 1992
www.booksforcooks.com

Books For Life

🖾 *Bethnal Green Mission Church, 305*
Cambridge Heath Road, E2 9LH
☎ *020 7729 4286*
✒ *www.bethnalgreenmissionchurch.co.uk*
🚌 *Bethnal Green LU*
🕒 *Mon-Fri 9.30am-5.30pm*

Located just by the entrance hall of the church and extending over two storeys, this shop is well-stocked with magazines, books, DVDs and CDs covering almost every aspect of Christian life and worship. The store also offers a selection of general as well as Christian second-hand books. The church is just opposite the Museum of Childhood.

Books Plus

🖾 *401 Edgware Road, W2 1BT*
☎ *020 7723 9888*
✒ *www.ukbooksplus.com*
🚌 *Edgware Road LU*
🕒 *Mon-Fri 9am-9.30pm,*
Sat 10am-9.30pm, Sunday 12noon-6pm

An Arabic bookshop specialising in Islamic material including children's books and Arabic learning materials.

Book Warehouse

✒ *www.thebookwarehouse.co.uk*

An established London discount chain with several London branches offering long opening hours, plenty of choice across all subject areas and a rapid turnover of stock. They are especially strong on glossy, coffee-table books on art, architecture, design, photography, cookery and gardening but are worth a visit for more or less any topic. There are also bargain CDs plus cards and stationery.

Branches at:

🖾 *38 Golders Green Rd, NW11 8LL*
☎ *020 8458 0032*
🚌 *Golders Green LU*
🕒 *Daily 9.30am-9pm, (Fri closes at 8pm)*

🖾 *72-74 Notting Hill Gate, W11 3HT*
☎ *020 7727 4149*
🚌 *Notting Hill Gate LU*
🕒 *Mon-Fri 9am-10pm,*
Sat 8.30am-10pm, Sun 10am-10pm

🖾 *120 Southampton Row,*
WC1B 5AB
☎ *020 7242 1119*
🚌 *Russell Square LU*
🕒 *Mon-Fri 8.30-10pm,*
Sat 9am-10pm & Sun 10am-10pm

🖾 *28 Upper Street, N1 0PN*
☎ *020 7226 8779*
🚌 *Angel LU*
🕒 *Daily 8.30am-8.30pm*

🖾 *155 Camden High Street, 347JY*
☎ *020 7482 4375*
🚌 *Camden LU*
🕒 *Mon-Sat 9am-8pm, Sun 10.30am-*
7.30pm

🖾 *104 Lower Marsh Street, SE1 7AB*
☎ *020 7620 2318*
🚌 *Waterloo LU*
🕒 *Mon-Sat 9.30am-7,30pm,*
Sun 11am-5pm

Bookworm

⌨ *1177 Finchley Road, NW11 0AA*
☎ *020 8201 9811*
✑ *www.thebookworm.uk.com*
🚌 *Golders Green LU (then bus)*
🕓 *Mon-Sat 9.30am-5.30pm,*
   Sun 10am-1.30pm

A lovely little shop specialising in books for children and young adults, packed with an extensive and interesting stock plus greetings cards, wrapping paper and audio CDs. There are regular events such as parties involving favourite characters and visits by authors. Storytelling takes place at 2pm every Tuesday and Thursday for toddlers.

Brick Lane Bookshop

⌨ *166 Brick Lane, E1 6RU*
☎ *020 7247 0216*
✑ *www.bricklanebookshop.org*
🚌 *Shoreditch High Street Overground*
🕓 *Daily 11am-6.30pm*
See full review on p.37

British Geological Survey

⌨ *London Information Office,*
   Natural History Museum,
   Cromwell Road, SW7 5BD
☎ *020 7589 4090*
✑ *www.bgs.ac.uk*
🚌 *South Kensington LU*
🕓 *Mon-Fri 10am-5pm (ring in advance)*

The BGS, next to the Lasting Impressions Gallery of the Natural History Museum, sells Survey publications including geological maps, guides, popular and academic books and posters. While many of the books are highly academic, a surprising number will be of interest to general readers and anyone who enjoys the countryside.

Brick Lane Bookshop

Brick Lane Bookshop
(Eastside Books Ltd)
166 Brick Lane
London
E1 6RU

Open every day 11am-6.30pm
020 7247 0216
info@bricklanebookshop.co.uk
@bricklanebooks
www.bricklanebookshop.org

15% OFF WITH THIS ADVERT

166 Brick Lane Bookshop 166

Brick Lane Bookshop

📖 *166 Brick Lane, E1 6RU*
☏ *020 7247 0216*
✎ *www.bricklanebookshop.com*
🚆 *Shoreditch High Street Overground*
🕐 *Daily 11am-6.30pm*

Brick Lane Bookshop is one of London's busiest independents, located in the heart of one of London's most fashionable areas surrounded by cafés, vintage stores, markets and Indian restaurants.

The shop is long established with a well-chosen general stock, a keen eye for the latest publications and a fantastic London section. First time visitors might assume this successful bookshop is a hard-nosed commercial venture, but Brick Lane Bookshop has its origins in 1970's radical politics and was originally called Tower Hamlets Arts Project (THAP) and began selling books from a small room in Watney Market Law Centre. One of the founders of the shop, Denise Jones, has lost none of her campaigning zeal and still keeps the original hand painted 'THAP' sign on a wall at the back of the store. She explains:

" It was possible in those days to get funding for arts projects and radical causes and our bookselling and publishing started in this very favourable environment ... Now things are a lot tougher and we have to be commercial to survive."

The gradual evolution of a radical bookseller trading from a table to the well organised Brick Lane Bookshop is a long one, involving several moves and in recent years a change in name from Eastside to Brick Lane Bookshop. Over the last 30 years of trading the company has also been involved in publishing books about local history including the autobiography of local boxer Stephen 'Johnny' Hicks

and 'Across Seven Seas' a compilation of memoirs by Bangladeshi immigrants to this part of London. This interest and involvement in the area's history helps explain Brick Lane's extensive London section which contains all kinds of obscure and mainstream publications, and its strong ties with local authors such as Alan Gilbey who worked at the shop for many years and whose book 'East End Backpassages' has a prominent display.

Kalina and Kate have joined Denise in recent years and helped build the business and develop the store's social media presence. The helpful staff are also on hand to deal with actual customers with so many tourists, students, artists and workers now thronging the main thoroughfare of Brick Lane. The team also run regular reading and writing groups, host small literary events and book launches at the shop and occasionally participate in larger literary events at the nearby RichMix Art Centre.

Brick Lane Bookshop is thriving in the new east end but still tries to keep a memory of its old radical roots alive, as Denise puts it:

"We're doing what we love and, fingers crossed, things are going well. We're so lucky to be in an area that's booming, but we are also a place committed to London's past. It's a tricky balance to make, but we seem to be managing it ..."

If you want to experience Brick Lane at its busiest, this shop is best visited on a Sunday when the markets are in full swing, although these days the street is busy throughout the week. There are lots of cafés in the area, but Brick Lane Coffee (at 157) with its motto of 'come happy leave edgy' is worth the trek to the top of the road.

British Library Bookshop

📖 *96 Euston Road, NW1 2DB*
☎ *020 7412 7735*
✎ *www.bl.uk*
🚇 *King's Cross/St Pancras LU & Rail*
🕐 *Mon-Fri 9.30am-6pm, Tues until 8pm,*
  Sat 9.30am-5pm, Sun 11am-5pm

The British Library is one of the largest libraries in the world and attracts over 2 million book-loving visitors annually (see page 38). The bookshop attached to the library is therefore in a fortunate position and has thrived while keeping books at the heart of what it's doing.

The bookshop caters to the literary interests of visitors to the library with a large area dedicated to all things related to books. If you are one of those readers who cares about point size, typography and the aesthetic appeal of a well designed book, then this shops will definitely merit a visit with its shelves of books about bookbinding, collecting, guides about how to write and research, calligraphy and even books about the history of paper.

The shop also has a newly expanded children's section with lots of new titles and low tables to encourage younger browsers. Adults are also well catered for with a substantial fiction section and a good choice of reference books covering history, biography and culture. The store also has a well-stocked London section which has proved a hit with the many tourists who visit the shop.

Despite its success in recent years, the shop is not letting the grass grow under its feet. In 2013 the retail team undertook a major refurbishment which saw the old

British Library Bookshop

> ❝ *We attract a lot of people who love books ... the printed book is very much be at the heart of what we are doing*"

purple colour scheme replaced by white walls, and display units removed from windows to allow more light in and giving the shop a much more contemporary feel. A few tough decisions were made and CDs and art books are no longer sold here, but the expanded children's section and a wider range of literary gifts have more than compensated.

The entrance to the shop is usually given over to the latest exhibition or event at the library and the retail team also run a pop-up shop which can materialise at book signings and readings throughout the building (see page 232 for more about the library's exhibitions).

The library has a great café and restaurant next to the glass tower where the Library of George III ascends to the roof of this spectacular interior space. If the weather is fine you might prefer the vast central courtyard of the library with its outdoor seating and café.

The British Museum Bookshop

⊞ *Great Russell Street, WC1B 3DG*
☎ *Museum switchboard 020 7323 8000*
   Direct number 020 7323 8179
✍ *www.thebritishmuseumshoponline.org*
🚉 *Russell Square LU*
🕐 *Mon-Thurs & Sat-Sun 9am-6pm,*
   Fri 9.30am-8.30pm

The British Museum has recently opened this new bookshop which is designed to look as impressive as the surrounding Great Court. The bookshop mirrors the curves of the court and has vast windows which allow light into this elegantly furnished retail space. The window displays are dominated by huge circular book sculptures which are a major feature of the store. Inside, the stock is largely given over to publications relevant to the Museum's collections with sections dedicated to ancient Egypt, ancient Greece, Rome, Mesopotamia, archaeology, mythology and religion. The stock does include some British and European history, food history, classic novels and Folio Society publications, but all other books are stocked in the museum's general gift shop. This is very much a boutique approach to book selling with the style of the shelving and colour schemes taking precedence over a comprehensive range of books, but as a gesture in the direction of supporting the sale of books it is to be commended. The store also sells DVDs and additional book related items such as bookmarks and lights. For rest and refreshment climb the stairs to reach the Court Restaurant or for a quick snack try the café on the same level as the shop.

The Broadway Bookshop

⊞ *6 Broadway Market, E8 4QJ*
☎ *020 7241 1626*
✍ *wwww.broadwaybookshophackney.com*
🚉 *London Fields Rail*
🕐 *Mon-Sat 10am-6pm, Sun 11am-5pm*

This dinky local bookshop has definite Tardis-like qualities. It extends onwards and downwards over three levels with books adorning every wall and surface. The stock is general and all subjects are covered but literary fiction, travel, local interest and history are especially strong. There is original art displayed on the walls, some second-hand books as well as new titles and there are even a few chairs for browsers. Join the mailing list to keep up to date on their many literary events and check the website for the latest recommendations. Broadway Market is full of great cafés and lunch spots and bursts into life at the weekends, particularly on Saturdays when the street market is in full swing.

THE BROADWAY BOOKSHOP

INDEPENDENT BOOKSELLER SINCE 2005

6 Broadway Market
Hackney
E8 4QJ

020 7241 1626

Monday – Saturday 10 am – 6 pm
Sunday 11 am – 5 pm

www.broadwaybookshophackney.com
email: books@broadwaybookshophackney.com

C

Calder Bookshop

- 51 The Cut, SE1 8LF
- 020 7620 2900
- www.calderbookshop.com
- Waterloo LU
- Mon-Sat 11am-9pm, Sun 12noon-8pm

Across the road from the Young Vic Theatre, this is an attractive bookshop that is also part of the Calder Theatre. The Calder Theatre is largely dedicated to staging radical plays and performances and its not-for-profit bookshop concentrates on new books about politics and theatre, although it now has a second-hand department with a more general stock. Definitely a shop that deserves to be better known.

Camden Arts Centre

- Arkwright Road, NW3 6DG
- 020 7472 5500
- www.camdenartscentre.org
- Finchley Road LU, Finchley Road, Frognal Overground
- Tues-Sun 10am-6pm, Wed 10am-9pm

The bookshop is based in CAC's reception area and stocks a good selection of books on art and critical theory, artists' monographs, magazines and exhibition catalogues. In addition there's a lovely range of illustrated children's books to keep the kids happy. The Centre hosts art exhibitions, courses, events and talks and its popular café is a great place to relax.

Camden Lock Books

- Old Street Station, 4 St Agnes Well, EC1Y 1BE
- 020 7253 0666
- www.camdenlockbooks.com
- Old Street LU/Rail
- Mon-Fri 8.30am-7pm, Sat 12noon-5.30pm

Formerly located in Camden Lock (hence the name), this amazing cavern of delights is located in the underground shopping arcade of Old Street station. There is a vast general stock, both full price and discount, but specialising in art, photography and fashion. In recent years they have added a selection of rare and collectable books to their range. Additional gift ideas include song books, maps, World Music CDs and cards. A surprising little gem of a shop.

John Carpenter Bookshop

- City of London School, Queen Victoria Street, EC4V 3AL
- 020 7332 0223
- www.johncarpenterbookshop.co.uk
- Blackfriars LU/Rail, St Paul's LU
- Ring to arrange to visit

Located in a boys' secondary school, this shop sells titles of interest to that age-range: everything from the latest fiction to revision guides, as well as calculators, greetings cards and stationery. The shop accepts orders from local businesses and members of the public, selling through www.hive.co.uk (see John Carpenter Bookshop website for details). Members of the public, should they wish to visit, need to telephone to arrange access as the shop is located within the school grounds.

The Cartoon Museum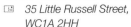

- 35 Little Russell Street, WC1A 2HH
- ☎ 020 70 8155
- ✎ www.cartoonmuseum.org
- 🚇 Tottenham Court Road LU, Holborn LU
- 🕓 Mon-Sat 10.30am-5.30pm, Sun 12noon-5.30pm

The Cartoon Museum is dedicated to British cartoons, caricatures, comics and animation. The attached bookshop stocks titles on these subjects including a good range of alternative comics, graphic novels and how-to-draw titles. There are also plenty of gift items and cards.

The Catholic Truth Society

- 25 Ashley Place, SW1P 1LT
- ☎ 020 7834 1363
- ✎ www.ctsbooks.org
- 🚇 Victoria LU/Rail
- 🕓 Mon-Fri 9.30am-5.30pm, Sat 10am-5pm

Just opposite Westminster Cathedral, this small shop offers a comprehensive range of books on all aspects of Catholic spirituality from theological texts to children's books, as well as a selection of religious gifts.

Chapter Two

- 199 Plumstead Common Road SE18 2UJ
- ☎ 020 8316 4972
- ✎ www.chaptertwobooks.org.uk
- 🚇 Woolwich Arsenal DLR/Rail, Plumstead Common Rail
- 🕓 Mon-Fri 9.30am-5.30pm (closed 1pm-2.30pm), Sat 10.30am-1pm

A specialist on the Plymouth Brethren and Dispensational Christianity, this shop stocks new and second-hand books and Christian literature including many foreign editions.

Chener Books

- 14 Lordship Lane, SE22 8HN
- ☎ 020 8299 0771
- 🚇 East Dulwich Rail
- 🕓 Mon-Sat 10am-6pm

A good-sized local bookshop with an excellent general selection of fiction and reference titles and displays to encourage browsing. Fiction, travel, biography and history are especially well-represented. The back room is now a dedicated children's area with a great selection of books within easy reach of junior readers. The local notice board is a useful resource and there are plenty of eateries on Lordship Lane and North Cross Road to keep hungry bibliophiles happy.

Chess & Bridge

- 44 Baker Street, W1U 7RT
- ☎ 020 7486 7015
- ✎ www.chess.co.uk
- 🚇 Baker Street LU
- 🕓 Mon-Sat 9.30am-6pm (Thurs until 7pm), Sun 11am-5pm

A specialist shop with a huge range of books and other items focusing on chess, bridge, poker and, to a lesser extent, backgammon, Go, draughts and mah-jong. The book section is extensive and there are also magazines, DVDs, chess and bridge computers and software. The shop stocks a fine selection of chess sets and publishes a yearly catalogue.

Children's Bookshop

⊡ *29 Fortis Green Road, N10 3HP*
☎ *020 8444 5500*
✑ *www.childrensbookshoplondon.com*
🚌 *Highgate LU*
☉ *Mon-Sat 9.15am-5.45pm*
   Sun 11am-4pm

Situated just opposite the Muswell Hill Bookshop (see p.85), this specialist shop has a huge stock of books for youngsters from baby's first books through to teenage fiction. Young bookworms can keep themselves up to the minute with the shop's recommendations, which include a useful list of new books. The staff know their stuff, there's a weekly storytime and the shop holds frequent author events.

Christian Books and Music

⊡ *Kensington Temple,*
   Kensington Park Road, W11 3BY
☎ *020 7727 8684*
🚌 *Notting Hill Gate LU*
☉ *Tues, Wed & Sat 12noon-7pm,*
   Sun 10am-7pm

A well-stocked bookshop in the basement of the church featuring contemporary Christian literature, music, cards, DVDs and magazines.

Christian Books Plus

⊡ *386 Brixton Road, SW9 7AW*
☎ *020 7737 1089*
✑ *www.christianbooks-plus.com*
🚌 *Brixton LU/Rail*
☉ *Mon-Sat 10am-6.30pm*

A Christian bookshop selling a wide range of books on Christian religion and life, plus devotional music and a wide range of gift items.

Rainbow Theatre

⊡ *232 Seven Sisters Road, N4 3NX*
☎ *020 7686 6006 Ext.6150*
🚌 *Finsbury Park LU/Rail*
☉ *Mon-Fri 10am-6pm*

Branch of the Christian bookshop Plus (see above).

Church House Bookshop

⊡ *31 Great Smith Street, SW1P 3BN*
☎ *020 7799 4064*
✑ *www.chbookshop.co.uk*
🚌 *Westminster & St James's Park LU*
☉ *Mon-Fri 9am-5pm, Thurs 9am-6pm*

A long-established religious bookshop just around the corner from Westminster Abbey and known as the 'official bookshop of the Church of England'. Recently refurbished, it sells a wide range of Christian books with an outstanding selection of greeting cards.

The Cinema Store

⊡ *4b Orion House,*
   Upper St Martin's Lane,
   WC2H 9NY
☎ *020 7379 7838*
✑ *www.thecinemastore.co.uk*
🚌 *Leicester Square LU*
☉ *Mon-Sat 10am-6.30pm,Sun 12noon-6pm*

A shop selling a wide range of books, DVDs, photographs and other paraphernalia associated with the cinema. The book stock covers all aspects of cinema from technical manuals to film biographies.

Clapham Bookshop

- 26 The Pavement, SW4 0JA
- 020 7627 2797
- www.claphambooks.com
- Clapham Common LU
- Mon-Fri 10am-7pm, Sat 10am-6pm, Sun 12noon-6pm

Nikki and Ed took over in 2006, when the shop was under threat of closure, having both worked here as temporary staff. They revitalised this Clapham institution, and have now secured its future by moving from the High Street to this new location on The Pavement opposite Clapham Common. The local community got behind the business during the transition and the Clapham Society has helped promote the new location just off the main strip but closer to the local market and Clapham Common. The basement of the shop is still used by the picture framers that once shared the space with a gallery and this arrangement has given the store a secure and affordable base from which to trade for years to come. Roy – one of a small team of booksellers at the store – explains:

"We had a really stressful year when the future of the store was uncertain and we let the stock rundown... This new shop is smaller, but with our future secure we have been able to increase our stock and business has improved since we opened in April (2014)... The local community has really rallied round and are determined to support us and keep their local bookshop rather than buy on-line ..."

The new shop has re-used the shelving from the old premises and now looks smart and modern with a great selection of contemporary fiction complemented by a well-chosen stock covering most important subject areas from London guides to cookery books. There is plenty here to keep the adult reader entertained but one of the shop's main strengths is the large children's section housed in a raised room at the back of the store. The shop hosts a Storytime event every Thursday which is proving popular with young customers.

Margherita is another of the team who started working here as a student but who has continued to be involved and loves the store:

"There are five regulars here and we all have different interests and enthusiasms and that's reflected in our choice of stock. We can't stock everything, but we have a really efficient ordering system in store and have found www.hive.co.uk a great way for people to order on line while supporting their local bookshop".

Clapham Bookshop is still a work in progress and there are lots of plans for improvements to the space as they get settled, but with a long tenancy and a supportive community this shop has a bright future.

There are some great cafés on the street and Venn Market is just around the corner if you visit at the weekend; on fine days Clapham Common offers an excellent place to sit and enjoy your new books. Clapham Books is the sister shop of Herne Hill Books (see page 64).

> The local community
> has really rallied round
> and are determined to
> support us and keep
> their local bookshop
> rather than buy on line"

Clapham Bookshop

Cornerstone

🏠 *299-301 Lavender Hill, SW11 1LN*
☎ *020 7924 2413*
🚌 *Clapham Junction Rail*
🕐 *Mon-Tues & Thurs 9.30am-6pm,*
   Wed 9.30am-1pm, Fri 9.30am-7pm,
   Sat 9.30am-3pm

This is an evangelical Christian bookshop with many books relating to this branch of the Christian faith. They also stock CDs, DVDs and gifts.

Courtauld Gallery Shop

🏠 *Somerset House, Strand,*
   WC2R 0RN
☎ *020 7848 2579*
✐ *www.courtauld.ac.uk*
🚌 *Covent Garden LU, Holborn LU,*
   Temple LU
🕐 *Daily 10am-6pm*

The Courtauld is one of the finest galleries in London with a world class collection of art (most notably Impressionist and Post-Impressionist works) and a busy programme of temporary exhibitions. The main shop at the gallery's entrance offers a wide selection of books on art, art history and culture as well as children's books and London guides. They also stock an attractive choice of postcards, prints, stationery, assorted gifts and souvenirs related to the Courtauld collection. There is a smaller store within the courtyard of Somerset House that stocks titles relevant to the gallery's current exhibitions as well as gifts.

D

Dar Al-Hikma

- 88 Chalton St, NW1 1HJ
- ☎ 020 7383 4037
- www.hikma.co.uk
- Euston LU/Rail
- ☼ Mon-Sat 10am-6pm

A publisher and seller of books in Arabic covering all subjects and all aspects of the Arab world including a selection of books for children. They also stock a range of Arabic-English dictionaries.

Dar Al-Taqwa

- 7A Melcombe Street, NW1 6AE
- ☎ 020 7935 6385
- daral_taqwa@hotmail.com
- Baker Street LU
- ☼ Mon-Sat 10am-7pm

This Islamic bookshop has a huge stock of books in English and Arabic on religion, philosophy, politics, history, art, society and culture, economics, language and travel. There is a range of children's books and also books for Arabic learners. The shop stocks English and Arabic magazines and newspapers, some published in the UK and some imported from the Middle East and the Gulf, as well as gift items.

Darussalam

Darussalam is the largest distributor, wholesaler and retailer of Islamic books and products in the UK. Most of its stock is in English but there are also Arabic, Urdu, Spanish, French, Bengali, Hindi, Albanian, Chinese, Farsi and Pashto volumes.

- 226 High Street, Walthamstow, E17 7JH
- ☎ 020 8520 2666
- www.darussalam.co.uk
- Walthamstow LU
- ☼ Mon-Sat 10am-6pm & Sun 11am-5pm

and

- Regent's Park Mosque,
  146 Park Road, NW8 7RG
- ☎ 020 7725 2246
- www.darussalam.mobi
- Baker Street LU, St John's Wood LU
- ☼ Daily 10am-10.30pm

Daunt Books

DAUNT BOOKS

Daunt Books

✍ www.dauntbooks.co.uk

Having made their reputation as sellers of
travel-related books in Marylebone High
Street, Daunt are now general booksellers
with several atmospheric shops notable
for their literary but accessible character
and enticing displays. All subjects are well
represented but travel remains a particular
strength with sections arranged by country
including guides, travel accounts, history
and literature. Daunt also have very well
chosen and extensive fiction departments
with plenty of reviews on display and
knowledgeable staff to offer advice.

Branches at:

📖 83/84 Marylebone High Street,
W1U 4QW
☎ 020 7224 2295
🚇 Baker Street LU, Bond Street LU,
Regent's Park LU
🕓 Mon-Sat 9am-7.30pm, Sun 11am-6pm

Behind the dark green facade of Daunt's
flagship store is a large and beautifully
designed interior which boasts a balconied
rear room flooded with light from above.
The stunning basement is lined floor to
ceiling with books and scattered with
comfortable chairs. The back of the shop
remains dedicated to travel titles, arranged
by country.

📖 158-164 Fulham Road, SW10 9PR
☎ 020 7373 4997
🚇 South Kensington LU
🕓 Mon-Sat 9am-9pm, Sun 11am-7pm

Pan Bookshop used to occupy these
premises and it's great to see Daunt has
brought a quality independent bookshop
back onto Fulham Road. The store has a
well-chosen general stock and a particularly
good children's department and regularly
hosts literary events and book launches.

📖 112-114 Holland Park Avenue,
W11 4UA
☎ 020 7727 7022
🚇 Holland Park LU
🕓 Mon-Sat 9am-7.30pm, Sun 11am-6pm

Just 100 metres from the tube station,
this is a great branch, with lots of tables
displaying the latest titles, a large travel
section and a welcoming children's area
at the rear. There are lots of cafés in the
area, the best being Cyrano, and Portobello
Market is nearby (see p.211).

📖 193 Haverstock Hill, NW3 4QL
☎ 020 7794 4006
🚇 Belsize Park LU
🕓 Mon-Sat 9am-9pm, Sun 11am-7pm

This is an appealing neighbourhood
bookshop, set in the heart of Belsize
Park's bustling shopping street. Despite
its compact size there is a good choice of
stock and an efficient ordering service.

📖 51 South End Road, NW3 2QB
☎ 020 7794 8206
🚇 Hampstead Heath Rail
🕓 Mon-Sat 9am-6pm, Sun 11am-6pm

This branch carries a good-quality, general
stock but with particular emphasis on
children's books. The picture books are
housed in a beautifully painted grotto with
small chairs and bean bags.

📖 61 Cheapside, EC2V 6AX
☎ 020 7248 1117
🚇 St Paul's LU, Bank LU
🕓 Mon-Fri 8am-7.30pm,
Sat 10am-6pm, Sun 11am-5pm

Behind the deceptively small entrance,
this branch is one of the largest in the
Daunt group. Over its two floors there is a
broad stock with particular strengths being
business and sport. The huge basement
is devoted to fiction and there is also a
substantial travel section.

Davenports

🖃 *7 Charing Cross Underground Arcade, Strand, WC2N 4HZ*
☎ *020 7836 0408*
🖉 *www.davenportsmagic.co.uk*
🚌 *Charing Cross LU/Rail*
🕓 *Mon-Fri 9.30am-5.30pm, Sat 10.30am-4.30pm*

Davenports has produced conjuring equipment and published books on magic since 1898, and over one hundred years later it's still a prime destination for magicians. The huge stock of magic equipment and props caters to beginners and experts alike (the 'Demon Arm-Chopper', anybody?) and the shop carries an equally extensive choice of DVDs and magic books, including many foreign titles. Davenports is located in the underground shopping arcade attached to Charing Cross tube station. The London Society of Magicians meets here every fortnight on Friday evenings.

Design Museum Bookshop

🖃 *28 Shad Thames, SE1 2YD*
☎ *020 7940 8753*
🖉 *www.designmuseum.org*
🚌 *London Bridge LU/Rail, Tower Hill LU*
🕓 *Daily 10am-5.45pm*

This shop, located on the ground floor of the museum, although not enormous, sells a range of books and magazines on design including fashion, architecture and graphic design and there's an interesting and unusual selection of books for children. There are always volumes relating to current exhibitions as well as a brilliant selection of gifts and stationery. In 2016 the Design Museum is going to up sticks from its current site and occupy the fully refurbished Commonwealth Institute building on Kensington High Street. Refer to their website for more information on the move.

Dominion Centre Bookshop

🖃 *9 The Broadway, High Road, Wood Green N22 6DS*
☎ *020 3441 8150*
🖉 *www.dominioncentre.org*
🚌 *Wood Green LU*
🕓 *Mon-Sat 9am-7pm, Sun 1pm-4pm*

A Christian bookshop operated by the Universal Prayer Group Ministries selling books on religion, the Christian life, prayer and worship as well as a range of Christian music.

Donlon Books

🖃 *75 Broadway Market, E8 4PH*
☎ *020 7684 5698*
🖉 *www.donlonbooks.com*
🚌 *London Fields Rail*
🕓 *Sun-Fri 11am-6pm, Sat 10am-6pm*

Donlon Books is a company on the rise among London's art bookshops. This Broadway shop has recently moved one door along to larger premises but still sells a great mix of books, journals and magazines on art, photography, music, counter culture and cultural theory including books by artists. They also stock a more limited selection of rare and hard to find titles. The new store is stylishly decorated with dark shelving, plain wood floors and enticing book displays. Broadway Bookshop (see p.40) and Artwords (see p 16) are both on this road and on Saturdays there's a further bookstall trading from the market.

Dulwich Books

🖼 *6 Croxted Road, SE21 8SW*
☏ *020 8670 1920*
🖥 *www.dulwichbooks.co.uk*
🚃 *West Dulwich Rail*
🕓 *Mon-Sat 9.30am-5.30pm*

This excellent local book store won the 2014 Independent Bookshop of the Year award. They pay a good deal of attention to new publications and display the latest newspaper reviews. The shop offers all the general subject areas you'd expect but is especially strong on art, travel, fiction and cookery as well as having a good children's section with suitably Lilliputian table and chairs. There's also a great selection of greetings cards and audiobooks. Join the e-mail list to receive a regular newsletter and special offers. The store runs a reading group and hosts regular events. La Gastronomia II, is just around the corner and a great place for a post-browse coffee.

Dulwich Picture Gallery

🖼 *Gallery Road, SE21 7AD*
☏ *020 8693 5254*
🖥 *www.dulwichpicturegallery.org.uk*
🚃 *West Dulwich or North Dulwich Rail*
🕓 *Tues-Fri 10am-5pm,*
   Sat-Sun & Bank Hols 10am-5pm

The book and gift shop is located at the exit of this historic south London art gallery designed by Sir John Soane. The shop is small but perfectly formed, stocking a range of books and unique gifts which reflect the DPG's paintings, architectural heritage and exhibition programme. There is also a selection of beautifully illustrated children's books and quirky guides to London and the local area. The garden café/restaurant is a complete delight.

Design Museum Bookshop

E

European Bookshop

⌨ *5 Warwick Street, W1B 5LU*
☎ *020 7734 5259*
✍ *www.europeanbookshop.com*
🚇 *Piccadilly Circus LU*
🕐 *Mon-Fri 9.30am-6.30pm,*
   Sat 10am-6.30pm

This is a gem of a bookshop featuring materials in French, German, Spanish, Russian, Polish, Romanian and Portuguese. They stock fiction and non-fiction books for readers of every level as well as language courses, self-study texts, dictionaries, audio materials and DVDs. In addition there are materials for learning a wide range of other European languages from English. The children's section at the rear of the ground floor is attractive and welcoming. The shop now also incorporates The Italian Bookshop, previously in Cecil Court (see page 68).

F

Farhangsara

⌨ *4 Ashbourne Parade, 1261 Finchley Road,*
   Temple Fortune, NW11 0AD
☎ *020 8455 5550*
✍ *farhangsara@aol.com*
🚇 *Golders Green LU*
🕐 *Daily 9am-11pm*

A specialist Persian book, music and film shop with a selection of CDs, DVDs and books in Farsi and English.

Fielders

⌨ *54 Wimbledon Hill Road, SW19 7PA*
☎ *020 8946 5044*
✍ *www.fielders.co.uk*
🚇 *Wimbledon LU/Rail*
🕐 *Mon-Fri 9am-6pm,*
   Sat 9.30am-5.30pm,
   Sun 11.30-4.30pm

Booksellers in Wimbledon for over seventy years, the Fielders of today is predominantly a well-stocked stationery, art and craft store but with a good selection of art books as well.

The Folio Bookshop

- 44 Eagle Street, WC1R 4FS
- 020 7400 4321
- www.foliosociety.com
- Holborn LU
- Mon-Fri 10am-5pm

Since it was founded just after World War I, The Folio Society has become well known for producing lovely illustrated and limited edition books. Quentin Blake, Vernon Lord and Tom Phillips are among the artists whose work has graced the pages of Folio Society editions. All the publications are designed with great care and printed on fine quality paper in hardback and come with their own slipcase.

The company's bookshop occupies the ground floor of their offices and although it is in a back street close to Red Lion Square and easily missed, it is worth the effort to track down. The shop only sells their own publications but there are books covering most subjects from poetry to history, classic fiction to philosophy, politics and sci-fi. Prices start at around £25 and go up to about £45 for a beautiful edition of Darwin's 'On the Origin of Species'. They also have great boxed sets and a Limited Edition range. The books make wonderful gifts and you can also browse and buy from their website.

Fopp

- 1 Earlham Street, WC2H 9LL
- 020 7845 9770
- www.fopp.com
- Leicester Square LU
- Mon-Wed 10am-10pm,
  Thurs-Sat 10am-11pm,
  Sun 12noon-6.30pm

Fopp are primarily a discount CD and DVD retailer which also offers a more limited range of discounted remainder books. The books comprise only about 10% of the stock, but there are usually some interesting titles with an emphasis on large coffee table tomes and contemporary fiction. This sort of shop might not appeal to traditional book lovers, but with prices starting from just £2 for a literary classic like Karouac's 'On the Road' and plenty of multi-buy deals, Fopp is always worth a visit.

Forbidden Planet – the Cult Entertainment Megastore

- 179 Shaftesbury Avenue,
  WC2H 8JR
- 020 7420 3666
- www.forbiddenplanet.com
- Tottenham Court Road or
  Leicester Square LU
- Mon-Tues 10am-7pm, Thurs till 8pm,
  Wed, Fri-Sat 10am-7.30pm,
  Sun 12noon-6pm

One of a nationwide chain, this is a huge and comprehensively stocked shop specialising in science fiction, fantasy, horror and cult material. The book department is downstairs and has mind-boggling selections in all these areas plus art (including digital, cult, street and fantastical art), counterculture, UFOlogy and books based on role play games. There is also a vast range of comics, graphic novels, manga and DVDs with plenty of rare imported material.

Foyles

🖎 www.foyles.co.uk

Foyles has been a major presence in the London book trade since brothers William and Gilbert opened their first store on Charing Cross Road in 1906. During the reign of William's daughter, Christina Foyle, the store acquired a reputation both for its vast stock and the Byzantine way in which books were categorised and customers were obliged to pay at central tills before returning to collect their books. Since Christina's passing in 1999 the company has changed beyond recognition and has even opened new branches beyond the bounds of Charing Cross Road, which would have seemed inconceivable under the old management. In 2014 the new flagship store was opened by Hilary Mantel in the former home of Central Saint Martins art college, marking the final transformation of the company into one destined to continue the Foyles brand into the 21st century.

🖳 *107 Charing Cross Road, WC2H 0DT*
☎ *020 7434 1574*
🚌 *Tottenham Court Road LU*
🕓 *Mon-Sat 9.30am-9pm, Sun 12noon-6pm (open 11.30am to 12 noon for browsing on Sundays) Public holidays 11am-8pm*

Designed by architects Lifschutz Davidson Sandilands with a lofty central atrium leading to four floors, the new Foyles flagship store remains dedicated to bookselling on a grand scale with over six kilometres of bookshelves and at least 200,000 titles in stock. The new store is a heartening place for any book lover to visit, making a commitment to book selling on the high street in a way that no other company has been able to match. Despite the transformation Foyles' longstanding commitment to holding stock on every conceivable subject remains, the shop for example carries over 200 books about acting and at least 12 titles on boat-building. If all the book hunting gets too much the store also boasts a great café where customers can relax and peruse their latest purchases. The new store is also a major literary venue with a busy itinerary of book launches and readings by major figures such as Haruki Murakami and there are even music events held in the auditorium. William Foyle once declared the store that bears his name to be 'the world's greatest bookshop' and he may well now be right.

Branches at:

🖳 *Royal Festival Hall, Southbank Centre, Riverside, SE1 8XX*
☎ *020 7440 3212*
🚌 *Waterloo LU/Rail*
🕓 *Daily 10am-10pm*

This modern glass-fronted store is compact but has a reasonable stock with particular strengths being fiction and children's books. It's a great place to browse with views across the Thames.

🖳 *Waterloo Station, Unit 22 Lower Concourse, SE1 8SW*
☎ *020 3206 2680*
🚌 *Waterloo LU/Rail*
🕓 *Mon-Sat 7am-9.30pm, Sun 9am-9.30pm*

This is the latest addition to the Foyles' stable, offering customers a good selection of fiction and recent best sellers in preparation for their travels.

🖳 *Westfield Stratford City, 74-75 Lower Ground Floor, E20 1EH*
☎ *020 3206 2671*
🚌 *Stratford LU/Rail*
🕓 *Mon-Fri 10am-9pm, Sat 9am-9pm, Sun 12noon-6pm*

This branch of Foyles remains a literary oasis amid the chaotic consumerism of the Westfield shopping centre.

Foyles, Charing Cross Road

Christina Foyle began working for Foyles aged 17 in 1928, and ran the company from the 1960s until her death in 1999. She left a bookshop displayed by publisher rather than author or subject, and a payment procedure that entailed queuing twice, at two separate tills, to make one purchase, charmed and antagonised the customers in equal measure.

Freedom Press Bookshop

⌨ *Angel Alley,*
84b Whitechapel High Street, E1 7QX
☎ *020 7247 9249*
✑ *www.freedompress.org.uk*
🚌 *Aldgate East LU*
🕐 *Mon-Sat 12noon-6pm,*
Sunday 12noon-4pm

This anarchist publisher's bookshop is located two doors down from the Whitechapel Art Gallery and is reached via a pedestrian alleyway off the main road. It has a huge stock of books (mostly new but with a few second-hand), journals and magazines (including The Freedom Press's own), about every aspect of anarchism including anarchist history, sociology, politics and ecology, with many titles that you won't find elsewhere. They also have an excellent selection of radical postcards on offer.

The French Bookshop

⌨ *28 Bute Street, SW7 3EX*
☎ *020 7584 2840*
✑ *www.frenchbookshop.com*
🚌 *South Kensington LU*
🕐 *Mon-Fri 8.15am-6.30pm,*
Sat 9am-6.30pm

Close to the Institut Français, this shop specialises in French books on almost every subject, including dictionaries, language courses and children's books. There are also extensive selections of French newspapers (supplied on the day of publication), maps, magazines, DVDs, stationery, greetings cards and even French versions of Monopoly and Trivial Pursuit. Another French bookshop, Librairie La Page (see p.56) is around the corner in Harrington Road. Bute Street is awash with lovely little patisseries and coffee shops and now hosts a popular farmers' market on Saturday mornings.

French's Theatre Bookshop

⌨ *52 Fitzroy Street, W1T 5JR*
☎ *020 7255 4300*
✑ *www.samuelfrench-london.co.uk*
🚌 *Warren Street LU*
🕐 *Mon-Fri 10am-6.30pm,*
Sat 11am-5pm

This large, well laid out and welcoming shop stocks scripts (including musicals) and books on every aspect of theatre and performance art. The selection encompasses everything from writing through to auditions and improvisation to performance itself. Here you can find guides to acting, lighting, make-up, costume and stage management as well as books on the great figures of the theatre. There's a folder of audition suggestions for aspiring actors and there are free booklists on all aspects of the stock which are also available on the website. The books are supplemented by DVDs of performances and CDs of musicals and more technical things like voice work.

G

Garden Museum Shop

⌨ *Lambeth Palace Road, SE1 7LB*
☎ *020 7401 8865*
✍ *www.gardenmuseum.org.uk*
🚌 *Lambeth North LU, Westminster LU,*
Vauxhall LU, Waterloo LU/Rail
🕐 *Closed for major refurbishment -*
due to reopen in 2017

The gift shop within this charming specialist museum has acquired a reputation for its extensive and fascinating range of horticultural titles on the history of gardens, writing about gardens, biographies of eminent gardeners and general reference books about plants and gardening. They also sell seeds, cards and gifts related to the museum. The Garden Museum has acquired significant funding for a major refurbishment and will be closed, along with its shop and excellent café until some undisclosed time in 2017. For more information about the museum's transformation and reopening, take a look at their website.

Gay's the Word

⌨ *66 Marchmont Street,*
WC1N 1AB
☎ *020 7278 7654*
✍ *www.gaystheword.co.uk*
🚌 *Russell Square LU*
🕐 *Mon-Sat 10am-6.30pm, Sun 2pm-6pm*

Gay's the Word (est.1979) is London's iconic independent queer bookshop and houses the most comprehensive selection of gay, lesbian and trans books in the UK. GTW has a relaxed and welcoming atmosphere and regularly hosts author events, signings, and group discussions. Stock-wise they have books on everything from lesbian literary fiction to underground 1950s gay erotic art; from pro-diversity children's books to obscure titles about homosexual life in revolutionary Russia. Their non-fiction covers a wide range of issues from cutting-edge queer theory, through to how to tell your mother you are gay. Located two minutes' walk from Russell Square tube, they are a straight-friendly, gay family business that offers a world-wide mail order service. Cards, DVDs and magazines are also available.

Geffrye Museum

⌨ *136 Kingsland Road, E2 8EA*
☎ *020 7739 9893*
✍ *www.geffrye-museum.org.uk*
🚌 *Hoxton Overground*
🕐 *Tues-Sun (& Holiday Mondays) 10am-5pm*

The Geffrye Museum offers a fascinating insight into English interiors through a series of rooms depicting the evolution of interior design over 400 years. At the end of your exploration you will find a book and gift shop covering many of the museum's interests including interior design, architecture, crafts, gardening and London guides and history. The books are carefully chosen and well displayed and the shop also offers a range of notebooks, cards and gift items, some of which relate to the permanent exhibition. The shop is right next to the museum's café and restaurant and there is an incredible herb garden which is open during the spring and summer months.

Stanley Gibbons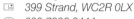

- 399 Strand, WC2R 0LX
- ☎ 020 7836 8444
- www.stanleygibbons.com
- Charing Cross LU/Rail
- Mon-Fri 9am-5.30pm, Sat 9.30am-5.30pm

This famous stamp dealer is the biggest stamp shop in the world with a stock of over 3 million stamps. They also have a large book section devoted to stamp catalogues and new and rare books on philately.

Good News Shop

- 654 High Road, Leyton, E10 6RN
- ☎ 020 8539 2906
- www.goodnewsleyton.co.uk
- Leyton Midland Rail
- Mon-Sat 9am-6.30pm

This award-winning shop specialises in Christian literature including children's books plus Christian music and greetings cards. There is a daily praise and worship service at 8.45am open to all.

Gosh! Comics

- 1 Berwick Street, W1F 0DR
- ☎ 020 7636 1011
- www.goshlondon.com
- Tottenham Court Road LU, Holborn LU
- Daily 10.30am-7pm

There is a huge range of old and new graphic novels, children's books, manga and American comic books on offer in this well-organised store. There's also a rolling programme of signings and events to pique fans' interest.

Greenwich Book Time

- 277 Greenwich High Road, SE10 9NB
- ☎ 020 8293 0096
- Cutty Sark DLR, Greenwich Rail
- Daily 9.30am-9pm

Located in the centre of Greenwich, this shop sells a broad and ever-changing range of discounted new books including fiction, art, cookery, history, biography and children's titles. They are particularly good when it comes to heavyweight coffee table books some of which are sold for a fraction of their original price. A visit at the weekends can be combined with Greenwich Market and Halcyon Books (see p.144) is just along the road.

Guanghwa

- 112 Shaftesbury Avenue, W1D 5EJ
- ☎ 020 7437 3737
- www.guanghwa.com
- Leicester Square LU
- Mon-Sat 10.30am-7pm, Sun 11am-7pm

Located in London's bustling Chinatown district, this bookshop offers an extensive collection of books in Chinese plus dictionaries, materials for adults and children learning Chinese and some books in English on popular Oriental subjects such as Tai Chi, Chinese medicine, martial arts, cookery and Feng Shui. Downstairs is a specialist art department with books on Chinese arts and crafts as well as all the papers, brushes and inks necessary for Chinese painting and calligraphy.

H

Harrods Children's Book Department

🔲 *87 Brompton Road, SW1X 7XL*
☎ *020 7730 1234*
✍ *www.harrods.com*
🚇 *Knightsbridge LU*
🕐 *Mon-Sat 10am-7pm, Sun 11.30am-6pm*
Located on the fourth floor, the Harrods Children's Book Department is vast with all ages catered for from first books up to teenage. They also sell DVDs, CDs and audio books. However, this is clearly a bookshop in which adults buy books for children; many of the shelves are very high, there are no toys, only a few small tables and if you want to browse, it's lucky that the carpet is so thick and plush.

Harrods

🔲 *87 Brompton Road, SW1X 7XL*
☎ *020 7730 1234*
✍ *www.harrods.com*
🚇 *Knightsbridge LU*
🕐 *Mon-Sat 10am-7pm, Sun 11.30am-6pm*
On the third floor of the world famous store (best reached by the hugely kitsch Egyptian Escalator), this large book department in a stunning shop is run by WH Smith. The range of books is extensive, although the arts and design are especially strong. The books are well-displayed, but this being a WH Smith's, there is a focus on bestsellers and little room for independent publications with nearly all books coming from the big publishing houses. To counterbalance the lack of diversity, at least customers get their purchases in a distinctive green and gold Harrods'bag.

Hatchards

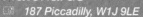

📷 *187 Piccadilly, W1J 9LE*
☎ *020 7439 9921*
✎ *www.hatchards.co.uk*
🚇 *Piccadilly Circus LU*
🕐 *Mon-Sat 9.30am-7pm,*
   Sun 12noon-6pm

John Hatchard founded this bookshop in 1797, making Hatchards the oldest surviving bookshop in London. The store has undergone several changes of ownership since the 1950s and was bought by Waterstones in 2002, but has managed to keep its comforting, refined atmosphere with dark wood panelling and winding oak staircase which connects five floors of books.

Gladstone and Disraeli could agree about very little, but shared a love of Hatchards

The portrait of Mr Hatchard still looks down benignly from the stairs on the ground floor – he would no doubt be pleased to see that traditions are being upheld in the bookshop that bears his name.

The store has a labyrinthine layout with plenty of the nooks and crannies so beloved of book worms and enough seating to encourage a quiet browse. Hatchards is one of London's largest bookshops and holds a stock of over 100,000 titles covering every conceivable subject, all displayed on dark wood shelving that extends floor to ceiling.

Gladstone and Disraeli could agree about very little, but shared a love of Hatchards – later illustrious patrons have included Lord Bryon, Oscar Wilde and Rudyard Kipling. The store is still popular with today's literary fraternity with a busy itinerary of book events and signings – details of which can be found on Hatchard's website.

Hatchards is located next to Fortnum and Mason and opposite the Royal Academy and is the proud holder of three royal warrants. Those wanting to acquire their reading material in the grand style will enjoy visiting this historic bookshop.

Hatchards

📷 *St Pancras International,*
   Euston Road, N1C 4QP
☎ *020 7278 1238*
✎ *www.hatchards.co.uk*
🚇 *St Pancras International Rail*
🕐 *Mon-Sat 7.30am-9pm, Sun 8am-8pm*

The neon Hatchards sign outside this newly established store gives a clue that this is a modern take on London's oldest bookshop. This mix of old and new is continued within the store with Hatchard's traditional circular tables dislaying books alongside contemporary light wood, wall to ceiling shelving and modern concealed lighting.

At 2,000 sq ft and carrying 15,000 books this is a relatively small shop but aims to punch well above its weight with regular deliveries from the flagship Hatchards on Piccadilly, allowing customers to order titles by 3pm, with collection by 5pm on the same day. With so many tourists passing through St Pancras the emphasis here is on paperback fiction, travel guides, children's books and selected gift items, but there is also the good choice of hardbacks for which Hatchards is renowned.

Helios Homeopathic Pharmacy

- 8 New Row, Covent Garden, WC2N 4LJ
- ☎ 020 7379 7434
- ✎ www.helios.co.uk
- 🚇 Leicester Square LU, Covent Garden LU
- ⏱ Mon-Fri 9.30am-5.30pm, Sat 10am-5.30pm

This homeopathic pharmacy sells homeopathic remedies plus a small, specialist selection of books about homeopathy, complementary therapies and health – there's a great range of carefully sourced toiletries as well.

The Hellenic Bookservice

- 89 Fortess Road, NW5 1AD
- ☎ 020 7267 9499
- ✎ www.hellenicbookservice.com
- 🚇 Tufnell Park LU, Kentish Town LU
- ⏱ Mon-Fri 9.30am-5.30pm, Sat 10am-5pm

Specialists in books on anything to do with Greece and Ancient Rome from prehistoric to modern times including titles on art, literature, language, theology, mythology, religion and travel.

Thomas Heneage Art Books

- 42 Duke Street St James's, SW1Y 6DJ
- ☎ 020 7930 9223
- ✎ www.heneage.com
- 🚇 Green Park LU, Piccadilly Circus LU, St James's Park LU
- ⏱ Mon-Fri 9.30am-6pm (or by appointment)

An extensive range of new and out-of-print books on all aspects of art including monographs on individual artists and fine and applied arts worldwide. The stock is colossal, with many items that are unavailable elsewhere. Enthusiasts can join the email list for regular updates about new stock and events. Thomas Heneage is a short walk from the Royal Academy and just across the road from Sims Reed, another specialist art bookseller (see p.108).

Herne Hill Books

- 289 Railton Road, SE24 0LY
- ☎ 020 7998 1673
- ✎ www.hernehillbooks.com
- 🚇 Herne Hill Rail
- ⏱ Mon-Fri 10am-7pm, Sat 10am-6pm, Sun 10am-4pm

Herne Hill Books has been open since August 2009, and is the small but perfectly formed sister of Clapham Books (see p.44); it is situated a stone's throw from Herne Hill train station at the pedestrianised end of Railton Road. The shop offers a condensed choice of eclectic titles echoing that of Clapham and cleverly displays its stock using every inch of available space. The shop has a fantastic selection of fiction, art titles, popular culture, biography, children's books and interesting gifts. The staff are friendly and skilled at researching and ordering hard-to-find and imported books. A treasure trove for the present-seeker, a paradise for the browser.

Heywood Hill

⊞ *10 Curzon Street, W1J 5HH*
☎ *020 7629 0647*
✎ *www.heywoodhill.com*
🚌 *Green Park LU*
🕓 *Mon-Fri 9.30am-6pm, Sat 9.30am-5pm*

Located to the rear of Shepherd Market, off Piccadilly, this is a new, second-hand and antiquarian bookshop combined. The books are stacked on tables, reach from floor to ceiling and spill over every surface. There's a good general stock but the best coverage is in literature, history, biography, travel and children's books. The shop was established in 1936 and retains an old-fashioned, refined air that makes a visit feel like a step back in time. Staff are justifiably proud of their ability to provide recommendations for customers based on their own extensive reading and they issue a list of recommended new titles four times a year. A blue plaque on the front wall testifies to the fact that Nancy Mitford worked here from 1942-1945. Just across the road a covered passageway leads into Shepherd Market where there are plenty of places for refreshment.

The Highgate Bookshop

⊞ *9 Highgate High Street, N6 5JR*
☎ *020 8348 8202*
🚌 *Archway LU*
🕓 *Mon-Sat 10am-6pm, Sun 12noon-5pm*

Situated on the corner of Bisham Gardens, this is a lovely, light, airy local shop serving a literary part of London. The stock is general but extensive and well laid out with plenty of shelf space devoted to the latest titles to keep readers up to date. The children's section at the back is welcoming and staff are friendly and helpful. Waterlow Park and Highgate Cemetery (see p.294) are both easily reached from here. The charity shops on the High Street are also worth a browse.

Hobgoblin

⊞ *24 Rathbone Place, W1T 1JA*
☎ *020 7323 9040*
✎ *www.hobgoblin.com*
🚌 *Tottenham Court Road LU*
🕓 *Mon-Sat 10am-6pm*

Specialist folk music shop selling instruments, CDs, DVDs and a wide range of magazines and printed music for a vast array of instruments including accordion, Celtic harp, pipes, dulcimer and tin whistle. The emphasis is on the traditions of the British Isles but also includes some World Music. The shop carries a huge number of adverts of interest for folk lovers including tuition and events.

Holloway Stationers and Booksellers

⊞ *357 Holloway Road, N7 0RN*
☎ *020 7607 3972*
🚌 *Holloway Road LU*
🕓 *Mon-Fri 9am-6pm, Sat 9.30am-6pm*

This is a stationers which also stocks a good selection of academic titles catering for the student population at the nearby Metropolitan University Campus. There is also a selection of books for children.

Houses of Parliament Shop

⌂ 12 Bridge Street,
 Parliament Square, SW1A 2JX
☎ 020 7219 3890
✐ www.shop.parliament.uk
🚇 Westminster LU
🕒 Mon-Fri 9.30am-5.30pm

Right opposite the Houses of Parliament this is the place to pick up official parliamentary publications including bills, acts, Hansard, Select Committee Reports and the House of Commons papers. The shop also stocks a range of material on UK politics, biographies, the constitution, parliamentary procedure, politics and political history. The store also does a roaring trade in parliamentary gifts such as the mug of UK Prime Ministers and House of Commons branded notebooks.

Housmans

⌂ 5 Caledonian Road, King's Cross, N1 9DX
☎ 020 7837 4473
✐ www.housmans.com
🚇 King's Cross LU/Rail
🕒 Mon-Fri 10am-6.30pm,
 Sat 12noon-6pm, Sun 12noon-6pm

Housmans is London's oldest radical bookshop, having stood at its current premises in the heart of King's Cross since 1945. With its roots in the British pacifist movement the shop offers a unique range of books and periodicals of political interest, taking in current affairs, socialism, anarchism, feminism, ecology and a great deal more besides. Housmans also has a weekly events programme and a well-stocked £1 second-hand basement.

I

I Knit London

⌂ 106 Lower Marsh, SE1 7AB
☎ 020 7261 1338
✐ www.iknit.org.uk
🚇 Waterloo LU/Rail
🕒 Mon, Fri-Sat 10.30am-6pm,
 Tues-Thurs 10.30am-8.30pm

After nearly dying out as a craft, knitting is back in fashion and this shop is a knitter's paradise stocking an enormous and exotic range of wool (the undercoat of the Arctic musk ox included), equipment and patterns to suit enthusiasts at every level. The stock of books is equally diverse and takes in crotchet and other wool crafts alongside knitting. Many of the projects detailed are gorgeous and require a lot of work, but there is something for everyone – a book on knitted toilet roll covers for example. There are knitting groups on Wednesday and Thursday evenings and classes are available.

Indian Bookshelf / Star Books

⌂ Suite 4b, Floor 15, Wembley Point
 1 Harrow Road, Wembley HA9 6DE
☎ 020 8900 2640
✐ www.starbooksuk.com
🚇 Stonebridge Park LU/Rail
🕒 Mon-Fri 9.30am-5pm

This company is a bookseller, library supplier and distributor of English books from India and foreign language books in over 30 languages. They supply books in various Asian, Indic, Middle Eastern (Arabic, Farsi), East European (Polish, Romanian, Latvian, Lithuanian), and West European (French, German, Spanish, Italian, Portuguese) languages. They also publish foreign language dictionaries and bilingual books.

Inner Space

- 36 Shorts Gardens, WC2H 9AB
- ☎ 020 7836 6688
- 🖎 www.innerspace.org.uk
- 🚌 Covent Garden LU
- ○ Mon-Sat 10.30am-6pm
  (Fridays until 5pm)

Based in the heart of bustling, commercial Covent Garden, Inner Space sells books on meditation, personal growth, relationships and relaxation. The store also provides a free Quiet Room, where visitors can practice meditation or simply relax and enjoy some peace and quiet. Also on offer are free courses in meditation, positive thinking, self esteem, and free talks at various locations in London.

The Imperial War Museum Shop

- Lambeth Road, SE1 6HZ
- ☎ 020 7416 5000
- 🖎 www.iwm.org.uk
- 🚌 Lambeth North LU
- ○ Daily 10am-6pm

This large London museum has reopened after a major re-development that includes three new shops, with one specialist shop focusing on books and audio visual titles. The shops have now refocused on all things related to war and the experience of war and the more general guides that formerly graced the bookshop's shelves have now largely gone. The new museum shops now concentrate on both World Wars, more recent global conflicts, warfare on land, sea and air, as well as poetry, autobiography and fiction relating to war. The shop has a particularly good stock of books about wartime life, art, fashion and food in Britain and there is an especially strong Holocaust section.

There are also smaller shops in the IWM's London outposts:

The Churchill Museum and Cabinet War Rooms

- Clive Steps, King Charles Street, SW1A 2AQ

Strong on Churchill.

HMS Belfast

- Morgan's Lane, Tooley Street, SE1 2JH

Strong on naval material.

HMS Belfast

Institute of Contemporary Arts Bookshop

The Mall, SW1Y 5AH
020 7766 1452
www.ica.org.uk/shop
Charing Cross LU, Piccadilly Circus LU
Tues-Sun 11am-9pm

Founded in 1947, the ICA is at the cutting edge of the contemporary arts scene in London. The bookshop occupies an area in the ICA foyer, offering a stock that concentrates on contemporary culture and ideas. Here you will find the latest books about art theory, radical politics, cinema, philosophy and feminism, as well as promotions related to the ICA's current programme. They also offer a great choice of magazines, DVDs and even greetings cards. Towards the back of the building the ICA has a great café where you can relax and browse your latest acquisitions.

Italian Bookshop ②

5 Warwick Street, W1B 5LU
020 7240 1634
www.italianbookshop.co.uk
Leicester Square LU
Mon-Fri 9.30am-6.30pm,
Sat 10am-6.30pm

An outpost of the language specialist European Bookshop (see p.52) featuring a superb stock of books in Italian, this is the only Italian bookshop in the country. Students of Italian are also well-served here as the shop specialises in learning materials for children and adults from the very first stages to advanced. There is also a selection of Italian DVDs and some books in English about Italy.

Jamyang Buddhist Centre

J

Jamyang Buddhist Centre

⊡ *The Old Courthouse,*
43 Renfrew Road, SE11 4NA
☎ *020 7820 8787*
✍ *www.jamyang.co.uk*
🚌 *Kennington LU, Elephant & Castle LU*
🕘 *Mon-Fri 10am-5pm*

Inside this converted courthouse can be found books on all aspects of Buddhism including Buddhist thought and philosophy, biography and art. There are also beautiful cards, gifts, statues, posters, religious hangings and crafts from Asia. The Courtyard Café at the Centre serves delicious meals and snacks.

Japan Centre Bookshop

⊡ *19 Shaftesbury Ave,*
W1D 7ED
☎ *020 3405 1246*
✍ *www.japancentre.com*
🚌 *Piccadilly Circus LU*
🕘 *Mon-Sat 10am-9.30pm, Sun 11am-8pm*

This store offers an extensive range of books and magazines in Japanese and also a selection of books in English about Japan, as well as Japanese literature in translation.

Jerusalem the Golden

⊡ *146-148 Golders Green Road,*
NW11 8HE
☎ *020 8455 4960*
✍ *www.jerusalemthegolden.com*
🚌 *Golders Green LU*
🕘 *Sun-Thurs 9.30am-6.30pm,*
Fri 9.30am-2.30pm

A long-established specialist bookseller of books in English and Hebrew on all aspects of Jewish life and religion, gifts, silverware and religious items.

Joseph's Bookstore

⌨ 2 Ashbourne Parade,
 1257 Finchley Road, Temple Fortune,
 NW11 0AD
☎ 020 8731 7575
✍ www.josephsbookstore.com
🚌 Golders Green LU
🕓 Mon-Fri 9.30am-6.30pm,
 Sun 10am-5pm (closed Saturdays)

As well as being a publisher, Joseph's is also a lovely local bookshop with a pleasant atmosphere and an en-suite café. Joseph's features a good general stock alongside a broad choice of Jewish interest titles, many sold at a discount. Magazines and a selection of original art are also on sale here. Events are organised in the bookshop and there's a noticeboard with details of other goings-on in the area. Readers can join an email list to receive a monthly mailing about upcoming events.

Judd Books

⌨ 82 Marchmont Street,
 WC1N 1AG
☎ 020 7387 5333
✍ www.juddbooks.com
🚌 Russell Square LU
🕓 Mon-Sat 11am-7pm, Sun 12noon-6pm

See p.150.

K

Karnac Books

⌨ 118 Finchley Road, NW3 5HT
☎ 020 7431 1075
✍ www.karnacbooks.com
🚌 Finchley Road LU
🕓 Mon-Fri 9.30am-6pm, Sat 10am-6pm

A huge, largely academic stock concentrating on psychology, psychotherapy, psychoanalysis and related fields. This long-established company also publishes books and translations in these fields, for which it has an international reputation. Every 4 to 6 months 'The Karnac Review' details new publications that might be of interest to customers.

Kensington Chimes Music

⌨ 9 Harrington Road, SW7 3ES
☎ 020 7589 9054
✍ www.chimesmusic.com
🚌 South Kensington LU
🕓 Mon-Sat 9am-5.30pm

The sister shop of Barbican Chimes (see p.18), this is a one of the largest music shops in London and jammed full of classical and modern music scores for every instrument at every level. The shop also stocks books on all aspects of music and is a friendly place for music lovers to browse with classical music playing in the background and approachable staff on hand for help and advice. The store also offers a selection of music-related gift items.

Judd Books

ALL BOOKS
£1.95
AND UNDER

Kew Bookshop

⌗ *1-2 Station Approach*
Richmond, Surrey ,TW9 3QB
☎ *020 8940 0030*
🖉 *www.kewbookshop.co.uk*
🚌 *Kew Gardens LU*
🕘 *Mon-Sat 9.30am-5.30pm,*
Sun 11am-5pm

The Kew Bookshop is adjacent to Kew Gardens tube station, and is part of a delightful parade of independent shops. The shop is well laid out and makes the most of its space. Since the demise of The Lion & Unicorn, a well-known children's bookshop in the area, Kew Bookshop supplies books for many local schools and nearly half the store is now dedicated to children's books and toys and the staff are particularly knowledgeable in this area. In both the adult and children's sections there is a wealth of staff reviews to consult and you are guaranteed to find some unusual books not necessarily stocked elsewhere. This is a quirky little shop with well-informed and helpful staff which is definitely worth a visit, especially if you are visiting Kew Gardens. Kew Bookshop has two sister stores, Barnes Bookshop (see p.21) and Sheen Bookshop (see p.107).

Kirkdale Bookshop and Gallery

⌗ *272 Kirkdale, SE26 4RS*
☎ *020 8778 4701*
🖉 *www.kirkdalebookshop.com*
🚌 *Sydenham Rail & Overground*
🕘 *Mon-Fri 9.30am-6pm,*
Sat 9am-5.30pm, Sun 12noon-3pm

A glorious local bookshop and art gallery that has been on this site since 1966. Visitors can read the paper and have a cup of tea or coffee. The book stock is pretty evenly split between new, second-hand and out of print books and the basement is a treasure trove for browsers. Second-hand prices are keen, and there is a large bargain selection outside starting from 40p. Naxos classical CDs, cards and gifts are also on sale. A book and writers' groups meet here, there's a Saturday morning storytime for children and they also run a loyalty card scheme. As if all this wasn't enough, Kirkdale also has a gallery which hosts a programme of exhibitions by local artists.

Koenig Books

🖎 *www.koenigbooks.co.uk*

This specialist modern art bookseller has three bases in the capital – all in excellent locations. The shops are attractive, well-stocked and the staff are knowledgeable and enthusiastic. Contemporary art, photography, design, architecture, theory and criticism are among the areas covered and all the shops stock full price books as well as remaindered titles. Branches at:

🔲 *80 Charing Cross Road,*
WC2H 0BB
☎ *020 7706 4907*
🚌 *Leicester Square LU*
🕒 *Mon-Sat 10am-8pm, Thurs to 9pm*
Sun 11am-6pm

The small ground floor displays a fabulous stock of newly published, up-to-the-minute art books and magazines and catalogues for current exhibitions. The more extensive basement is no less covetable with an excellent stock of remainder books on all aspects of art at competitive prices.

Koenig at the Serpentine Gallery

🔲 *Kensington Gardens, W2 3XA*
☎ *020 7706 4907*
🖎 *www.serpentinegallery.org*
🚌 *South Kensington LU, Lancaster Gate LU*
🕒 *Daily 10am-6pm (closed Monday in the winter months) – the bookshop remains open in the periods between exhibitions when the gallery is closed*

The Serpentine Gallery is located in the heart of Kensington Gardens and specialises in modern and contemporary art. The bookshop reflects this with a carefully curated stock of art books and magazines.

Koenig at the Whitechapel Gallery

🔲 *Whitechapel Gallery,*
80-82 Whitechapel High Street, E1 7QX
☎ *020 7522 7897*
🖎 *www.whitechapelgallery.org*
🚌 *Aldgate East LU*
🕒 *Tues-Sun 11am-6pm (Thurs until 9pm)*

This branch offers a great selection of books on art from the 1960's onwards. There's always a big display of material that relates to current shows in the gallery and a consistently fine selection of art magazines and postcards.

Krypton Komics

🔲 *94 Blackhorse Lane, E17 6AA*
☎ *020 8527 7558*
🖎 *www.keycomics.com or www.kryptonkomics.com*
🚌 *Blackhorse Road LU*
🕒 *Tues 10am-2.20pm, Wed-Sat 10am-6pm, closed Wed-Fri 2.20pm-3.30pm*

A colossal range of American comics from 1945 to the present with over 10,000 titles available and more than a quarter of a million comics listed on the website with prices from £2 upwards.

L

Librairie La Page

⌨ *7 Harrington Road, SW7 3ES*
☎ *020 7589 5991*
✎ *www.librairielapage.com*
🚌 *South Kensington LU*
🕐 *Mon-Fri 8.15am-6.30pm,*
Sat 9am-6.30pm
(shorter times during the French Lycée
holidays – ring to check)

Selling a fine assortment of mostly new and some second-hand French books, this small but well-stocked shop is especially strong on literature and the social sciences, but also stocks a range of French cookbooks, graphic novels and travel guides. Their great selection of children's books resides in a dedicated section at the back, which is furnished with a tiny table and chairs. The store hosts a monthly kid's book club for those aged 8-10 years old who want to learn French, and a Saturday Club for younger Francophiles aged between 3 and 5. Magazines, cards, CDs and DVDs plus a basement packed with Clairefontaine stationery and a noticeboard for local news complete the attractions of this lovely shop. The French Bookshop (see p.56) is just around the corner on Bute Street, as are plenty of cafés and patisseries.

London Buddhist Centre

⌨ *51 Roman Road, E2 0HU*
☎ *020 8981 1225*
✎ *www.lbc.org.uk*
🚌 *Bethnal Green LU*
🕐 *Mon-Fri 10am-5pm*

A specialist Buddhist bookshop with a small selection of about one hundred titles on Buddhism from most traditions. There are also meditation stools and cushions, statues, malas and cards. The Centre runs a range of courses, classes and retreats – contact them for information. Their second-hand bookshop, Jambala, is around the corner (see below) as is The Larder Restaurant for refreshment.

Jambala

⌨ 247 Globe Road, Bethnal Green, E2
☎ *020 8981 1225*
✎ *www.jambalacharityshop.com*
🚌 *Bethnal Green LU*
🕐 *Mon-Fri 11am-6pm, Sat 10am-6pm*
(Ring to check)

This is the second-hand bookshop attached to the London Buddhist Centre (see above), which sells a great selection of books and vinyl.

London City Mission Bookshop

⌨ *175 Tower Bridge Road, SE1 2AH*
☎ *020 7407 7585*
✎ *www.lcm.org.uk*
🚌 *London Bridge LU/Rail, Tower Hill LU*
🕐 *Mon-Fri 9am-3.30pm*

A small selection of books on Christianity and theology are available in the reception area of the Mission. Greetings cards are also on sale.

Lutyens & Rubinstein Bookshop

The London Review Bookshop

- 14 Bury Place, WC1A 2JL
- 020 7269 9030
- www.londonreviewbookshop.co.uk
- Tottenham Court Road LU, Holborn LU
- Mon-Sat 10am-6.30pm, Sun 12noon-6pm

In 2003 the team behind the highly esteemed literary publication, 'The London Review of Books', decided to open a bookshop. They found the perfect location just around the corner from their Bloomsbury offices and a great deal of thought was put into getting the new shop to look and feel just right. The final, simple, open-plan style of the shop is the work of the late Peter Campbell who designed many of the covers for the LRB over the years, and the high shelves, large pendant ceiling lights and plain wood floors still look good today despite the wear and tear of many years of successful trading.

David Lea has been one of the team of managers here since the shop opened and is acutely aware of the importance of atmosphere:

"The key thing is making the physical shop a nice place to visit, making it a different experience from shopping on the internet ... Here there are informed people to talk to and good books to look at and handle."

Manager Natalia Della Ossa and David work with four other full-time booksellers to provide an excellent service offering plenty of advice when required and a well-chosen stock of fiction, history, biography, politics, travel and probably one of the best poetry sections in the country. The London Review of Books is one of the world's leading literary publications, so it is no surprise that this shop is very aware of the latest releases and always has fascinating displays and recommendations. There is a great deal to keep the visitor entertained on the ground floor of the store, but it is worth remembering that they also have a large and well-stocked basement which is sometimes missed by the uninitiated.

> " *The key thing is making the physical shop a nice place to visit, making it a different experience from shopping on the internet...Here there are informed people to talk to and good books to look at and handle*"

The bookshop hosts about two literary events every week including book signings, poetry readings and book launches. The shop also has a wonderful café which is always busy and which serves delicious food and an extensive choice of teas and coffee. The café is a favourite meeting place for London-based publishers and authors, and many books have been commissioned over lunch in these elegant surroundings. It's a welcoming place to relax and peruse your bookshop purchases.

London Transport Museum Shop

🏠 *Covent Garden Piazza,*
   WC2E 7BB
☎ *020 7379 6344*
✎ *www.ltmuseum.co.uk*
🚌 *Covent Garden LU*
🕐 *Sun-Tues 10am-6.30pm,*
   Wed-Thurs & Sat 10am-7pm,
   Fri 11am-7pm

Reflecting the content of the museum, this shop sells books, magazines and DVDs covering most aspects of transport in the kind of detail that should satisfy the most pedantic train spotter with many titles from specialist publishers such as Aurum, Capital Transport, Oxford Publishing Company, Ian Allan and Middleton Press. The emphasis is British, but there is also some overseas material. For those with a more general interest there are London guides and a huge and fabulous selection of posters, cards and gifts. The London souvenirs here are among the most attractive to be found anywhere in the city, although a few veer towards the weird – London Underground map boxer shorts anyone?

Lutyens & Rubinstein Bookshop

🏠 *21 Kensington Park Road, W11 2EU*
☎ *020 7229 1010*
✎ *www.lutyensrubinstein.co.uk*
🚌 *Ladbroke Grove LU, Notting Hill Gate LU*
🕐 *Mon & Sat 10am-6pm,*
   Tues-Fri 10am-6.30pm, Sun 11am-5pm

For many years literary agents Sarah Lutyens and Felicity Rubinstein harboured dreams of owning their own bookshop. In 2009 they bought a former lingerie store and employed architects De Rosee Sa to create a space that could double as offices and a modern bookshop.

The result is a stylish mix of high, dark wood shelves with lower display units, clever lighting, a raised level for children's books and a spiral staircase that leads to a subterranean space dedicated to adult fiction. The really clever feature is the sliding bookshelves that conceal the offices of the agency and can be moved Bond movie style to create a larger space for literary events and readings.

The shop's lighting and use of space are really effective and they also have beautiful book sculptures which hang from the high ceiling and also regularly feature in the changing window display. Above all, Lutyens & Rubinstein offers a well-chosen stock of fiction, biography and popular reference titles, a good children's section as well as poetry and art books. The staff are an important part of the shop's appeal and they go out of their way to offer recommendations and order books quickly when not in stock.

Claire Harris is the manager here and her phenomenal appetite for reading has been put to good use in the 'Year in Books' gift scheme. Customers give Claire some idea of the favoured reading matter of the recipient and she uses her

Lutyens & Rubinstein Bookshop

knowledge to send them an appropriate book every month for a year. Her intuition is uncanny and the scheme has developed and acquired a loyal group of regular subscribers sending books across the world.

Notting Hill is popular with tourists, particularly on market days, but the majority of Lutyens & Rubinstein's customers are locals and really make an effort to support the shop. Tara, who takes responsibility for the children's section, explains:

"Our local customers are very supportive. I think it's because Elgin Books – which closed about ten years ago – was just around the corner, and people really remember how awful it was to lose a bookshop ..."

The fact that this is a new venture and has a successful company behind the bookshop, gives the place an incredible sense of optimism. Felicity Rubenstein comes up from her office and gives a very positive view of the future of books in the world of Amazon and Kindle :

"In the history of publishing every time a new format has come out everybody has wrung their hands and said 'oh the paperback will kill the industry, ahh book clubs, that's the death of the bookshop!' but that isn't the case, it just expands the ways in which people can read ..."

This optimistic and fresh approach to bookselling is most welcome and makes this a shop well worth going out of your way to visit. Their website is also a useful resource and gives information about the shop's busy itinerary of events and readings.

M

Maghreb Bookshop

▢ 45 Burton Street,
WC1H 9AL

☎ 020 7388 1840

✎ www.maghrebbookshop.com

🚌 Euston & King's Cross LU/Rail,
Russell Square LU

🕐 Opening hours vary, ring before visiting

A tiny shop specialising in new, rare and out of print books on the Maghreb countries of North Africa (Tunisia, Algeria, Libya, Morocco and Mauritania), the Arab World and Islam. Many of the books are unavailable elsewhere – the shop claims 'here you can find the unfindable'. They also offer a worldwide mail order service.

Magma

✎ www.magma-shop.com

These compact spaces stock a top-notch range of cutting edge design, photography, illustration, contemporary art (including street art), graphics, animation, media and architecture books plus magazines, DVDs, stationery, t-shirts and multi-media materials. Their product store, at 16 Earlham Street (tel: 020 7240 7571) has a selection of funky and desirable gift items.

Branches at:

▢ 117-119 Clerkenwell Road, EC1R 5BY

☎ 020 7242 9503

🚌 Farringdon LU/Rail, Chancery Lane LU

🕐 Mon-Sat 10am-7pm

▢ 29 Shorts Gardens,
WC2H 9AP

☎ 020 7240 7970

🚌 Covent Garden LU

🕐 Mon-Sat 10am-7pm, Sun 12noon-6pm

Magma, Covent Garden

Maison Assouline

⌗ *196A Piccadilly, W1J 9EY*
☏ *020 3327 9370*
🖋 *www.assouline.com*
🚇 *Piccadilly LU*
🕐 *Mon-Sat 10am-8pm, Sun 10am-7pm*

Assouline describes itself as 'the first luxury brand on culture' and its publications as 'the most sophisticated books in the world'. Their new flagship store on Piccadilly was launched with the help of several Hollywood A-listers and a great deal of Krug Champagne in the autumn of 2014. Now Londoners can enjoy the 'world of Assouline', where 'sophisticated' means big, colourful and expensive – most of their books are large coffee table tomes costing upwards of £40. The collection of antiques upstairs is limited and expensive. The café menu is limited and expensive. The range of books for sale is limited and expensive. If you have the cash and want to buy into the concept of building a 'luxury library', this store is a welcome addition to London's literary landscape.

Manor House Books / John Trotter Books

⌗ *80 East End Road, Finchley, N3 2SY*
☏ *020 8349 9484*
🖋 *www.manorhousebooks.co.uk*
🚇 *Finchley Central LU*
🕐 *Mon-Thurs 9am-4.30pm;*
Other times by appointment

A small but extremely well-stocked specialist shop selling academic Jewish and Middle East interest books, with around 5,000 new and over 20,000 rare and second-hand titles. The shop has a café and there is also free parking outside.

Manna Christian Centre

⌗ *147-149 Streatham High Road,*
SW16 6EG
☏ *020 8769 8588*
🖋 *www.mannachristiancentre.co.uk*
🚇 *Streatham Rail*
🕐 *Mon-Fri 9.45am-5.45pm,*
Sat 9.45am-5.30pm

A shop specialising in Christian material including books on theology, prayer, scripture and the Christian way of life. It also has a children's department.

Maison Assouline

Maritime and Insurance Books

🖳 *Unit 11 The High Cross Centre,*
Fountayne Road, N15 4QN
☏ *020 8275 4295*
🖋 *www.mandibooks.com*
🚇 *Tottenham Hale LU/Rail*
🕓 *Mon-Fri 9am-5pm*

A specialist shipping, marine, insurance and risk management bookseller offering an extensive range of professional books in these areas. Established in the City of London since 1740, when one Thomas Witherby opened a stationery shop, the business has moved from the City in recent years and is now primarily a mail order company – but visitors to the shop are welcome.

Maritime Books

🖳 *66 Royal Hill, SE10 8RT*
☏ *020 8692 1794*
🖋 *www.navalandmaritimebooks.com*
🚇 *Greenwich Rail/DLR*
🕓 *Wed-Sat 10am-6pm*

A specialist shop carrying 12,000-15,000 books including full-price, remainder, second-hand, and antiquarian books on all things maritime. This is the only shop with this specialism in London. It's a short walk from the town centre in Greenwich but definitely worth the trip if the sea is your thing.

Marylebone Books

🖳 *35 Marylebone Road, NW1 5LS*
🖋 *www.marylebonebooks.co.uk*
☏ *020 7911 5049*
🚇 *Baker Street LU*
🕓 *Mon-Thurs 9.30-6.30pm,*
Fri 9.30am-5.30pm
(Opening times vary at the start of
semesters and in vacations. Ring before
making a special journey.)

Located in the courtyard of the main University of Westminster campus, this independent bookshop only stocks academic titles relevant to the university's courses. Subjects covered include business, law, management, economics, construction, surveying, architecture and planning. Non University of Westminster customers need to report to Reception from where they will be escorted to the shop.

Branch at:

🖳 *115 New Cavendish Street, W1W 6UW*
☏ *020 7915 5432*
🚇 *Goodge Street LU, Regent's Park LU*
🕓 *Mon-Thurs 9.30-6.30pm,*
Fri 9.30am-5.30pm
(Opening times vary at the start of
semesters and in vacations. Ring before
making a special journey.)

Mega-City Comics

🖳 *18 Inverness Street, NW1 7HJ*
☏ *020 7485 9320*
🖋 *www.megacitycomics.co.uk*
🚇 *Camden Town LU*
🕓 *Daily 10am-6pm, Thurs to 7pm*

Situated in the Inverness Street Market just north of Camden Town tube station, this store features comics and a range of graphic novels, with a considerable selection of imported titles and back issues. The website contains a vast listing of material that simply won't fit into the shop and they claim to have the largest selection of back issues in London.

Mesoirah Books

⌧ *61-63 Oldhill Street, N16 6LU*
☎ *020 8809 4310*
🚌 *Stoke Newington Rail*
🕓 *Sun-Thurs 10am-9pm,*
   Fri 10am-3pm (1pm in winter)

Located at the Clapton Common end of Oldhill Street, this is a specialist Jewish bookseller whose stock includes books in Hebrew and English.

Mind Chakra

⌧ *4a Castletown Road, W14 9HE*
☎ *020 7386 8678*
✎ *www.mindchakra.com*
🚌 *West Kensington LU*
🕓 *Wed-Thurs 12noon-7pm, Fri 12noon-6pm,*
   Sat-Sun 11am-6pm

A specialist in books about the Indian subcontinent in English as well as books in Indian languages with a particular emphasis on Sanskrit. Music and dance also features strongly in the book stock, which is supplemented by music CDs, some instruments and artefacts. In recent years the focus has broadened to include books concerning Indian art, philosophy and spirituality, as well as offering a selection of Indian art. Mind Chakra is located next to the Institute of Indian Art and Culture which has a small art gallery and reference library (see p.242).

The Mosaic Rooms Bookshop

⌧ *Tower House*
   226 Cromwell Road, SW5 0SW
☎ *020 7370 9990*
✎ *www.mosaicrooms.org*
🚌 *Earl's Court LU*
🕓 *Tues-Sat 11am-6pm*
   (during exhibitions only)

The Mosaic Rooms is an exhibition space funded by the AM Qattan Foundation which promotes the culture of the Middle East. The organisation's bookshop is open in conjunction with exhibitions and stocks work by a carefully chosen selection of up-and-coming as well as established writers from the region as well as art books and films in both English and Arabic. Outside exhibition times their stock can be viewed and purchased via their excellent website.

Museum of Childhood Shop

⌨ *Cambridge Heath Road,*
   South Bethnal Green, E2 9PA
☎ *020 8983 5200*
✑ *www.vandashop.com*
🚇 *Bethnal Green LU*
🕓 *Daily 10am-5.30pm daily*

The Museum of Childhood shop in Bethnal Green carries over 200 children's titles as well as books relating to the collection. It is a shop that encourages reading and play and also stocks a great range of children's gifts and toys.

The Museum of London

⌨ *London Wall, EC2Y 5HN*
☎ *020 7814 5600*
✑ *www.museumoflondon.org.uk*
🚇 *St Paul's LU or Barbican LU*
🕓 *Daily 10am-6pm*

London's history is of course the raison d'être of this enjoyable museum. The shop unsurprisingly carries a range of books for adults and children concentrating on the city's history from Celtic, Roman and Viking times up to the present day including social history, art and architecture, food, fashion and transport. London-based fiction also features, as do specialist titles published by the Museum of London and the Museum of London Archaeology Service. There's a section concentrating on the history of the London suburbs, so it isn't all about the centre of the city. As well as books the shop offers a great selection of gifts and souvenirs.

The Museum of London Docklands

⌨ *No 1 Warehouse, West India Quay,*
   E14 4AL
☎ *020 7001 9844*
✑ *www.museumindocklands.org.uk*
🚇 *West India Quay DLR*
🕓 *Daily 10am-6pm*

The emphasis in this bookshop is the same as that of the museum, namely the story of London's river, port and people from pre-Roman times through to the recent regeneration of the Docklands area. The book stock includes both adult and children's titles and takes in the Thames, local history, shipping, pirates, slavery, engineering and trade as well as a more general selection of London guides.

Musicroom

⌨ *11 Denmark Street, WC2H 8TD*
☎ *020 7632 3950*
✑ *www.musicroom.com*
🚇 *Tottenham Court Road LU*
🕓 *Mon-Fri 10am-7.30pm, Sat 10am-6pm,*
   Sun 11am-5pm

Located in a street dedicated to music, this shop specialises in sheet music, mostly modern, plus books on contemporary music. Stock includes biographies as well as recording and production manuals for both analogue and digital technologies.

Museum of Childhood

Muswell Hill Bookshop

⌗ *72 Fortis Green Road, N10 3HN*
☎ *020 8444 7588*
✐ *www.muswellhillbookshop.com*
🚇 *Highgate LU, East Finchley LU*
🕒 *Mon-Sat 9.30am-6pm, Sun 11am-4pm*

In the main Muswell Hill shopping drag and opposite the Children's Bookshop (see p.43), this shop has recently down-sized but is still extremely well-stocked. It offers a wide selection of fiction and its reference books range across many academic subject areas, including philosophy, politics, cultural studies and psychology. Accompanying the books is a good selection of cards and stationery and the store also offers a community notice board as well as occasional literary events. The staff produce a weekly Top Ten List of new books which is always interesting reading.

Mysteries

⌗ *9-11 Monmouth Street,*
WC2H 9DA
☎ *020 7240 3688*
✐ *www.mysteries.co.uk*
🚇 *Leicester Square LU*
🕒 *Mon-Sat 10am-7pm, Sun 1pm-6pm*

A shop specialising in mind, body and spirit titles with an excellent range of books covering spirituality, personal development, meditation, dreams and symbols, yoga, health, numerology, palmistry, Tarot, Buddhism, astrology, shamanism and magic, among a great many other subjects. There are also CDs and DVDs for hypnosis, meditation and yoga plus huge numbers of accessories and gift items. Psychic readings using different media are available, as are a range of classes.

N

The National Gallery

- *Trafalgar Square, WC2N 5DN*
- *General 020 7747 2885,*
  Main shop 020 7747 5958
- *www.nationalgallery.org.uk*
- *Charing Cross LU/Rail*
- *Daily 10am-5.45pm*
  (Friday until 8.45pm)

The main shop of the National Gallery is vast and given due prominence at the at the main entrance of the museum's Sainsbury Wing. The range of books is excellent and includes guides to the collection, exhibition catalogues and gift books, with sections on individual artists, art history, conservation, art theory, museum studies, architecture and sculpture. Thames and Hudson, Phaidon, and Taschen publications are much in evidence. The shop also stocks magazines, DVDs, children's art books and London guides. Inspired by the gallery's permanent collection of paintings, as well as its temporary exhibitions, the store also has displays of jewellery, homewares, postcards, prints and stationery.

There are two other smaller shops in the gallery; one at Level 2 near the main entrance and one by the Getty entrance. However, neither have anywhere near the extensive book stock of the main shop. The best place for refreshment in situ is the National Gallery Café which can be accessed from the gallery or directly from St Martin's Place, and which serves good food and boasts one of the best views in London.

National Geographic

- *102 Brompton Road,*
  SW3 1JJ
- *020 7589 4583*
- *www.nglondonstore.co.uk*
- *Knightsbridge LU*
- *Mon-Wed 11am-8pm,*
  Thurs-Sat 9am-9pm, Sun 12noon-6pm

This is one of National Geographic's very few retail stores. It has pretty much everything for the traveller from travel books to travel gear, cameras and binoculars plus artefacts, jewellery and household items from near and far. The book selection is limited to National Geographic publications but these are extensive, occupying four shelving units at the back of the store. National Geographic travel guides cover most countries of the world and they also publish glossy books of their renowned travel photography. The store has an excellent café where you can enjoy your purchases over a cappuccino.

The National Maritime Museum

- *Park Row, SE10 9NF*
- *020 8858 4422*
- *www.rmg.co.uk*
- *Cutty Sark DLR*
- *Daily 10am-5pm*

This museum is dedicated to the adventure and drama of Britain's seafaring past. The gift shop features a selection of books for adults and children on all things maritime including exploration, the history of the navy and slavery, as well as more general titles. If books about the sea are your thing then nearby Maritime Books (see p.82), is also worth a look.

The National Portrait Gallery Bookshop ②

🏛 St Martin's Place, WC2H 0HE
☎ 020 7306 0055 ext 311
✎ www.npg.org.uk
🚌 Charing Cross LU/Rail,
   Leicester Square LU
🕓 Daily 10am-6pm, Thurs & Fri until 9pm

The prominent gift shop on the ground floor also sells a limited range of books, but the majority of book stock is displayed in the basement bookshop. Here they offer an extensive selection of art, history, costume, photography books and magazines in addition to the best selection of books on portraiture in London. There's also a good choice of children's books and gallery publications. The Portrait Café next door to the shop is an ideal place to rest weary feet and enjoy your purchases.

National Theatre Bookshop

🏛 South Bank, SE1 9PX
☎ 020 7452 3456
✎ www.shop.nationaltheatre.org.uk
🚌 Waterloo LU/Rail
🕓 Mon-Sat 9.30am-10.45pm,
   Sun 12noon-6pm

The bookshop at the National Theatre has always been a favourite haunt for thespians and those interested in the theatre, with a great range of play texts and DVDs of live performances. The shop has recently undergone a major refurbishment, moving to a more central location within the National Theatre and now becoming open plan, allowing visitors to browse in the main foyer of the theatre. The new design of the shop allows gifts, London guides and other items on promotion to take pride of place, but the number of serious theatre books and plays has not declined and occupies a large and continuous wall of shelving at the back of the shop. A store definitely worth visiting on the South Bank and very close to the Southbank Book Market (see p.212).

National Theatre Bookshop

The Natural History Museum Shop

- Cromwell Road, SW7 5BD
- 020 7942 5360
- www.nhmshop.co.uk
- South Kensington LU
- Daily 10am-5.50pm

The main shop of this renowned museum is close to the Cromwell Road entrance. Alongside all the usual museum gifts there is a selection of books for adults and children on subjects relevant to the museum including evolution, dinosaurs, geology and the whole of the plant and animal kingdoms. There are also a few books to be found at the other smaller retail outlets in the museum which include a specific dinosaur shop at the exit to the Dinosaur Gallery.

New Beacon Books

- 76 Stroud Green Road, N4 3EN
- 020 7272 4889
- www.newbeaconbooks.co.uk
- Finsbury Park LU
- Mon-Sat 1.30pm-6pm

A long-established and highly experienced specialist seller of new books on Black Britain and Europe, Africa, the Caribbean and African America. They also have plenty of titles on Asia, the Middle East and South America and well-stocked sections on cultural and women's studies. Fiction and non-fiction titles are sold here and there is a great children's section. The staff are knowledgeable, can produce specialist book lists to cater for individual interests and offer a worldwide mail order service. Cards and magazines are sold and there's information on events of interest.

Newham Bookshop

- 745-747 Barking Road, E13 9ER
- 020 8552 9993
- www.newhambooks.co.uk
- Upton Park LU
- Tues-Fri 9.30am-5pm, Sat 10am-5pm

Established in 1978, just around the corner from West Ham football ground, this bookshop is a real treasure. Its general stock includes excellent fiction, poetry and drama sections and in non-fiction it is strong on history, London history (for which it is especially renowned), social work, counselling, sociology, sport (especially football), education, business, multi-ethnic issues, and politics. The children's section takes up about half the shop with books for babies to teens and lots of educational literature, as well as welcoming little chairs for small visitors. Newham bookshop hosts events and readings and has recently helped launch a new book market – Book Wood Fair (see p.207). Over the years this friendly bookshop has acquired legions of fans, the poet Benjamin Zephaniah among them.

Nomad Books

- 781 Fulham Road, SW6 5HA
- 020 7736 4000
- www.nomadbooks.co.uk
- Parson's Green LU
- Mon-Fri 9am-6.30pm,
  Sat 9.30am-5.30pm, Sun 11am-4.30pm

A fabulous, welcoming shop with a café in the heart of it, for book buyers in need of sustenance. The downstairs houses the travel section with an excellent selection of guidebooks, maps, travel literature and fiction associated with destinations across the globe. The ground floor features the café and the general stock while the children's section at the rear is the location of the biggest, most inviting seats of any London bookshop. There are regular reading groups – one for modern books and one for classics – and also a children's reading group. Nomad Books now have a great selection of cards, wrapping paper and notebooks and also offer a loyalty scheme.

The Notting Hill Bookshop

- 🏠 13 Blenheim Crescent, W11 2EE
- ☎ 020 7229 5260
- ✎ www.thenottinghillbookshop.co.uk
- 🚇 Ladbroke Grove LU
- ☺ Mon-Fri 9am-7pm, Sat 8.30am-7pm, Sun 10am-6pm

This excellent general bookshop opened its doors for the first time back in 2011 on the site previously occupied by The Travel Bookshop, which had traded for over thirty years and was the inspiration for the shop presided over by William Thacker (Hugh Grant) in the 1999 film 'Notting Hill'. While the new store maintains a good deal of the unique atmosphere of its predecessor with high bookshelves and enticing table displays, it has developed a character of its own with a much broader stock range that includes fiction, the visual arts and children's books as well as travel writing and guide books. The staff are well informed and helpful and there is an efficient ordering service if they don't have what you want in stock. For those looking for a literary gift they also offer a range of cards and wrapping paper. There are plenty of local cafés for post-purchase refreshment including the excellent Books for Cooks (see p.32) café which is just opposite.

Nutricentre Bookshop

- 🏠 7 Park Crescent, W1B 1PF
- ☎ 020 7323 2382
- ✎ www.nutricentrebooks.com
- 🚇 Great Portland Street LU
- ☺ Mon-Fri 9am-7pm, Sat 10am-6pm

Situated in the basement of the Hale Clinic, this bookshop carries an enormous selection of books, magazines, CDs and DVDs on nutrition, alternative and complementary therapies, personal and spiritual development, and world medical traditions such as Chinese medicine. A great many of their titles are North American imports and hard to find elsewhere. The atmosphere is relaxed, with no shortage of tables and chairs for leisurely browsing. The staff are approachable and knowledgeable and will make every effort to order special requests. Furthermore, the basement is shared with the Nutricentre supplement shop, where one can consult qualified nutritionists for product advice.

Newham Bookshop

Serving the communities of east London since 1978

745-745 Barking Road E13 9ER
Tel: 020 8552 9993
www.newhambooks.co.uk

Nearest Tube: Upton Park

Tuesday-Friday 9.30 am-5 pm
Saturday 10 am-5 pm

O

Orbital

⌖ *8 Great Newport Street,*
WC2H 7JA
☎ *020 7240 0591*
✍ *www.orbitalcomics.com*
🚇 *Leicester Square LU*
🕓 *Mon-Sat 10.30am-7pm, Wed & Thurs*
until 7.30pm, Sun 11.30am-5pm

One of London's best-known comic shops, stocking everything to set the comic fan's heart racing. There are weekly shipments of imported comic books, rare back-issues, graphic novels and all the latest collected editions. Orbital has large sections dedicated to manga and independent comics as well as small press publications from around the world. The shop also has a number of shelves and cabinets displaying collectable toys, t-shirts, posters and other gift items of appeal to comic lovers – Spider-Man mug anyone?

Other Criteria

⌖ *14 Hinde Street, W1U 3BG*
☎ *020 7935 5550*
✍ *www.othercriteria.com*
🚇 *Bond Street LU*
🕓 *Mon-Sat 10am-6pm, Sun 12-6pm*

Other Criteria is artist Damien Hirst's publishing company and publishes his catalogues plus art monographs and artist-led books. Despite the expensive surroundings, books start from as little as £20. However, many of the titles come in limited editions and cost serious money. Anyone with an interest in contemporary art will enjoy a visit to this gallery and a browse of the books on offer from artists such as Sarah Lucas, Mat Collishaw and Paul Fryer.

Owl Bookshop

⌖ *209 Kentish Town Road, NW5 2JU*
☎ *020 7485 7793*
✍ *www.facebook.com/owlbooks*
🚇 *Camden Town LU & Kentish Town LU*
🕓 *Mon-Sat 9am-6pm,*
Sun & Bank Hols 11am-6pm

Owl Bookshop is a Kentish Town institution which has been supplying the locals of NW5 with their reading material and offering great service since 1974. In 2010 the store was taken over by Daunt Books, but the shop has maintained its own identity and unique atmosphere. The book stock is very broad with a great fiction selection while the middle of the store is occupied by promotional tables with the latest publications and staff recommendations. In recent years the already large children's section has been expanded and now about one third of the shop is dedicated to young readers, covering anything from baby picture books to teenage fiction. Owl Bookshop is a pleasant place to shop with friendly staff and lots of chairs for browsers. Customers buying a book gift will find an impressive range of cards and wrapping paper. There is also a good selection of DVDs for adults and children and a loyalty card offering a 5% discount. The store regularly hosts book readings, poetry evenings and other literary events, details of which can be found on their regularly updated Facebook page.

P

Pages of Hackney

🏛 *70 Lower Clapton Road, E5 0RN*

☎ *020 8525 1452*

✍ *www.pagesofhackney.co.uk*

🚌 *Hackney Central Rail*

🕐 *Mon-Fri 10am-7pm, Sat 10am-6pm,*
Sun 12noon-6pm

A delightful local bookshop that has been created on the site of a barber shop and which, like its predecessor, serves as a focal point for the local community. It's a small space but the stock covers a broad range – local interest and fiction are especially well represented. Downstairs is now dedicated to a great value selection of second-hand books. Far from being a dingy basement this area is stylishly modern and well-lit with comfy chairs to encourage browsing. Pages of Hackney also hosts regular literary events. Just a few doors along, at number 88, Biddle Bros, is a traditional pub and a great spot to recuperate from the exertions of book buying.

Pathfinder Bookshop

🏛 *1st Floor, 120 Bethnal Green Road, E2 6DG*

☎ *020 7998 0959*

✍ *www.pathfinderpress.com*

🚌 *Liverpool St LU/Rail,*
Shoreditch Overground

🕐 *Tues-Fri 10am-7pm, Sat 11am-5pm*
(times vary – check in advance)

The struggles of working people throughout the world and black and women's studies are the focus of this radical bookshop at the northern end of Brick Lane – the entrance is actually on Brick Lane. Their extensive stock features numerous titles on 'liberation' movements and their leaders. The shop also stocks current and back copies of New International – 'A Magazine of Marxist Politics and Theory'. If you join the Pathfinder's Readers Club (details on the website) you get at least 15% discount on books and 25% on their selected book of the month. There's a weekly programme of events relevant to the subjects covered by the bookshop.

Pages of Hackney

Persephone Books

⌨ *59 Lamb's Conduit Street,
WC1N 3NB*

☎ *020 7242 9292*

✐ *www.persephonebooks.co.uk*

🚌 *Holborn LU, Russell Sq LU*

🕑 *Mon-Fri 10am-6pm, Sat 12noon-5pm*

Persephone is a small, independent publisher that reprints forgotten classics by twentieth-century writers (mostly women) in beautifully produced volumes with colourful endpapers and bookmarks. Their best selling title is 'Miss Pettigrew Lives for a Day' by Winifred Watson, which was made into a film in 2008 with a stellar cast headed by Frances McDormand. Persephone don't rest on their laurels however, and publish three new books in spring and autumn each year. Their authors include Katherine Mansfield, Dorothy Whipple and Marghanita Laski. Their catalogue is a rewarding read and enthusiasts can join the mailing list.

Persephone Books is located in a beautiful early 18th-century building on the very charming Lamb's Conduit Street and sells only Persephone titles. The store is also the venue for literary lunches, book groups and film screenings organised by Persephone as well as being the offices for this active and engaged publishing company. This cosy shop also offers a good range of greetings cards, bookmarks and mugs related to the books. For those looking for a literary present there is also a gift-wrapping service. Lamb's Conduit Street is the ideal place to stroll after literary exertions with several excellent coffee bars including Sid's, which is next door.

Photographers' Gallery Bookshop

🖃 *16-18 Ramillies Street, W1F 7LW*
☎ *020 7087 9323*
✐ *www.tpg.org.uk*
🚌 *Oxford Circus LU*
🕐 *Mon-Wed, Fri & Sat 10am-6pm,*
   Thurs 10am-8pm, Sun 11.30am-6pm

A few yards from Oxford Street, this is a fabulous photography bookshop with several thousand titles. Stock includes an impressive range of photographic monographs and anthologies as well as books on art theory and a few technical publications. They also offer an excellent a range of magazines, postcards and gifts and stock some unusual cameras. If you are in need of refreshment there's a bright and welcoming café upstairs. The store hosts regular book launches and signings – check their website or Twitter for more information.

Photographers' Gallery Bookshop

Pickled Pepper Books

⌨ *10 Middle Lane, Crouch End, N8 8PL*
☎ *020 3632 0823*
✎ *www.pickledpepperbooks.co.uk*
🚌 *Finsbury Park LU - then bus W3 or W7*
🕓 *Mon-Fri 9.30am-5.30pm,*
   Sat 10am-6pm, Sun 11am-5pm

This specialist children's bookshop opened
in 2012 and, despite the current trend
toward online shopping, has proved a
success with Crouch End children and
their families. There are many reasons
for the shop's popularity, among them an
open-plan layout that is designed to be
pushchair friendly, plenty of seating and an
in-store café. The owners, Urmi & Steven,
are careful in their selection of stock with
lots of imaginative books for kids and plenty
of parenting books and adult fiction for
the grown-ups. The shop also has a busy
itinerary of events and readings throughout
the week, making this a place where pre-
school kids can enjoy a story and acquire
an interest in books and reading in a friendly
and comfortable environment. For older
children there is a popular fortnightly book
group and once a week there is a Young
Illustrators club for budding artists. The
weekends are busy with readings, visiting
authors and even puppet shows. Details
of all events can be found on their website.
Run with energy and enthusiasm, Pickled
Pepper Books is a great resource for North
London parents and children.

The Pitshanger Bookshop

⌨ *141 Pitshanger Lane, W5 1RH*
☎ *020 8991 8131*
✎ *www.pitshangerbooks.co.uk*
🚌 *Ealing Broadway LU (then E2 or E9 bus)*
🕓 *Mon-Sat 9.30am-5.30pm*

Located next to the public library, this is an
attractive and well laid-out local bookshop
offering a welcoming atmosphere for
browsers. The stock is comprehensive
and they have an efficient ordering system
that can usually source a title for next day
collection. There's also a selection of
greetings cards, gift stationery, audiobooks
and children's games and there are regular
literary events.

PMS Bookshop

⌨ *240 King Street, W6 0RF*
☎ *020 8748 5522*
✎ *www.polskamacierz.org*
🚌 *Ravenscourt Park LU*
🕓 *Mon-Sat 11am-6pm, Sun 12noon-5pm*

Located in POSK, the Polish Social and
Cultural Association, this shop specialises in
Polish books including children's titles and
magazines. There are also language
courses and dictionaries for those who
want to learn Polish and books in Polish
about all aspects of Poland. The shop
also stocks a selection of Polish gift and
souvenir items.

Pollock's Toy Museum

🏠 *1 Scala Street, W1T 2HL*

☎ *020 7636 3452*

✒ *www.pollockstoys.com*

🚇 *Goodge Street LU*

🕐 *Mon-Sat 10am-5pm*
    Closed Bank Holidays

The shop attached to this enchanting small museum has an old-fashioned charm. As well as being a toy shop, stocking traditional toys and an extensive selection of toy theatres, it also sells a range of new and antiquarian children's books, plus titles on the history of toys and toy collecting.

Potterton Books London

🏠 *93 Lower Sloane Street, SW1W 8DA*

☎ *020 7730 4235*

✒ *www.pottertonbookslondon.co.uk*

🚇 *Sloane Square LU*

🕐 *Mon-Sat 10am-6pm*

This store offers new, out-of-print, rare and vintage books on interior design, the fine and decorative arts, antiques, gardens, architecture, fashion, jewellery and lifestyle. As you would expect from a shop specialising in interior design, it is well laid out with plenty of room for browsing. Potterton Books don't just wait for antique enthusiasts and interior designers to come to them but also exhibit at many of London's antique fairs.

Primrose Hill Books

🏠 *134 Regent's Park Road, NW1 8XL*

☎ *020 7586 2022*

✒ *www.primrosehillbooks.com*

🚇 *Chalk Farm LU*

🕐 *Mon-Fri 9.30am-6pm,*
    Sat 10am-6pm, Sun 11am-6pm

A peach of a bookshop set on a popular local shopping street. There's a large general stock of nicely displayed hardbacks and paperbacks with fiction, travel and biography especially well represented. There are some enticing bargain shelves of second-hand books outside and there's a huge second-hand stock that is accessible via the website. The area abounds with cafés if you haven't come prepared for a picnic on nearby Primrose Hill.

Arthur Probsthain

🏠 *41 Great Russell Street,*
    WC1B 3PE

☎ *020 7636 1096*

✒ *www.apandtea.co.uk*

🚇 *Tottenham Court Road LU*

🕐 *Mon-Fri 9.30am-5.30pm,*
    Sat 12noon-4pm

Arthur Probsthain opened its doors for the first time in 1903 and is now run by the fourth generation of the family. The shop specialises in books on pretty much everything to do with Asian, Middle Eastern and African subjects including art, music, religion, language and culture. The stock combines new and second-hand books and features many titles that you are unlikely to find elsewhere. As well as stocking a collection of unique books, Probsthain's also contains a small art gallery hosting exhibitions of Oriental and African art as well as a popular tea room in the basement serving traditional afternoon tea. Arthur Probsthain also operate the bookshop in SOAS (see p.106). Their second-hand stock is also available online via AbeBooks.

Protestant Truth Society Bookshop

🏠 *184 Fleet Street, EC4A 2HJ*

☎ *020 7405 4960*

✒ *www.protestant-truth.org*

🚇 *Temple LU, Blackfriars LU/Rail*

🕐 *Mon-Fri 9.30am-5.30pm*

A Christian bookshop featuring a large selection of Protestant and Reformed literature including theology, the sermons of eminent preachers and inspirational works. They also sell children's books, greetings cards, music and DVDs.

Q

The Quaker Bookshop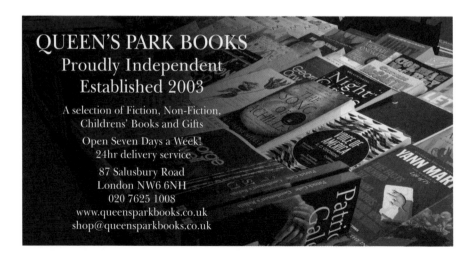

🖳 *Friends House, 173 Euston Road,*
NW1 2BJ
☎ *020 7663 1030*
🖎 *www.quaker.org.uk/bookshop*
🚆 *Euston LU/Rail*
🕓 *Mon-Fri 10am-5pm*

A bookshop operated by the Society of
Friends (Quakers) specialising in Quaker
books published in the UK and around
the world. They carry a large stock
on spirituality, liberal Christianity, social
responsibility, the environment, conflict
resolution and peace work. There is also a
selection of children's titles. The bookshop
is arranged around the café, thus making
browsing and refreshment easy to combine.

Queen's Park Books

🖳 *87 Salusbury Road, NW6 6NH*
☎ *020 7625 1008*
🖎 *www.queensparkbooks.co.uk*
🚆 *Queen's Park LU/Rail*
🕓 *Mon-Fri 9am-7pm,*
Sat 9.30am-6.30pm, Sun 10am-5pm

A friendly local independent bookshop
with a comprehensive range of books
covering all main subject areas. They
also stock a great range of books for
children and young adults. The staff
pride themselves on their ability to get
titles with speed and efficiency, including
foreign publications and hard-to-find, out
of print books. For those who want to
purchase a special gift, the store boasts a
handsome range of cards and stationery
and offers a gift-wrapping service. Queen's
Park Books regularly hosts readings and
book launches and is a big supporter of
community events and services. Caldo
(three doors down) is the place to go for
refreshments.

QUEEN'S PARK BOOKS
Proudly Independent
Established 2003

A selection of Fiction, Non-Fiction,
Childrens' Books and Gifts

Open Seven Days a Week!
24hr delivery service

87 Salusbury Road
London NW6 6NH
020 7625 1008
www.queensparkbooks.co.uk
shop@queensparkbooks.co.uk

R

Regent Hall

- 275 Oxford Street, W1C 2DJ
- ☏ 020 7629 5424
- ✍ www.regenthall.co.uk
- 🚌 Oxford Circus LU
- 🕓 Tues-Fri 11am-4pm and most Sundays after church service 12noon-1pm

A Christian bookshop, which also sells cards, gifts and CDs, in the Salvation Army's Regent Hall. This Christian centre is just a few yards away from Oxford Circus and also boasts an on site café.

Review

- 131 Bellenden Road, SE15 4QY
- ☏ 020 7639 7400
- ✍ www.reviewbookshop.co.uk
- 🚌 Peckham Rye Rail
- 🕓 Tues, Fri-Sat 10am-6pm, Wed 11am-6pm, Thurs 12noon-7pm, Sun 11am-5pm

At the junction of Bellenden Road and Choumert Road, this is a great local bookshop with an excellent, well-selected stock, displayed in welcoming surroundings. All subjects are covered but they are particularly strong on contemporary literary fiction and have a superb range of foreign fiction in translation. Another strength is the children's section which has lots of fiction and some lovely illustrated books to entice even the most reluctant reader. The bookshop helps organise the Peckham Literary Festival and also hosts regular readings and signings.

RIBA Bookshop

www.ribabookshops.com

- Royal Institute of British Architects 66 Portland Place, W1B 1AD
- ☏ 020 7307 3753
- ✍ www.ribabookshops.com
- 🚌 Regent's Park LU, Great Portland St LU, and Oxford Circus LU
- 🕓 Mon-Fri 9.30am-5.30pm Sat 10am-5pm

Located in the stunning Art Deco headquarters of the Royal Institute of British Architects, the RIBA Bookshop is Europe's leading architectural bookshop. The stock is wide-ranging, covering all aspects of the built environment both in Britain and overseas – subjects include theory, practice management, city guides, construction technology, contracts, interior design, landscape and sustainable architecture. There is an enormous selection of magazines, journals and monographs detailing the work of individual architects; as well as a great deal for the general reader who is interested in the built environment. RIBA also has an attractive range of notebooks, postcards and other stationery. Open to all, the adjoining café, bistro restaurant and new gallery space make RIBA, and its bookshop, a destination not to be missed.

RICS Bookshop

- 1st Floor, 12 Great George Street, Parliament Square, SW1P 3AD
- ☏ 020 7334 3776
- ✍ www.rics.org/bookshop
- 🚌 Westminster LU
- 🕓 Mon-Fri 9.30am-5.30pm

A specialist shop selling books related to the theory and practice of chartered surveying including topics such as building, construction, architecture, business, management, engineering, surveying and law.

Riverside Bookshop

🏠 *Unit 15 Hay's Galleria,*
   57 Tooley Street, SE21 2QN
☎ *020 7378 1824*
✎ *www.theriversideway.wordpress.com*
🚌 *London Bridge LU/Rail*
🕒 *Mon-Fri 9am-6pm, Sat 10am-6pm*
   Sun 11am-6pm

The Riverside Bookshop is a great independent with a wide range of stock, particular strengths being adult fiction, London books and local interest, a small but well chosen children's section and a reliable stock of biographical writing, cookery and reference books. Suzanne Dean has been the manager here for nearly 20 years and says that people often wrongly assume that Riverside is part of a chain because of the black shelving and red signs that are reminiscent of those in the old Books etc stores (which have now disappeared from the high street). Thanks to its corner location, Riverside Bookshop has a lot of window space relative to its size and staff regularly change the displays, giving due prominence to the latest titles.

One of the main reasons that Riverside continues to thrive when so many bookshops have hit the wall is partly its location in the busy Hays Galleria.

"We're lucky, I think this is why we've survived for so long, because we're not dependent on one type of customer, we've got lots of office trade, we've got the hospital and the courts, we've also got the visiting tourists and Londoners enjoying the river... So we're not a traditional type of community bookshop."

The shop changed hands about six years ago, but the new owners allow Suzanne and her team to run things and with over 80 years bookselling experience between them, they clearly know what they are doing. The book trade has changed but they are fighting the trend to online shopping with great service and a responsive approach to customer demand.

"You've definitely got to work harder these days to keep your customers and have more control of your stock and always have new things ... New titles have a much shorter shelf life, so you've really got to know your stock and keep in touch with your customers' needs ..."

Riverside has weathered a tough period in book retailing and it is heartening to hear a bookseller enthuse about the future. Suzanne and her staff are currently excited about the arrival of new companies taking office space in the nearby Shard and are busy working out ways to encourage the newcomers to visit. This enthusiasm, combined with the staff's knowledgeable recommendations and regularly changing displays make this one of the best independent book stores in London and well worth a visit.

Discover the home of British Architecture

Royal Institute of British Architects
66 Portland Place, London

▸ Europe's leading architectural bookshop
▸ Events and exhibitions
▸ The British Architectural Library
▸ Bistro and café
⊖ Oxford Circus

RIBA ᛘ **Bookshops**

RIBA ᛘ
Architecture.com

Rough Trade East

🗔 East 'Dray Walk', Old Truman Brewery
    91 Brick Lane, E1 6QL
☎ 020 7392 7788
🖉 www.roughtrade.com
🚌 Whitechapel LU, Aldgate East LU
🕓 Mon-Thurs 8am-9pm, Fri 8am-8pm,
    Sat 10am-8pm, Sun 11am-7pm

This flagship branch of Rough Trade is renowned for its range of CDs and vinyl and for all the ephemera (t-shirts, mugs etc) surrounding popular music. What is less well known is the increasing range of books the store now offers with a particular emphasis on publications about sex, drugs and rock 'n' roll, street art and protest, but with enough contemporary fiction, art books and London guides to appeal to a wider audience. Rough Trade supports local publishers, stocks a selection of books chosen by staff and hosts regular book launches and events. The store provides a spacious and energetic environment in which to browse – a rarity in the book world these days – and even has a café. Brick Lane Bookshop (see page 36) is just around the corner.

Claire de Rouen Books

🗔 First Floor,
    125 Charing Cross Road,
    WC2H 0EW
☎ 020 7287 1813
🖉 www.clairederouenbooks.com
🚌 Tottenham Court Road LU
🕓 Tues-Sat 12am-6.30pm

An amazingly diverse and wonderful collection of photography, fashion and art books perched high above the hustle and bustle of Charing Cross Road. The shelves are packed with gorgeous volumes from near and far that will fascinate and intrigue enthusiasts. A tiny gem and a required destination for anyone interested in photography and fashion. The store organises the Room&Book art bookfair at the ICA (see p.195).

The Royal Academy of Arts Shop

🗔 Burlington House, Piccadilly, W1J 0BD
☎ 020 7300 5757
🖉 www.royalacademy.org.uk/shop
🚌 Piccadilly Circus LU, Green Park LU
🕓 Daily 10am-6pm (Fri until 10pm)

As befits this most august of art institutions, even the RA's shop occupies a commanding position at the top of the grand staircase of the entrance hall – there is no admission fee to this part of the building. The shop offers a selection of books for adults and children on the history of art, art techniques and the work of individual artists, alongside exhibition catalogues and a selection of books on London. There are excellent gifts suitable for all ages, attractive greetings cards and a range of DVDs about art.

Royal Court Theatre

🗔 Sloane Square, SW1W 8AS
☎ 020 7565 5024
🖉 www.royalcourttheatre.com
🚌 Sloane Square LU
🕓 Mon-Fri 4pm-8pm,
    Sat (and weekday matinées) 2pm-8pm

Located at the mezzanine level on the way down to the bar, the books here are dedicated to twentieth and twenty-first-century plays and books on the theory and practice of modern drama. Playtexts for Royal Court Productions, past and present, are available for £3 and collections of five past productions are sold for just £10. Staff pride themselves on their ability to help with the selection of monologues and scenes for audition pieces and showcases.

Owner Alastair, Zoe and their ubiquitous dog, Bert, preside over an inspiring selection of books. Since the shop opened in 2011 they have turned Rye Books into an integral part of the local community.

Rye Books is a cafe and bookshop offering new & used books, outdoor seating and great coffee. Events include, author readings, film nights and children's story-time twice a week.

They also offer next day ordering, free local delivery and a gift wrapping service.

Rye Books
45 Upland Rd, SE22 9EF
Mon Sat: 10.00 18.00
Sun & Bank Hol: 13.00 18.00
tel. 020 3581 1850
www.ryebooks.co.uk

Royal Opera House Shop ②

🖥 Covent Garden, WC2E 9DD
☎ 020 7212 9331
✍ www.roh.org.uk
🚌 Covent Garden LU
🕓 Mon-Sat 10am-7.30pm

The Royal Opera House provides grand surroundings for this well organised bookshop. The shop is situated next to the Box Office, close to the entrance, with stock covering books and magazines on ballet and opera including history, personalities and individual works with some titles suitable for children. Enthusiasts will find the rest of the shop equally alluring with DVDs, CDs, clothing and gifts galore.

Ruposhi Bangla

🖥 220 Tooting High Street, SW17 0SG
☎ 020 8672 7843
✍ www.ruposhibangla.co.uk
🚌 Tooting Broadway LU
🕓 Open by appointment

This is a specialist shop selling a huge range of Bengali books (including children's titles) from Bangladesh and India. The choice is wide, taking in fiction and non-fiction and there is a large selection of educational materials. The stock also includes music and maps as well as English translations of Bengali texts, Bengali language courses and books in Bengali about learning English.

Rye Books

🖥 45 Upland Road, SE22 9EF
☎ 020 3581 1850
✍ www.ryebooks.co.uk
🚌 East Dulwich or Peckham Rye Rail
🕓 Mon-Sat 10am-6pm, Sun
   (and Bank Holidays) 1pm-6pm

Alastair Kenward founded this independent local bookshop back in 2012, transforming an old junk shop complete with mice infestation into this stylish and modern retail space. Since that time the store has gone from strength to strength, attracting many loyal customers who are drawn to the great selection of fiction, children's books, art and design, biography, history and food and drink, as well as gifts and cards.

The design of the shop shows an eye for detail – from the stylish shop counter and display units to the turquoise and green striped logo, which all give some hint of Alastair's art background. The look of the place is matched by the friendly service which includes free local deliveries, regular book events, kid's reading groups and even a matching striped book van which sells at schools and Northcross Road Market on Saturdays (see p.211).

The shop has added a small but interesting second-hand section and serves delicious tea, coffee and cake with seating outside on fine days. It's no surprise that Rye Books is becoming a much-loved institution among the book lovers of East Dulwich.

S

Saatchi Gallery

🖳 *Duke of York's HQ, King's Road, SW3 4RY*
☎ *020 7811 3079*
✎ *www.saatchigallery.com*
🚌 *Sloane Square LU*
🕓 *Daily 10am-6pm*

Admission is free to this major gallery devoted to contemporary art. The shop is located on the first floor and is well worth a visit with a diverse array of gifts but significant space given to a careful selection of books on contemporary art, photography and ideas, as well as books relating to current exhibitions. Children are not forgotten with titles to encourage creativity and enjoyment. Those on the hunt for bargains will not be disappointed as there is usually a selection of heavily discounted titles. The nearby Taschen (see p.118) and John Sandoe (see p.104) are also worth visiting if you are in the area.

St Christopher's Hospice Bookshop

🖳 *51-59 Lawrie Park Road, SE26 6DZ*
☎ *020 8768 4660*
✎ *www.stchristophers.org.uk*
🚌 *Sydenham & Penge East Rail*
🕓 *Ring for opening times*

A specialist shop selling books on hospices, palliative care and bereavement, including books for bereaved children.

St Paul's

🖳 *Morpeth Terrace, SW1P 1EP*
☎ *020 7828 5582*
✎ *www.stpauls.org.uk*
🚌 *Victoria LU/Rail*
🕓 *Mon-Sat 9.30am-6pm*

Situated next door to Westminster Cathedral, this is probably the largest Christian bookshop in London. Every aspect of Christianity is covered and they also stock a huge range of CDs, DVDs, cards and gift items.

John Sandoe

🖃 *10-12 Blacklands Terrace, SW3 2SR*
☎ *020 7589 9473*
🖉 *www.johnsandoe.com*
🚌 *Sloane Square LU*
🕒 *Mon-Sat 9.30am-6.30pm*
(until 7pm in Dec), Sun 11am-5pm

John Sandoe occupies a quaint Regency cottage just off the King's Road and has recently expanded to include the former vet's next door, increasing the held stock to around 28,000 titles spread over three floors. The place has been spruced up somewhat with the expansion, but the atmosphere of genteel calm remains. The winding stairs leading to the first floor are still decorated with neatly framed photos of writers that have visited the store over the years since the eponymous Mr Sandoe established a bookshop here in 1957.

Sandoe's is not a large store, but its reputation and loyal customers make it one of the giants of London's book scene with a well chosen range covering literature, art, architecture, history, biography, reference, travel and drama, as well as children's books and plenty of unusual editions and titles you're unlikely to find elsewhere. Every effort is made to utilise the available space, including an ingenious sliding shelving system upstairs that is unique to the store.

The friendly staff are on hand to offer help and advice, but are unobtrusive enough to let visitors enjoy a quiet browse. They are busy even when the store is quiet, with about one third of sales being mail order via their quarterly catalogue sent to customers across the world. A narrow storeroom is used to manage this side of the business with carefully labelled packages piled high and awaiting dispatch. Sandoe's website is a useful resource and the store is active in social media from where you can find out about the numerous book launches and events to which John Sandoe plays host.

John Sandoe

Sangeeta

🏠 22 Brick Lane, E1 6RF
☎ 020 7247 5954
🚇 Aldgate East LU
🕐 Daily 11am-9pm

In the heart of the restaurant area of Brick Lane, this shop specialises in Bangladeshi books, newspapers, magazines and dictionaries. Stock includes children's books and British Asian lifestyle magazines. There are also Bengali and Hindi music and films on CD and DVD.

Sao Paulo Imports

🏠 Casa Brasil, Queensway Market, 23-25 Queensway, WC2 4Q J
☎ 020 7792 2931
🖊 www.casabrasillondres.co.uk
🚇 Bayswater LU, Queensway LU
🕐 Mon-Sat 11am-8pm, Sun 12noon-6pm

Located inside this Brazilian supermarket, which sells all manner of Brazilian delicacies, this is a specialist importer of Brazilian books (fiction and non-fiction), magazines, DVDs and CDs. This isn't the easiest place to find – it is located at the back of the market, between Units D and F.

Sathya Sai Book Centre

🏠 19 Hay Lane, NW9 0NH
☎ 020 8732 2886
🖊 www.srisathyasaibookcentre.org.uk
🚇 Colindale LU, Kingsbury LU
🕐 Mon-Fri 11am-5pm,
    Sat & Sun 11am-3pm

A shop selling religious books about and by the Indian Guru, Sri Sathya Sai Baba (in English, Chinese, Gujarati and Hindi) plus books on spirituality, yoga and health. There are DVDs and CDs as well and a selection of artefacts and gift items.

School of Life

🏠 70 Marchmont Street, WC1N 1AB
☎ 020 7833 1010
🖊 www.theschooloflife.com
🚇 Russell Square LU
🕐 Mon-Sat 10am-6pm

The School of Life offers an imaginative approach to teaching the skills to live a good life. To this end the school runs a busy schedule of classes and events and also publishes a vast array of quirky self-help and popular philosophy books with titles such as 'How to Age' and 'How to Connect with Nature' which are sold from their small, smart shop on Marchmont Street.

School of Oriental and African Studies Bookshop

🏠 Brunei Gallery, Thornhaugh Street, WC1H 0XG
☎ 020 7898 4470
🖊 www.soas.ac.uk/visitors/bookshop
🚇 Russell Square LU
🕐 Mon-Tues, Thurs-Fri 9.30am-5.30pm, Wed 10.30am-5.30, Sat 12noon-4pm

Located in the foyer of the Brunei Gallery building just opposite the main SOAS entrance, this tiny shop (operated by Arthur Probsthain – see p.95) is amply stocked with books covering the school's areas of study. This includes Africa, South East Asia, China, Japan, the Middle East, Ethnomusicology and Islam. Academic titles on literature, history, economics, politics and culture are the core stock and for linguists there are dictionaries and language learning materials. Somehow they also manage to squeeze in some great greetings cards and a selection of World Music CDs. Take a few minutes to check out the current exhibitions at the Brunei Gallery – they have some fascinating shows. There is also a delightful Japanese-inspired roof garden.

Schott Music

⌨ *48 Great Marlborough Street, W1F 7BB*
☎ *020 7534 0710*
✍ *www.schott-music.co.uk*
🚇 *Oxford Circus LU*
🕐 *Mon-Fri 10am-6.30pm, Sat 10am-6pm*

Schott is a publisher of classical sheet music for all instruments and standards. The shop also stocks material from many other publishers and its vast selection includes scores for musicals and shows as well as the classical repertoire. There are tutors for all instruments, plus books about music and gifts with a musical theme.

Selfridges (Part of WH Smith)

⌨ *400 Oxford Street, W1A 1AB*
☎ *0800 123400 ext 13678 or 13670*
🚇 *Bond Street LU*
🕐 *Mon-Sat 9.30am-10pm, Sun 12am-6pm*

Selfrides boasts a large and beautifully designed book department, but it is now run as a branch of WH Smiths. This means that few books by independent publishers are to be found here and so there are significant gaps in its stock. That said, it is still an impressive retail space and it does have many fine books, so worth a browse.

Sheen Bookshop

⌨ *357 Upper Richmond Road, SW14 7NX*
☎ *020 8876 1717*
✍ *www.sheenbookshop.co.uk*
🚇 *Mortlake Rail*
🕐 *Mon-Sat 9.30am-5.30pm,
Sun 11am-5pm*

An appealing local shop in the East Sheen shopping area stocking a range of thoughtfully selected and well-displayed books. This is a great place to find books that might otherwise slip under the radar. There are especially strong children's, cookery, travel and London sections plus gifts, greetings cards and toys. The shop is part of a small chain including Kew Bookshop (see p.72) and Barnes Bookshop (see p.21).

The Shop at Bluebird

⌨ *350 King's Road, SW3 5UU*
☎ *020 7351 3873*
✍ *www.theshopatbluebird.com*
🚇 *Fulham Broadway LU, Sloane Square LU*
🕐 *Mon-Sat 10am-7pm, Sun 12noon-6pm*

This shop occupies a large ground floor space beneath the famous Chelsea restaurant. It features a fine book selection among its array of furniture, fashion and accessories. The book stock is eclectic and includes fashion, photography, travel, art, architecture, design, film and food with an emphasis on big, glossy volumes. Browsing is aided by handy sofas and great music playing in the background. The children's book section is at a distance from the adult books and contains some very beautiful books that are perhaps wasted on the sticky-fingered young. There's also a small range of top-quality first and limited edition books which should definitely be kept out of childrens' reach.

The Shop at St Martin's

⌨ *St Martin-in-the-Fields,*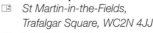
   Trafalgar Square, WC2N 4JJ
☎ *020 7766 1122*
✍ *www.smitf.org*
🚇 *Charing Cross LU/Rail*
🕐 *Mon-Wed 10am-7pm, Thurs-Sat 10am-
9pm, Sun 11.30am-6pm*

This central London church holds regular services but also stages concerts, and has a brass-rubbing centre in its crypt with an attached restaurant and shop. Alongside an excellent range of gifts, cards and stationery, the shop also has a selection of books on Christianity, comparative religion, history, natural history and cookery. There's also a range of titles for children.

Silverprint

- 120 London Road, SE1 6LF
- ☎ 020 7620 0169
- www.silverprint.co.uk
- Elephant & Castle Rail/LU
- ◷ Mon-Fri 9.30am-5.30pm,
  Thurs 9.30am-8pm

A specialist photographic supply shop par excellence. Photographers make pilgrimage here from near and far. The stock of books is quite small but highly selective and specialised, covering darkroom, studio and photographic techniques, experimental processes and digital photography. In recent years Silverprint has expanded its range of photographers' monographs and also hosts regular photography exhibitions. The staff are knowledgeable and helpful and the store has all the equipment, materials and software you'll need to apply the techniques referred to in the books.

Slightly Foxed on Gloucester Road

- 123 Gloucester Road, SW7 4TE
- ☎ 020 7370 3503
- www.foxedbooks.com
- Gloucester Road LU
- ◷ Mon-Sat 10am-7pm,
  Sun 11am-5pm

Formerly The Gloucester Road Bookshop, charming shop is now run by the same people who publish the literary quarterly, 'Slightly Foxed'. The new team have kept a substantial second-hand and antiquarian stock, but have added to it a well-chosen range of new books with a particularly strong children's section. As well as books, the store also offers an appealing range of gifts such as mugs, tea towels and greetings cards. Awarded 'Vintage Independent Bookshop of the Year' in 2014, this little shop is well worth adding to your book buying itinerary.

Sims Reed

- 43a Duke Street,
  St James's, SW1Y 6DD
- ☎ 020 7930 5566
- www.simsreed.com
- Green Park LU
- ◷ Mon-Fri 10am-6pm

A specialist art and architecture bookseller with many volumes at the very top of the quality and price range. Sims Reed deal in a heady mixture of new, out-of-print, rare and antiquarian volumes that cover areas including architecture, applied arts, photography, exhibition catalogues and Asian and Islamic, European and American art. Their stock (usually around 4,000 book titles plus catalogues) is detailed on their website. The shop is located just across the road from the other major art bookseller in the area, Thomas Heneage (see p.108), and is a few minutes' walk from the Royal Academy of Art.

BOOKS ARE MY BAG #BAMB

LOVE BOOKS
LOVE BOOKSHOPS

Sims Reed

JOHN SMITH'S BOOKSHOPS

🖃 *www.johnsmith.co.uk*

This national chain operates a number of academic bookshops based in universities in the capital. They, not unreasonably, specialise in the subjects covered by the academic institution. Opening times can vary during vacation times, so it is always worth checking before making a journey to visit. Second-hand books are available as they operate a textbook buy back service, which enables students to get a bit of money back on text books they no longer need.

Branches at:

London Metropolitan University

🖃 *The Basement, Calcutta House, Old Castle Street, E1 7NT*
☎ *020 7426 0442*
🚌 *Aldgate East LU*
🕒 *Mon-Fri 9am-5.30pm term times only.*

Specialising in law, psychology, business and economics.

Queen Mary, University of London

🖃 *329 Mile End Road, E1 4NT*
☎ *020 8981 7942*
🚌 *Stepney Green LU / Mile End LU*
🕒 *Mon-Fri 9am-5.30pm*

Business, law, economics, history, English, accounting and finance.

Regent's College

🖃 *Inner Circle, Regent's Park, NW1 4NS*
☎ *020 7935 0183*
🚌 *Baker Street LU*
🕒 *Mon-Fri 9am-5.30pm*

Business, languages, psychotherapy and counselling.

University of East London

Specialising in education, law, psychology, business and social studies.

Stratford Campus

🖃 *Conference and Computer Centre, Water Lane, E15 4LZ*
☎ *020 8223 4602*
🚌 *Stratford LU/DLR*
🕒 *Mon-Fri 9am-5.30pm, extended to 7pm during peak times.*

Docklands Campus

🖃 *The Atrium, East Wing, 4-6 University Way, E16 2RD*
☎ *020 8223 7193*
🚌 *Cyprus DLR*
🕒 *Mon-Fri 9am-5.30pm, extended to 7pm during peak times.*

University of Greenwich

Specialising in business, law, economics, education and politics.

Main Campus

🖃 *Mews Building, College Way, Old Royal Naval College, SE10 9NN*
☎ *020 8465 5740*
🚌 *Cutty Sark DLR*
🕒 *Mon-Fri 9am-5.30pm, Sat 10am-4pm term times only.*

Avery Hill Campus

🖃 *Mansion Site, Bexley Road, Eltham, SE9 2PQ*
☎ *020 8331 7584*
🚌 *Falconwood Rail*
🕒 *Mon-Thurs 9am-5.30pm, Fri 9am-5pm Open August to June only.*

Soho Original Books

✑ www.sohobooks.co.uk
🕐 Mon-Sat 10am-1am, Sun 11am-11pm

Soho Original started life as a single shop in the heart of the Soho back in 1993. There are now two stores in London specialising in art, architecture, design, photography and erotica. The stores offer a good value selection of general books in a bright, modern environment with sexually explicit titles tucked away downstairs.

Branches at:
🖃 12 Brewer Street, W1F 0SF
☎ 020 7494 1615
🚌 Piccadilly / Leicester Square LU

🖃 121 Charing Cross Road, WC2H 0EW
☎ 020 7734 4121
🚌 Tottenham Court Road LU

Shalimar Books

🖃 38 Kennington Lane, SE11 4LS
☎ 020 7735 2101
✑ www.indianbooksuk.com
🚌 Kennington LU
🕐 Mon-Fri 10.30am-6pm

Shalimar are importers and distributors of books from India, agents for a number of Indian publishers, and a great source of Indian titles that you're unlikely to find elsewhere. Their range includes books on Indian politics, history and culture as well as fiction and children's books by Indian authors. They welcome visitors to their bookshop, but also have an efficient online ordering system via their website. Shalimar Books is a member of the Association of Radical Booksellers (ARB).

Society of Genealogists

🖾 *14 Charterhouse Buildings,*
Goswell Road, EC1M 7BA
☎ *020 7702 5483*
✑ *www.sog.org.uk*
🚇 *Barbican LU*
🕓 *Tues-Thurs and Sat 10am-5.30pm*
(Thurs until 7.30pm)

The bookshop here supplements the work of the library (see p.255), which enables people to trace their family history. The Society is one of the foremost publishers of books on family history and the shop sells books published by the Society and other publishers on all aspects of genealogy. The shop is a wonderful resource for anybody interested or involved in the subject, with information about how to embark on the whole process plus books on local and social history. The Society also hosts many lectures and courses of interest to enthusiasts.

The South Kensington Bookshop

🖾 *22 Thurloe Street, SW7 2LT*
☎ *020 7589 2916*
✑ *www.kensingtonbooks.co.uk*
🚇 *South Kensington LU*
🕓 *Mon-Fri 10am-8pm,*
Sat 11am-7pm, Sun 12noon-7pm

This store is far more attractive and pleasant to explore than a typical discount bookshop. Tastefully decorated with careful displays and helpful staff, the shop offers a good selection of books with particular strengths being history and large format, glossy art, design, architecture and photography titles, plus quality contemporary and classic fiction. The only indication that this is a discount bookshop is the price with all books offered at considerable discounts. A great shop just a few minutes' walk from the Victoria and Albert Museum.

South Kensington Books

Independent Bookseller

www.kensingtonbooks.co.uk

22 Thurloe St
London SW7 2LT
0207 589 2916

Mon–Fri: 10.00 - 20.00
Sat: 11.00 - 19.00
Sun: 12.00 - 19.00

Visual Arts • Architecture • Photography • History
Poetry • Music • Biography • Cookery • Fiction

Souvenir Press

🖾 *43 Great Russell Street,*
   WC1B 3PD
☎ *020 7580 9307*
✒ *www.souvenirpress.co.uk*
🚌 *Tottenham Court Road LU*
🕔 *Mon-Fri 9.30am-5.15pm*

This independent publisher of reference
books has been trading for over 60 years
and runs this small shop from its offices in
Bloomsbury. They only sell Souvenir Press
publications but their list of over 500 titles
is pretty comprehensive, including anything
from 'The Joy of Allotments' to 'A Natural
History of the Piano'. Their website is a
useful resource which allows you to view
their latest catalogue but the bookshop is
well worth a visit if you are in Bloomsbury,
particularly as Jarndyce (see page 148) and
Arthur Probsthain (see page 95) are also on
the same street.

Spink

🖾 *69 Southampton Row,*
   WC1B 4ET
☎ *020 7563 4000*
✒ *www.spink.com*
🚌 *Holborn LU, Russell Square LU*
🕔 *Mon-Fri 9.30am-5.30pm*

This specialist dealer and auctioneer of
coins, medals, stamps, banknotes and
wine has been trading since 1666. Spink's
grand auction house in central London
has a bookshop in the reception area
with a considerable new, out of print and
antiquarian stock of titles covering all its
specialisms. They also publish books
concerning their key subject areas and a
regular newsletter that keeps subscribers
informed about future auctions and events.

Stanfords

🖾 *12-14 Long Acre, WC2E 9LP*
☎ *020 7836 1321*
✒ *www.stanfords.co.uk*
🚌 *Leicester Square LU*
🕔 *Mon-Sat 9am-8pm;*
   Sun 12noon-6pm

Stanfords is the World's biggest map and
travel bookshop covering pretty much
every inch of the known world for all kinds
of travellers from explorers to tourists.
Here you will find an impressive selection
of guidebooks, travelogues, glossy photo
books, maps and fiction based in foreign
climes. Complementing all this you can
also expect to find fantastic displays of
stationery, atlases, globes, magazines, travel
accessories, gifts for adults and children
alike and a carefully chosen range of travel
themed furniture and home accessories.

Stanfords was established by Edward
Stanford in 1853 and the shop has been
in the same building since 1901. Many
famous travellers have bought their maps
from Stanfords including Captain Scott,
Ernest Shackleton, Florence Nightingale,
Michael Palin and Sir Ranulph Fiennes.
Stanfords also appears in The 'Hound of
the Baskervilles', so even Sherlock Holmes
was a customer!

The vast shop stocks the largest range of
maps in the world, importing them from
every corner of the globe. The selection
includes reproduction antique maps,
nautical charts, international maps and the
full Ordnance Survey range. If they don't
have exactly what you want, there is a Map
Room where bespoke maps are printed
exactly to your specifications. As you walk
around the store, don't forget to look down
where vast maps even line the floors. The
store also has a café on the ground floor
where you can relax with your purchases
and start planning your next adventure.

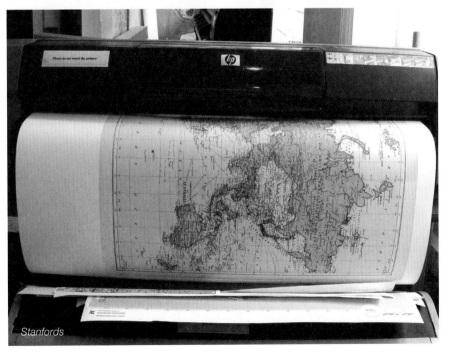

Stanfords

Rudolf Steiner Bookshop

🖃 *Rudolf Steiner House, 35 Park Road, NW1 6XT*

☎ *020 7724 7699*

✍ *www.rsh.anth.org.uk*

🚌 *Baker Street LU*

🕓 *Mon-Fri 12noon-2pm & 4pm-7.45pm Sat 10am-2pm & 3pm-6.30pm*

This bookshop specialises in texts by Rudolf Steiner and associated authors which develop the ideas of Steiner and the Anthroposophical movement. Subjects covered include spiritual development, art, education, child development, parenting, medicine, gardening and architecture, plus there is a selection of children's books. The shop also sells a range of biodynamically produced foods and body care products from Weleda and Dr Hauschka.

Stepping Stones Mind Body & Soul

🖃 *97 Trafalgar Road, SE10 9TS*

☎ *020 8853 2733*

✍ *www.steppingstonesgreenwich.co.uk*

🚌 *Maze Hill Rail*

🕓 *Daily 10am-7pm*

This small shop primarily sells healing crystals, crystal jewellery, spiritual gifts and books on magic and spirituality. There's a Mind, Body and Soul Centre attached where clients can choose from a menu of therapies. The shop is situated fifteen minutes' walk from Greenwich centre or two minutes from Maze Hill rail station.

Stoke Newington Bookshop

Stoke Newington Bargain Bookshop

- 153 Stoke Newington High Street, N16 ONY
- ☎ 020 7249 8983
- ⌨ www.stokenewingtonbookshop.co.uk
- 🚌 Stoke Newington Rail
- ⏱ Mon-Sat 10am-5.30pm

A discount bookshop belonging to Stoke Newington Bookshop (see below), just a few doors down. They offer a good range at fair prices and are especially strong on art, cookery, gardening, reference, fiction and children's titles. As well as bargain books, the shop also carries a range of traditional wooden toys which have proved a big success with the buggy pushing denizens of Stokie. Greetings cards, art supplies and stationery complete the stock of this long-established bargain shop.

Stoke Newington Bookshop

- 159 Stoke Newington High Street, N16 ONY
- ☎ 020 7249 2808
- ⌨ www.stokenewingtonbookshop.co.uk
- 🚌 Stoke Newington Rail
- ⏱ Mon-Sat 9.30am-6pm, Sun 11am-5pm

Soothing music, well-displayed stock and tempting special offers greet visitors to this spacious local bookshop. Their fiction and children's sections are particularly impressive but non-fiction and newly published books also have a strong presence, most notably local interest and local history books. The store also offers a selection of cards, music CDs and they now stock a range of adult jigsaws. The bookshop regularly hosts author readings and is the sole bookseller for the annual Stoke Newington Literary Festival which takes place in June (see page 307). For bargain books, look out for their sister shop – Stoke Newington Bargain Bookshop (see above) a few doors away.

Steimatzky Hasifira

- 46 Golders Green Road, NW11 8LL
- ☎ 020 8458 9774
- ⌨ www.theisraelishop.co.uk
- 🚌 Golders Green LU
- ⏱ Mon-Thurs 10am-7pm, Fri 10am-3pm, Sun 10.30am-7pm

A Jewish bookseller with a large selection of books in English and Hebrew on all aspects of Jewish religion, life and experience. The stock includes publications for English speakers learning Hebrew, Jewish and Israeli music and DVDs, plus guidebooks to Israel.

Henry Stokes and Co

- 58 Elizabeth Street, SW1W 9PB
- ☎ 020 7730 7073
- ⌨ www.hrstokes.com
- 🚌 Victoria LU/Rail, Sloane Square LU
- ⏱ Mon-Fri 9am-6pm, Sat 9am-4pm

This local shop has traded on Elizabeth Street for over 150 years, producing its own range of fine stationery, but also selling gifts and a well-chosen selection of novels, reference and children's books. They offer an efficient ordering service to supplement the stock and run a book club which offers discounts on purchases as well as participation in their monthly online literary discussion. Elizabeth Street is also the location of two fabulous bakeries Poilâne and Baker & Spice.

Swedenborg Society Bookshop

- 20-21 Bloomsbury Way, WC1A 2TH
- ☎ 020 7405 7986
- ⌨ www.swedenborg.org.uk
- 🚌 Tottenham Court Road LU, Holborn LU
- ⏱ Mon-Fri 9.30am-5pm

A publisher and bookseller of the philosophical writings of Emanuel Swedenborg (in English, the original Latin and a range of foreign languages) and books and journals about his life and works. There is also a selection of second-hand and antiquarian books.

T

Tabernacle Bookshop

🖃 *Metropolitan Tabernacle, Pastor Street, Elephant and Castle, SE1 6SD*

☎ *020 7735 7076*

✑ *www.tabernaclebookshop.org*

🚇 *Elephant & Castle LU*

🕓 *Mon-Fri 9am-5pm, Sat 10am-1pm*

The Tabernacle Bookshop is one of the UK's oldest reformed Christian bookshops and the largest distributor of Christian Sunday School lessons. The history of the bookshop stretches back to Mrs Spurgeon's book fund which was started in 1875 to supply theological books to ministers. The Metropolitan Tabernacle is just opposite the huge shopping centre at the Elephant and Castle.

Tales on Moon Lane

🖃 *25 Half Moon Lane, SE24 9JU*

☎ *020 7274 5759*

✑ *www.talesonmoonlane.co.uk*

🚇 *Herne Hill Rail*

🕓 *Mon-Fri 9am-5.45pm, Sat 9am-6pm, Sun 10.30am-4pm*

This specialist children's bookshop has recently celebrated its tenth birthday and remains a popular bookstore with local parents and children. The reasons for the store's continued success are clear: it has a fabulous range of books, highly knowledgeable staff and lots of sofas and chairs to make book shopping a comfortable and relaxing experience. The book stock is supplemented by gifts and toys and enticing displays.

The books are arranged in helpful ways and the staff are always on hand with tips and recommendations if you get stuck. There is a storytelling session every Tuesday at 11am during term-time and half-term activities and author events are also a feature. This part of Half Moon Lane now has several children's shops including ones selling toys, shoes and dancing clothes. There are lots of places for a post-purchase coffee and Brockwell Park is just around the corner if a picnic is more your thing.

TASCHEN

🖃 *12 Duke of York Square, SW3 4LY*

☎ *020 7881 0795*

✑ *www.taschen.com*

🚇 *Sloane Square LU*

🕓 *Mon-Sat 10am-6pm (Thurs and Sat until 7pm), Sun 12noon-6pm*

Just opposite the entrance to the Saatchi Gallery, a few yards from King's Road, this is Taschen's only dedicated London store. It showcases the books of the eponymous publisher whose titles cover art in its broadest sense including modern art, design, fashion, architecture, photography, lifestyle and film. This modern shop is the flamboyant work of Philippe Starck and displays Taschen's glossy titles to perfection. It also has a gallery space in the basement which is well worth exploring. The shop has occasional sales when display and slightly damaged stock is sold for 50-75% discount – check their website for details. The Saatchi Gallery Bookshop (see p.103) and John Sandoe (see p.104) are both just a short stroll away.

Tate Britain Shop

⌨ *Tate Britain, Millbank, SW1P 4RG*
☎ *020 7887 8888*
🖉 *www.tate.org.uk*
🚌 *Pimlico LU*
🕓 *Daily 10am-5.50pm*

The main shop near the Millbank entrance, although smaller than its sister in Tate Modern (see opposite) still stocks an impressive number of books on the Tate's collections. British art from 1500 to the present day is the emphasis here and the art essays and monographs are supplemented by art magazines and journals, books on recent exhibitions, children's books and more general titles on British history and culture and London. It's a good place to look for unusual gifts, art materials and stationery items too and there's a huge array of postcards and posters of works in the collection. There is also a small shop just off the main hallway, selling goods relating to the current show and the Manton shop, near the Manton Street entrance, which sells items related to the exhibition there.

Tate Modern Shop

⌨ *Tate Modern, Bankside, SE1 9TG*
☎ *020 7401 5167*
🖉 *www.tate.org.uk*
🚌 *Blackfriars LU/Rail*
🕓 *Sun-Thurs 10am-6pm,*
   Fri & Sat 10am-10pm

From power station to powerhouse art gallery, Tate Modern is one of London's cultural success stories. It's also home to the most extensive art bookshop in London, situated just next to the towering main Turbine Hall, and boasting over 10,000 titles. The stock reflects the enormous scope of the Tate's art holdings and caters for all levels of knowledge and interest – art techniques, art history, art and critical theory, design, painting, sculpture, installation art, photography and lens-based media and architecture are just some of the subjects covered. There are posters and postcards galore as well, and a natty range of designer gifts. There are smaller shops on Level 2 (River Shop, which includes books on the local area) and Level 4 (the Exhibition Shop with items connected to the current exhibition). Be sure to journey to the upper floors of the gallery for stunning views across London.

Tennis Gallery

⌨ *112 Arthur Road, SW19 8AA*
☏ *020 8715 8866*
✎ *www.tennisgallerywimbledon.com*
🚍 *Wimbledon Park LU*
🕔 *Tues-Sat 10am-5pm (extended hours during Wimbledon fortnight)*

Just across the park from the All England Lawn Tennis Club, this is a must-see destination for all tennis fans. They stock around 6,000 titles published in the UK, USA and Australia covering all aspects of the game including history, coaching, players, tournaments, health and fitness, yearbooks and related fiction. Allied to this there are tennis related posters, greetings cards, DVDs, calendars, gifts, paintings and other collectables. The shop also produces a monthly newsletter and an annual catalogue.

The Theosophical Society in England

⌨ *50 Gloucester Place, W1U 8EA*
☏ *020 7935 9261*
✎ *www.theosophical-society.org.uk*
🚍 *Baker Street LU*
🕔 *Mon-Thurs 2pm-6.30pm,*
   Sun 4.30pm-8.30pm (during lectures)

This bookshop is based in the foyer of the British headquarters of the Theosophical Society, which is a centre for lectures and meditation and has a library. The bookshop has mostly new, full price, books concerning Theosophy but also sells publications about other religions, and has some discounted and second-hand titles.

Tintin Shop

⌨ *34 Floral Street,*
   WC2E 9DJ
☏ *020 7836 1131*
✎ *www.thetintinshop.uk.com*
🚍 *Leicester Square LU, Covent Garden LU*
🕔 *Mon-Sat 10.30am-5.30pm,*
   Sun 12noon-4pm

This store sells books, posters, cards, clothing, watches, crockery ... actually everything and anything to do with Tintin, his adventures and his creator.

Torah Treasures

⌨ *16 Russell Parade,*
   Golders Green Road, NW11 9NN
☏ *020 8458 8289*
✎ *www.torahtreasures.co.uk/*
🚍 *Brent Cross LU*
🕔 *Sun-Wed 9.30am-6pm,*
   Thurs 9.30am-4pm,
   Fri 9.30am-3pm (1pm in winter)

Specialist Jewish bookseller with a good stock of Hebrew and English books on all aspects of Jewish religion, history, culture and life.

Treadwell's

See page 164.

V

Victoria and Albert Museum Shop

🏛 *Cromwell Road, SW7 2RL*
☎ *020 7942 2000*
✎ *www.vandashop.com*
🚇 *South Kensington LU*
🕓 *Daily 10am-5.30pm, Friday until 9.40pm*

The V&A Shop sells all sorts of accessories, textiles and gifts inspired by the collections and exhibitions of the museum. The world of books is not forgotten with a dedicated bookshop with particular strengths in design, photography, fashion, architecture, jewellery, sculpture and textiles. The store has a good general stock, but is particularly popular with the trendy design and fashion students who trawl the museum for inspiration and are drawn to the shop's extensive display of fashion magazines. As well as selling the work of other publishers, the V&A also offers over 180 of its own publications which are beautifully illustrated and feature the collections and exhibitions of the museum. The V&A's historic café is a real treat and a great way to conclude your visit and peruse your purchases.

Village Books

🏛 *1d Calton Avenue, SE21 7DE*
☎ *020 8693 2808*
✎ *www.village-books.co.uk*
🚇 *North Dulwich Rail*
🕓 *Mon-Sat 9am-5.30pm, Sun 11am-5pm*

The bright red shop front and imaginative window displays make this award-winning local bookshop difficult to miss. Inside, visitor are assured a warm welcome and a well-chosen selection of adult fiction, biography, travel and children's books spread over two floors with enticing displays and recommendations for those looking for inspiration. Former Waterstones directors Hazel Broadfoot and Julian Toland acquired the business in 1996, continuing a tradition of bookselling from the premises that goes back to before the war. Village Books has changed with the times and now has an active social media presence and efficient ordering system which has allowed the store to keep a loyal local following who also enjoy the literary events and book signings that are a feature here. The store offers a good selection of cards and wrapping paper and will gift wrap any purchase for those looking for a literary present. The delicious Au Ciel patisserie is just a few doors away if you require refreshment after your exertions.

Village Games

🏛 *65 West Yard, Camden Lock, NW1 8AF*
☎ *020 7485 0653*
✎ *information@villagegames.com*
🚇 *Camden Town LU*
🕓 *Wed-Sun 10am-5.30pm*

This tiny shop specialises in games and puzzles of all sorts. Its limited book selection covers mainstream games like chess, Go and Mah Jong as well as more esoteric mathematical and geometric puzzles.

W

The Wallace Collection

🏛 *Hertford House, Manchester Square, W1U 3BN*

☎ *020 7563 9522*

✎ *www.wallacecollection.org.uk*

🚇 *Bond Street LU, Baker Street LU*

🕐 *Daily 10am-5pm*

The Wallace Collection houses the extraordinary art collection amassed by the Hertford family and is especially renowned for its eighteenth-century French pictures, porcelain, furniture and armoury. It is also home to impressive collections of Old Masters and Renaissance treasures. The museum shop sells a classy range of gift items inspired by the collection as well as a carefully selected stock of books about art, arms and armour and fashion including scholarly catalogues relating to the museum's collection. There is also a reasonable choice of children's books. Refreshment is available in The Wallace Restaurant and Café, located in the glass-covered courtyard.

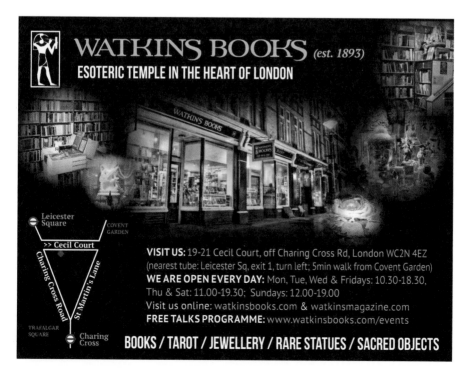

WATKINS BOOKS *(est. 1893)*

ESOTERIC TEMPLE IN THE HEART OF LONDON

VISIT US: 19-21 Cecil Court, off Charing Cross Rd, London WC2N 4EZ (nearest tube: Leicester Sq, exit 1, turn left; 5min walk from Covent Garden)
WE ARE OPEN EVERY DAY: Mon, Tue, Wed & Fridays: 10.30-18.30, Thu & Sat: 11.00-19.30; Sundays: 12.00-19.00
Visit us online: watkinsbooks.com & watkinsmagazine.com
FREE TALKS PROGRAMME: www.watkinsbooks.com/events

BOOKS / TAROT / JEWELLERY / RARE STATUES / SACRED OBJECTS

123

WATERSTONES

🖳 www.waterstones.com

Waterstones are shops with a serious literary feel to them with an emphasis on books rather than peripherals. The staff are generally pretty clued up about their subject and always willing to locate a book in another store if it isn't on their shelves. With well over twenty shops across the capital, you'll not have to travel far to reach one. Waterstones run a loyalty card scheme which offers discounts and special promotions and that is worth joining.

Branches at:

Canary Wharf Cabot

🖃 Cabot Place East, Canary Wharf, E14 4QT

☎ 020 7513 0060

🚌 Canary Wharf LU/DLR

🕓 Mon-Fri 8.30am-8pm, Sat 10am-6pm, Sun 11am-6pm

A medium-sized store located in the heart of Canary Wharf.

Canary Wharf Jubilee

🖃 Unit 1, Jubilee Place, 45 Bank Street, Canary Wharf, E14 5NY

☎ 020 7719 0688

🚌 Heron's Quay DLR

🕓 Mon-Fri 8.30am-8pm, Sun 12noon-6pm

Camden

🖃 128 Camden High Street, NW1 7JR

☎ 020 7284 4948

🚌 Camden Town LU

🕓 Mon-Fri 9.30am-7pm, Sat 9.30am-6pm, Sun 11.30am-6pm

Chiswick

🖃 220-226 Chiswick High Road, W4 1PD

☎ 020 8995 3559

🚌 Turnham Green LU

🕓 Mon-Fri 9am-7pm, Sat 9am-6.30pm, Sun 11am-5pm

Clapham

🖃 70 St John's Road, SW11 1PT

☎ 020 7978 5844

🚌 Clapham Junction Rail

🕓 Mon-Sat 9am-7pm, Sun 11am-5pm

This branch offers the usual broad range with an especially extensive children's section towards the rear of the store.

Covent Garden

🖃 9-13 Garrick Street, WC2E 9BA

☎ 020 7836 6757

🚌 Covent Garden LU

🕓 Mon-Sat 9.30am-8pm, Sun 12noon-6pm

Fiction, travel and art related titles are prominent on the ground floor but the usual extensive Waterstones stock can be found in the basement.

Ealing

🖃 64 Ealing Broadway Centre, W5 5JY

☎ 020 8840 5905

🚌 Ealing Broadway LU

🕓 Mon-Sat 9am-7pm, Sun 11am-5pm

A small, two-storey branch in the heart of Ealing's shopping centre.

Economists' Bookshop

London School of Economics,

🖃 Clare Market, Portugal Street, WC2A 2AB

☎ 020 7405 5531

🚌 Holborn LU

🕓 Mon-Fri 10am-6.30pm, Sat 12noon-6pm

A specialist academic shop.

Finchley Road (O2)

🖃 Unit 5, O2 Centre, Finchley Road, NW3 6LU

☎ 020 7433 3299

🚌 Finchley Road LU

🕓 Mon-Fri 10am-8pm, Sat 10am-8pm, Sun 11am-5pm

Waterstones, Piccadilly

Finchley

🖃 *782 High Street, North Finchley,*
N12 8JY
☎ *020 8446 9669*
🚇 *Finchley Road LU*
🕒 *Mon-Sat 9.30am-6pm, Sun 11am-5pm*

Gower Street

🖃 *82 Gower Street, WC1E 6EQ*
☎ *020 7636 1577*
🚇 *Goodge Street LU*
🕒 *Mon-Fri 8.30am-8pm, Sat 9.30am-7pm,*
Sun 12noon-6pm

The best academic bookstore in London
– just around the corner from London
University. Hundreds of thousands of titles
are ranged over five floors. The second-
hand and discount sections are extensive.
(see p.168)

Greenwich

🖃 *51 Greenwich Church Street, SE10 9BL*
☎ *020 8853 8530*
🚇 *Cutty Sark DLR, Greenwich Rail/DLR*
🕒 *Mon-Sat 9.30am-7pm,*
Sun 12noon-5.30pm

Hampstead

🖃 *68-69 Hampstead High Street, NW3 1QP*
☎ *020 7794 1098*
🚇 *Hampstead LU*
🕒 *Mon-Sat 9am-8pm,*
Sun 11.30am-5.30pm

A large, well-stocked and bustling branch of
this chain with two floors packed with every
subject under the sun. As befits a store in
the heart of literary Hampstead, there are
regular readings and signings.

Hatchards

✎ *www.hatchards.co.uk*
🖃 *187 Piccadilly, W1J 9LE*
☎ *020 7439 9921*

🖃 *St Pancras International,*
Euston Road, N1C 4QP
☎ *020 7278 1238*
See review p.62

Islington

🖃 *11 Islington Green, N1 2XH*
☎ *020 7704 2280*
🚇 *Angel LU*
🕒 *Mon-Sat 9.30am-8pm,*
Sun 11am-5.30pm

This branch extends over two floors
and since the closure of Borders is now
Islington's largest bookstore. There's a
well-stocked children's section and a good
general stock. The shop overlooks Islington
Green which is a pleasant place to relax
when the weather is fine.

Kensington

🖃 *193 Kensington High Street, W8 6SH*
☎ *020 7937 8432*
🚇 *High Street Kensington LU*
🕒 *Mon-Sat 9am-8pm,*
Sun 11.30am-5.30pm

A large branch with a wide selection
of books over three floors. The art,
photography and design sections upstairs
are extensive and there's a welcoming
children's section with browsing beanbags
to invite a longer stay. The travel and
history coverage in the basement is pretty
comprehensive as is the ground floor fiction
stock. This branch often hosts readings
and signings.

King's Road

☐ *150-152 King's Road, SW3 3NR*

☎ *020 7351 2023*

🚇 *Sloane Square LU*

🕓 *Mon-Sat 9am-7pm,*
Sun 11.30am-5.30pm

There are two floors in this bustling and justifiably popular branch in the heart of the King's Road shopping drag. The shop itself is spacious, well-stocked and attractively laid out and there is an especially welcoming children's section with low tables and chairs for little browsers.

Leadenhall

☐ *1-3 Whittington Avenue,*
Leadenhall Market, EC3V 1PJ

☎ *020 7220 7882*

🚇 *Monument LU*

🕓 *Mon-Fri 8am-6.30pm*

The market itself is lovely – a tiny characterful haven in the midst of the impersonal City. This branch of Waterstones is spread over two storeys with a wide-ranging stock including the more serious subjects of management, finance and law appropriate for a branch surrounded by City institutions.

London Wall

☐ *54-55 London Wall, EC2M 5RA,*

☎ *020 7628 9708*

🚇 *Moorgate LU/Rail, Liverpool Street LU/Rail*

🕓 *Mon-Fri 8.30am-7pm*

Notting Hill

☐ *39-41 Notting Hill Gate, W11 3JQ*

☎ *020 7229 9444*

🚇 *Notting Hill Gate LU*

🕓 *Mon-Fri 9am-7.30pm,*
Sat 9.30am-7pm, Sun 12noon-6pm

Busy two-storey branch just a few minutes' walk from Portobello Road market.

Oxford Street Plaza

☐ *6-17 The Plaza, Oxford Street, W1D 1LT*

☎ *020 7436 9145*

🚇 *Oxford Circus LU,*
Tottenham Court Road LU

🕓 *Mon-Sat 9am-8pm, Sun 12noon-6pm*

Oxford Street West

☐ *421 Oxford Street, W1C 2PQ*

☎ *020 7495 8507*

🚇 *Bond Street LU, Marble Arch LU*

🕓 *Mon-Sat 9am-8pm, Sun 11am-6.30pm*

Piccadilly

☐ *203-206 Piccadilly, W1J 9HD*

☎ *020 7851 2400*

🚇 *Piccadilly Circus LU*

🕓 *Mon-Sat 9am-10pm,*
Sun 11.30am-6.30pm

Occupying the former premises of Simpson's department store with its grand art deco stone shop front and concave ground floor windows, Waterstones' flagship store is an impressive example of bookselling on a grand scale. The foyer of the shop with its high ceilings and marble floors is equally majestic. With stock spread over six floors every conceivable subject is covered with over 150,000 books displayed on some eight miles of shelving. The range of books is incredible but helpful staff are on hand to help you navigate around this vast emporium. As you would expect from Waterstones' largest store there is a busy itinerary of events and book signings and the walls of the staircase are lined with photos of the literary greats and famous names who have attended events here from Ian McEwan to David Beckham. The store has two cafés, a restaurant and plenty of comfy seating, making browsing and relaxing here a real pleasure. The store also includes:

The Russian Bookshop

☐ *30 Jermyn Street, SW1Y 6WW*

☎ *020 7851 2483*

🕓 *Mon-Sat 9am-10pm,*
Sun 12noon-6.30pm

Putney

🖳 *6/6a Exchange Centre, SW15 1TW*
☎ *020 8780 2401*
🚌 *Putney Bridge LU*
🕒 *Mon-Sat 9am-6pm, Thurs until 7pm,*
Sun 11am-5pm

A large branch, which positively invites browsing with comfy chairs, intelligently selected and displayed stock, and a coffee shop upstairs.

Trafalgar Square ②

🖳 *The Grand Building,*
Trafalgar Square, WC2N 5EJ
☎ *020 7839 4411*
🚌 *Charing Cross LU/Rail*
🕒 *Mon-Fri 9am-9pm, Sat 9.30-9pm,*
Sun 12noon-6pm

This three-storey branch has fairly limited floor space on the ground and first floors, but a massive basement. The branch has the usual extensive general stock, but has a particularly good travel section upstairs, where you will also find the in-store café.

Walthamstow

🖳 *Unit 30-31 Selborne Walk*
Shopping Centre,
26 Selborne Walk, Walthamstow, E17 7JR
☎ *020 8521 3669*
🚌 *Walthamstow LU*
🕒 *Mon-Sat 9.30am-6pm,*
Wed from 10am, Sun 11am-5pm

Wandsworth

🖳 *Unit 5, Southside Shopping Centre,*
SW18 4TF
☎ *020 8874 4597*
🚌 *Wandsworth Town Rail*
🕒 *Mon-Sat 10am-6pm, Sun 11am-5pm*

Wimbledon

🖳 *12 Wimbledon Bridge, SW19 7NW*
☎ *020 8543 9899*
🚌 *Wimbledon LU*
🕒 *Mon-Sat 9am-6.30pm, Sun 11am-5pm*

Opposite the station in the main Wimbledon shopping area, the store is not one of the largest but carries an extensive range displayed over two storeys.

Outskirts

Barnet

🖳 *2 The Spires, EN5 5XY*
☎ *020 8449 8229*
🚌 *High Barnet LU*
🕒 *Mon-Sat 9am-5.30pm,*
Sun 10.30am-4pm

Bromley

🖳 *100 The Glades Shopping Centre,*
BR1 1DJ
☎ *020 8460 6037*
🚌 *Bromley North Rail*
🕒 *Mon-Sat 9am-6pm, Thurs till 9pm,*
Sun 11am-5pm

Croydon

🖳 *1063/4/7 Whitgift Centre, CR0 1UX*
☎ *020 8686 7032*
🚌 *West Croydon LU*
🕒 *Mon-Sat 9am-6pm, Thurs till 8pm,*
Sun 11am-5pm

Harrow

🖳 *60/62 St Ann's Road, HA1 1JX*
☎ *020 8863 4578*
🚌 *Harrow-on-the-Hill LU/Rail*
🕒 *Mon-Sat 9.30am-6pm, Thurs till 7pm,*
Sun 11am-5pm

Ilford

🖾 *158-160 High Road, IG1 1LL*
☎ *020 8478 8428*
🚌 *Ilford Rail*
🕓 *Mon-Sat 9.30am-6pm, Sun 11am-5pm*

Kingston Bentalls Centre

🖾 *Unit 59 Wood Street, KT1 1TR*
☎ *020 8974 6811*
🚌 *Hampton Wick Rail*
🕓 *Mon-Fri 9am-6pm, Thurs till 9pm,*
    Sat 9am-7pm, Sun 11am-5pm

Richmond

🖾 *2-6 Hill Street, TW10 6UA*
☎ *020 8332 1600*
🚌 *Richmond Rail*
🕓 *Mon-Sat 9am-6.30pm,*
    Sun 11.30am-5.30pm

Teddington

🖾 *65-67 High Street, TW11 8HA*
☎ *020 8977 6883*
🚌 *Teddington Rail*
🕓 *Mon-Fri 9.30am-6pm, Sat 9am-5.30pm,*
    Sun 11am-5pm

Twickenham

🖾 *19 King Street, TW1 3SD*
☎ *020 8744 2807*
🚌 *Twickenham Rail*
🕓 *Mon-Sat 9.30am-5.30pm,*
    Sun 10.30am-4.30pm

Waterstones, Piccadilly

Watkins

🖃 *19-21 Cecil Court, Charing Cross Road, WC2N 4EZ*
☎ *020 7836 2182*
🖋 *www.watkinsbooks.com*
🚌 *Leicester Square LU*
🕒 *Mon-Sat 10.30am-6.30pm, Sun 12noon-7pm*

Established in 1893, Watkins claims to be the world's oldest esoteric bookshop. It carries a huge and varied stock of books, magazines, CDs and DVDs on ancient and modern philosophy, astrology, spirituality, religion and alternative therapies. Staff are knowledgeable and helpful and a mail order service is also available. The 'Watkins' Mind Body Spirit' magazine is published in-house and features articles by contemporary spiritual teachers. As well as new titles, magazines and journals they also stock a good selection of second-hand books, religious artefacts, jewellery, Tarot decks, essential oils and gift items.

Wellcome Shop

🖃 *Blackwell's at Wellcome Collection 183 Euston Road, NW1 2BE*
☎ *020 7611 2160*
🖋 *www.blackwell.co.uk/wellcome*
🚌 *Euston LU/Rail, Euston Square LU, Warren Street LU, Kings Cross LU*
🕒 *Mon-Sat 10am-6pm, Thurs till 10pm, Sun 11am-6pm*

The Wellcome Collection has become a popular visitor attraction in recent years with major exhibitions concerning just about anything relating to the Collection, including brains, death, sexuality and the human condition. As the collection has become better known so has this branch of Blackwell's grown in prominence with a wide range of stock covering science, the humanities and the connection between art and science, but also including books with broader appeal, such as art and psychology, children's books with

Wellcome Shop

a particular emphasis on the human body and creativity, and a well-stocked section dedicated to London. Situated in the atrium of the Wellcome Collection, the shop has large windows facing onto Euston Road which let light into this open-plan, modern retail space. The service here is excellent and there are plenty of gift items, wrapping paper and postcards supplementing the book stock. Situated right next to the Wellcome Café and with the world-renowned Wellcome Library (see p.258) in the same building, this store is well worth exploring. For more Blackwell's branches see p.24.

West End Lane Books

⌨ 277 West End Lane, NW6 1QS
☎ 020 7431 3770
✍ www.westendlanebooks.co.uk
🚌 West Hampstead LU
☾ Mon-Fri 9am-7pm, Sat 9.30am-6.30pm, Sun 12noon-5pm

West End Lane Books is a lovely, family-owned, independent bookshop. The shop is well laid out with many books facing out for easy browsing. There's an extensive fiction section, strong biography, history, business, politics, culture and travel sections and a delightful children's section with an array of classics and contemporary fiction and some real gems from smaller publishers. The shop also sells a good selection of beautiful stationery and has become well known for its regular author talks and readings. You can sign up for their chatty monthly newsletter on the website or follow them on Twitter for news on their two book groups (general and crime), visiting authors, special offers and competitions. Their sister shop is Queen's Park Books (see p.96).

Wilde Ones

⌨ 283 King's Road, SW3 5EW
☎ 020 7352 9531
✍ www.wildeones.com
🚌 South Kensington LU, Sloane Square LU
☾ Mon-Fri 10am-6pm, Sat 10am-7pm, Sun & Bank Hols 12noon-6pm

This self-styled 'ramshackle emporium' sells a large selection of books including subjects such as Tibetan Buddhism, Taoism, Tarot, crystals and healing, Sufism, esoteric Christianity and reincarnation. For those who want to look the part the store also offers jewellery and textiles, and a range of artefacts for the new age home from crystals to essential oils.

Wildy & Sons Ltd

✍ www.wildy.com

This company was established on the Lincoln's Inn site in 1830 but was almost certainly selling books in London before that date. They have two specialist law bookshops in the centre of legal London.

⌨ Lincoln's Inn Archway, Carey Street, WC2A 2JD
☎ 020 7242 5778
🚌 Chancery Lane LU
☾ Mon-Fri 8.45am-6pm

This branch also sells second-hand and antiquarian law books.

⌨ 16 Fleet Street, EC4Y 1AU
☎ 020 7353 3907
🚌 Chancery Lane LU
☾ Mon-Fri 9am-6pm

This branch also sells London guide books for general readers.

Wimbledon Books and Music

📖 *40 The High Street, Wimbledon Village, SW19 5AU*

☎ *020 8879 3101*

✎ *www.wimbledonbooksandmusic.co.uk*

🚌 *Wimbledon LU*

🕓 *Mon-Sat 10am-5.30pm, Sun 11am-5pm*

This small but well-stocked bookshop has a loyal following among the denizens of SW19 and is very much engaged with the community, being the chosen bookseller for the annual Wimbledon Bookfest (see p.132). The stock covers most subjects but particular strengths are children's books and a local section with titles dealing with Wimbledon, Richmond and the Thames. There are regular readings for children during term-time and occasional book signings and events by local authors. The shop is located in the heart of Wimbledon Village, with the Common just 50 metres away and plenty of coffee shops in which to relax and enjoy your purchases.

The Works

📖 *Unit 24, Lewisham Centre, SE13 7HB*

☎ *020 8297 9265*

✎ *www.theworks.co.uk*

🚌 *Lewisham DLR/Rail*

🕓 *Mon-Sat 9am-6pm & Sun 10am-5pm*

A nationwide discount retail chain with a few London branches. The Works sells heavily discounted books with an emphasis on glossy cookery, gardening, interior design, reference and art books. The stores are modern and charmless but there are plenty of bargains. They also sell plenty of children's books, stationery, DVDs and art materials.

Branches:

📖 *Unit 10 London Designer Outlet, Empire Way, HA9 0WS*

☎ *020 8900 2216*

🚌 *Woolwich Arsenal LU*

🕓 *Mon-Sat 10am-8pm, Sun 12noon-6pm*

and

📖 *97-99 Powis Street, Woolwich, SE18 6JB*

☎ *020 8317 1848*

🚌 *Wembley Stadium Rail*

🕓 *Mon-Sat 9am-5.30pm, Sun 10am-4pm*

WEST END LANE BOOKS

Dream of browsing beautiful books in a welcoming, tranquil spot? It's what we're here for.

Extensive selection of the best new and classic fiction, non fiction, children's, travel, stationery & a great deal more.

Join our mailing list for news of our regular author readings, book groups and promotions.

Independent bookselling since 1994. Time Out Love London Best Shop winner 2014
www.welbooks.co.uk info@welbooks.co.uk 0207 431 3770 @WELBooks

Y

Yamaha Music London

- 152-160 Wardour Street, W1F 8YA
- 020 7432 4400
- www.yamahamusiclondon.com
- Tottenham Court Road LU, Oxford Circus LU
- Mon-Fri 9.30am-6pm (Thurs till 8pm), Sat 10am-5.30pm

Formerly Chappell of Bond Street, but other than a change in name this long established store continues to provide an excellent range of musical instruments alongside a wide choice of scores for classical and modern music. Virtually every instrument, style of playing and level of competence is covered and there are also instrumental tutors for aspiring musicians. Backing tracks, music for ensemble playing and books on music, complete the stock of this wonderful shop.

Yogamatters

- 32 Clarendon Road, N8 0DJ
- 020 8888 8588
- www.yogamatters.com
- Turnpike Lane LU
- Mon-Fri 9am-6pm (Thurs till 8pm), Sat 9am-4pm

A specialist yoga shop that prides itself on being the yoga community's best kept secret. This place sells everything that anyone involved in yoga from beginner to teacher level could possibly need, including a great range of books (they estimate to have about 1,200 titles). The subjects covered include yoga practice, yoga therapy, meditation, ayurveda, philosophy as well as religion as it relates to yoga. There are also DVDs, yoga clothing and equipment. The shop is just off Hornsey Park Road in an industrial estate. Despite the unspiritual surroundings the staff are welcoming and helpful, making the journey more than worthwhile.

1, 2, 3...

30th Century Comics

- 18 Lower Richmond Road, SW15 1JP
- 020 8788 2052
- www.30thcenturycomics.co.uk
- Putney Bridge LU
- Mon-Sat 10.30am-6pm

A specialist in new and vintage UK and US comics and annuals including Superman, Spider-Man, Batman and X-Men (from the US) and Beano, Dandy, Bunty, Rupert and Eagle (from the UK). Their vintage stock dates largely from the 1930's to 1980's with a few titles from even earlier. They also stock some comic-related merchandise such as action figures and carry a selection of second-hand books in the science-fiction, horror, mystery and 'sleaze' genres.

Second-hand
& Antiquarian

Second-hand & Antiquarian Bookshops

A

Adanami Bookshop

- 30 Brewer Street, W1F 0SS
- ☎ 020 7437 5238
- Piccadilly Circus LU
- ☺ Daily 12noon-10pm

A few minutes' walk into Soho from Piccadilly Circus, this tiny shop is piled floor to ceiling with second-hand Japanese language books and magazines.

Al Saqi Books

See p.15

Altea Antique Maps

- Altea Gallery, 35 St George Street, W1S 2FN
- ☎ 020 7491 0010
- www.alteagallery.com
- Oxford CircusLU, Green Park LU, Bond Street LU
- ☺ Mon-Fri 10am-6pm, Sat 10am-4pm

Antique maps, charts and plans are the main stock of this shop but antiquarian atlases, travel books and cartography reference are also available. Many of the maps are beautiful objects in their own right and a few are available for under £100 – not bad for a special gift.

Any Amount of Books

- 56 Charing Cross Road, WC2H 0QA
- ☎ 020 7836 3697
- www.anyamountofbooks.com
- Leicester Square LU
- ☺ Daily 10.30am-9.30pm

A long-standing Charing Cross Road favourite with an excellent general stock of second-hand books and a high turnover. They are especially good for review copies of newly published titles at low prices. It's always busy and the basement houses a huge number of special bargains. Their entire stock of over 42,000 books is listed on Abebooks, so start there if you're searching for a particular book. Other good second-hand bookshops can be found a short walk away on Charing Cross Road and also on Cecil Court, closer to Trafalgar Square.

Archive Books and Music

- 83 Bell Street, NW1 6TB
- ☎ 020 7402 8212
- www.archivebookstore.co.uk
- Edgware Road LU, Marylebone LU
- ☺ Mon-Sat 11.00am-6pm

Probably one of the most disorganised, overwhelming bookshops in London – and an absolute delight. Books are stacked floor to ceiling and tottering piles occupy every surface. Stepladders are provided for the exploration of the heights while venturing down to the music cellar is rather like an expedition to a virgin jungle peopled with the ghosts of composers past (there's even a piano down there if you can excavate sufficiently far). With bargains galore spilling from boxes outside, this shop carries a general stock but is especially strong on sheet music (popular and classical) and books about music. An eccentric gem of a shop.

B

Black Gull

There are two shops, separated by quite a distance but both with a similar feel and stock, despite one being in the heart of a frantic market and the other in the genteel suburbs. They both feature a wide-ranging and fast-changing general stock but are especially strong on quality fiction, history, philosophy, psychology, art, photography, fashion and textiles, film and children's books. Black Gull are always looking to buy new stock and will collect when larger quantities are involved. Branches at:

⌂ 70-71 The West Yard,
    Camden Lock Place, NW1 8AF
☎ 020 7267 5005
🚌 Camden Town LU
🕒 Daily 10am-6pm

⌂ 121 High Road, East Finchley, N2 8AG
☎ 020 8444 4717
✎ black.gull.finchley@gmail.com
🚌 East Finchley LU
🕒 Daily 9.30am-7pm

Book and Comic Exchange

⌂ 14 Pembridge Road, W11 3HL
☎ 020 7229 8420
✎ www.mgeshops.co.uk
🚌 Notting Hill Gate LU
🕒 Daily 10am-8pm

This is a large nationwide chain that trades in all kinds of second-hand goods. This branch is the only one that continues to deal in books. It operates a system by which the longer a book stays on the shelf the lower it is priced. The shop is usually busy and there's a fast turnover of stock, but the shops are quite shabby and the staff not particularly helpful.

BLACK GULL BOOKS

art • photography • film • history • philosophy
psychology • music • drama • folklore • fiction

new • used • antiquarian / open 7 days 10am - 6pm

121 High Rd, East Finchley
London, N2 8AG
020 8444 4717
077907 86351

70 West Yard, Camden Lock Place
London, NW1 8AF
020 7267 5005
077907 86351

The Book and Record Bar at the Gypsy Queen

20 Norwood High Street, SE27 9NR
020 8670 9568 / 07971 265 228
www.facebook.com/thebookandrecordbar
West Norwood Rail
Tues-Sun 10.30am-6pm

Mike started off selling records from a stall, at West Norwood's monthly market, The Feast, before opening his own coffee shop that also sells vinyl and books. The book stock is pretty extensive and includes a great kid's section, poetry, crime, lots of interesting reference books and a great range of paperback fiction with prices starting from just £2. Mike has also acquired a large collection first edition fiction and most of these titles are available for £8-£10, with the more expensive, rare books available to view on request. This is a real haven for Norwood's bibliophiles and vinyl collectors, and also serves great coffee – who could ask for more?

Bookmongers

439 Coldharbour Lane, SW9 8LN
020 7738 4225
www.bookmongers.com
Brixton LU/Rail
Mon-Sat 10.30am-6.30pm, Sun 11am-4pm

There's much for the bargain minded book lover to appreciate at this brilliant second-hand bookshop just around the corner from the Ritzy Cinema in Brixton. The stock is wide ranging and keenly priced and well organised with sections on business and commerce, books by Irish and Scottish writers and foreign language titles, as well as mainstream fiction and more academic books on history and science. This is undoubtedly one of the best second-hand bookshops south of the river. Head up and into Market Row to find the excellent Rosie's Café or Franco Manca for a post-purchase pizza.

The Bookshop on the Heath

74 Tranquil Vale, Blackheath, SE3 0BW
020 8852 4786
www.bookshopontheheath.co.uk
Blackheath Rail
Mon-Tues, Thurs-Fri 11.00am-5.30pm Sat 10am-6pm, Sun 11am-5pm

Located on the corner of Blackheath Village near to the Heath, a short walk from Greenwich, this long-established shop carries antiquarian and second-hand books in most subject areas, including local history and guidebooks, as well as modern first editions. The shop is particularly known for general literature, crime, science fiction, religious/spiritual, biography, poetry and children's books. The price range extends from a £1.80 paperback to a first edition James Bond for considerably more. In addition to the excellent book stock there is also a selection of prints, maps and original art. There are plenty of coffee shops and restaurants nearby, and a picnic on the Heath is an appealing option on fine days.

Bryars & Bryars 2

7 Cecil Court, WC2N 4EZ
020 7836 1910
www.paralos.co.uk
Leicester Square LU
Mon-Sat 11am-6pm

This store specialises in atlases, maps and charts of all regions, dating from the fifteenth century to the twentieth. They offer a selection of topographical and natural history prints as well as general antiquarian books on subjects such as early printing, classics, history, literature, detective fiction, art and travel.

C

Marcus Campbell Art Books

⊞ 43 Holland Street, Southwark, SE1 9JR
☎ 020 7261 0111
✍ www.marcuscampbell.co.uk
🚌 Southwark LU, Blackfriars LU/Rail
🕓 Mon-Sat 10.30am-6.30pm,
Sun 12noon-6pm

Handily located next to Tate Modern and close to the River Thames, this shop deals in out-of-print, rare and second-hand books on twentieth-century and contemporary art. Stock includes books on important movements, monographs, catalogues, artists' books, magazines and ephemera. There's also a selection of exhibition catalogues from £1.

Church Street Bookshop

⊞ 142 Stoke Newington Church Street,
N16 0JU
☎ 020 7241 5411
🚌 Stoke Newington Rail
🕓 Daily 11am-6pm

An excellent second-hand bookshop located in the heart of Stoke Newington. Small but amply stocked, the shop veers towards serious subjects including literary criticism, history, health, politics, psychology, philosophy, art, design and literary fiction. There's also an extensive range of children's books. They always have plenty of recently published review copies and well-stocked bargain boxes with books for as little as 50p. You can survey their more expensive stock on www.abebooks.com.

Classic Rare Books

⊞ 61 Cambridge Street, SW1V 4PS
☎ 020 7834 5554
✍ www.classicrarebooks.co.uk
🚌 Pimlico LU, Victoria LU/Rail
🕓 By appointment

This company has been established for over 20 years and specialises in fine and rare books with prices ranging from £18 for a recent hardback to a selection of rare leather bound books for many thousands of pounds. The stock covers English and French literature, history, bound sets, first editions, voyages, travel, illustrated books and fine bindings.

Collinge and Clark

⊞ 13 Leigh Street, WC1H 9EW
☎ 020 7387 7105
✍ www.collingeandclark.co.uk
🚌 Russell Square LU
🕓 Mon-Fri 11am-6.30pm,
Sat 11am-3.30pm

A small, high quality, second-hand, antiquarian and rare bookshop which specialises in volumes from private presses and books on arts and crafts, literature and typography. Much of the stock is leather-bound and in mint condition with price tags to match, but there are some leather-bound volumes for as little as £30. Fans of the television series 'Black Books' still visit Collinge and Clark as it was the location for the fictional bookshop.

They will probably be disappointed to discover that the staff here are friendly and helpful and even go to the trouble of producing a catalogue twice a year.

Copperfield's

🖃 *37 Hartfield Road, SW19 3SG*
☎ *020 8542 0113*
⌨ *www.copperfieldbooks.co.uk*
🚇 *Wimbledon LU/Rail*
🕘 *Mon-Wed 9.30am-7pm,*
Thurs & Fri 9.30am-8pm,
Sat 8.30am-7pm, Sun 11am-5pm

A gem of a second-hand bookshop a few minutes' walk from the main Wimbledon shopping centre. The shop is jam-packed with titles in all subject areas with an estimated 42,000 books in the shop plus another 8,000 in storage. It's hard to select any area in particular for special mention but they are particularly strong on philosophy, poetry, fiction, travel, biography and history. The children's section is very good and effort is made to make it accessible and comfortable for young browsers. The themed window displays here are always interesting and the annual January sale is a real event. It's a hard-hearted book lover who leaves empty-handed.

Daniel Crouch Rare Books

🖃 *4 Bury Street, St James's, SW1Y 6AB*
☎ *020 7042 0240*
⌨ *www.crouchrarebooks.com*
🚇 *Green Park LU*
🕘 *Mon-Fri 10am-6pm, Sat by appointment*

Daniel Crouch Rare Books has been dealing in antique atlases, maps and sea charts from this smart Mayfair shop since 2010. The business may be relatively new, but Daniel Crouch and his business partner Nick Trimming have a wealth of experience in this field and have already established a reputation as purveyors of rare atlases and fine bindings. Prices start from £60 for a 1975 edition of Printer Maps of Victorian London and go up to as much as £110,000 for John Speed's first English world atlas dating from 1676. Their website is excellent and contains details of most of their current stock.

E

Francis Edwards

🖃 *72 Charing Cross Road, WC2H 0BE*
☎ *020 7379 7669*
⌨ *www.francisedwards.co.uk*
🚇 *Leicester Square LU*
🕘 *Mon-Sat 9am-9pm, Sun 12noon-8pm*

Sharing an entrance with Quinto (see p.160) and close to the tube station and the other bookshops on Charing Cross Road, this shop has a general antiquarian stock although it is especially strong on art, military history, first editions, natural history, science and travel. Large weekly deliveries of books keep the shelves replenished and make this store worth a regular visit. They issue catalogues on various subjects and a glance at these will reassure buyers that the stock here is of good quality and fairly priced with many collectable books starting at £20.

Peter Ellis Bookseller

🖃 *18 Cecil Court, WC2N 4HE*
☎ *020 7836 8880*
⌨ *www.peter-ellis.co.uk*
🚇 *Leicester Square LU*
🕘 *Mon-Fri 10.30am-7pm,*
Sat 10.30am-5.30pm

A small Cecil Court shop specialising in modern literature, modern first editions, history, travel and illustrated books. They have some rare and wonderful titles on their shelves, making this a shop worth exploring on a visit to Cecil Court.

F

Keith Fawkes

⌨ *1-3 Flask Walk, NW3 1HJ*
☎ *020 7435 0614*
🚇 *Hampstead LU*
🕓 *Daily 10am-5.30pm*

Just around the corner from the underground station, this is a quintessential second-hand bookshop, with a massive stock ranged high on shelves and in piles that would take days rather than hours to sift through. The stock covers all general subjects and is especially strong on art, literature, music and first editions. The store has a fair selection of more expensive antiquarian books, but for those on a budget they also offer a well-stocked discount table outside on Mondays with all books for £2 or less. The table is used from Tuesday to Sunday for the sale of antiques and collectables, complementing the genteel atmosphere of the bookshop which is now a Hampstead institution having traded for over 40 years.

Sam Fogg

⌨ *15D Clifford Street, W1S 4JZ*
☎ *020 7534 2100*
🖳 *www.samfogg.com*
🚇 *Bond Street LU, Green Park LU, Oxford Circus LU*
🕓 *Mon-Fri 9.30am-5.30pm*

This gallery specialises medieval, Islamic and Indian art and manuscripts. You ring the bell for entry but the staff here are approachable, so don't be put off. Exhibitions change every month or two and are accompanied by scholarly catalogues that are works of art in their own right.

Fosters' Bookshop

⌨ *183 Chiswick High Road, W4 2DR*
☎ *020 8995 2768*
🖳 *www.fostersbookshop.co.uk*
www.stephenfoster.co.uk
🚇 *Turnham Green LU*
🕓 *Mon - Sat 10.30am-5.30pm*
most Sundays – 11.00am-5pm

A lovely little second-hand bookshop with an eclectic stock – anything that appeals to the owners finds shelf space, anything that doesn't is rejected. This makes for a highly attractive and personal selection encompassing everything from bargains on the table outside to rare, antiquarian, leather-bound and highly-collectible books inside. Try to categorise their interests and staff will tell you, "We see it as our remit to stock the books that Waterstones should, but don't". There's a great sign in the window 'Children, Dogs and Mad Grannies welcome' – but from experience, the welcome extends far beyond this. If you can't make it all the way to Chiswick to visit this fabulous bookshop, they also exhibit at the major London book fairs (see p.189).

Robert Frew Ltd

⌨ *8 Thurloe Place, SW7 2RX*
☎ *020 7590 6650*
🖳 *www.robertfrew.com*
🚇 *South Kensington LU*
🕓 *Mon-Fri 10am-6pm, Sat 11am-5pm*

A long-established antiquarian book dealer, now with premises opposite the Victoria and Albert Museum. They have specialisms in travel, colour plate and illustrated books, atlases, fine bindings and collectable sets of literary books. Staff are friendly and prices start from £50 upwards. The shop also sells a handsome selection of prints and maps.

G

Natalie Galustian Rare Books

⌸ *22 Cecil Court, WC2N 4HE*
☎ *020 7240 6822*
✎ *www.nataliegalustian.com*
🚇 *Leicester Square LU*
🕓 *Mon-Wed 10am-6pm,*
   Thurs-Sat 11am-7pm

A relatively recent arrival on Cecil Court offering first editions of nineteenth and twentieth-century English and American books as well as African, African American and Caribbean literature, poetry and history. Poker and gambling books form another speciality, as do Beat and avant-garde literature and contemporary art books.

R A Gekoski

⌸ *13 Bathurst Mews, W2 2SB*
☎ *020 7706 2735*
✎ *www.gekoski.com*
🚇 *Paddington LU*
🕓 *Mon-Fri 10am-5.30pm*

Specialists in twentieth-century literature and modern first editions at the very top end of the market. Gekoski also stock important letters and manuscripts from authors including Conrad, Henry James, Joyce and Plath to name just a few. Prices can be reasonable but rise to £150,000 – they sold an inscribed first edition of 'Ulysses' in 2002 for US$460,000. The eponymous Rick Gekoski is also an author and broadcaster.

Slightly Foxed on Gloucester Road

⌸ *123 Gloucester Road, SW7 4TE*
☎ *020 7370 3503*
✎ *www.foxedbooks.com*
🚇 *Gloucester Road LU*
🕓 *Mon-Sat 10am-7pm, Sun 11am-5pm*

What was formerly Gloucester Road Bookshop was taken over by the good folk at the literary quarterly Slightly Foxed in 2009. They have continued their predecessor's tradition of second-hand and antiquarian bookselling and combined this side of the business with a more limited, but carefully chosen range of new books with a particularly good selection of children's titles and many unusual independent publications you will not find in a typical high street bookshop. The shop has a light and airy atmosphere and the staff are friendly, enthusiastic and knowledgeable. As well as their quarterly literary magazine room is also found for an appealing selection of gift items, cards and stationery, making this a great place to hunt down a gift for the book lover in your life.

Goldsboro Books

⌸ *23-27 Cecil Court, WC2N 4EZ*
☎ *020 7497 9230*
✎ *www.goldsborobooks.com*
🚇 *Leicester Square LU*
🕓 *Mon-Sat 10am-6pm*

This store is the UK's largest specialist in signed modern first editions, including recently published crime and historical fiction alongside literary titles, fantasy and children's books. Like many of the bookshops on Cecil Court there's an excellent choice of bargain books on display outside. The Goldsboro Book of the Month Club offers discounts for regular purchasers.

Greenwich Book Place & Gallery

📖 *258 Creek Road, SE10 9SW*
☎ *020 8177 9209*
✑ *www.wordsandimagesforall.com*
🚃 *Cutty Sark DLR*
🕐 *Mon-Sat 2pm-6pm, Sun 2pm-5.30pm*

Mr Herbert has been running this second-hand bookshop for nearly 30 years and continues to offer visitors a good selection of academic literature, popular reference books and an extensive choice of paperback fiction. Prices start from just 90p and most fiction is available for a modest £2. The shop is located in a long-closed pub and the remnants of the bar and some of the fittings can still be seen among the bookshelves. The shop sells its wares online (www.abebooks.co.uk) and also offers a reasonable selection of collectable first editions. The shop is a short walk from the centre of Greenwich, and is well worth taking a detour to explore.

H

Halcyon Books

📖 *1 Greenwich South Street, SE10 8NW*
☎ *020 8305 2675*
✑ *www.halcyonbooks.co.uk*
🚃 *Greenwich Rail/DLR*
🕐 *Daily 10am-6pm*

A fantastic shop close to the main tourist sights in Greenwich and offering a large selection of second-hand, out-of-print and discounted new books in all subject areas. There's a particularly broad range of fiction, literary criticism, history, art and travel but keep an eye out too for books in foreign languages including French, Spanish and Japanese. There's a busy, literary atmosphere with restful music playing in the background.

Peter Harrington

📖 *100 Fulham Road, SW3 6HS*
☎ *020 7591 0220*
✑ *www.peterharrington.co.uk*
🚃 *South Kensington LU*
🕐 *Mon-Sat 10am-6pm*

A book lover's dream selling fabulous rare and antiquarian books. Most subjects are covered but the specialisms are bound sets, English literature, science, philosophy and the history of ideas, children's books, travel, voyages, photography, natural history and fine bindings. This is a shop dealing in quality books at the top end of the market. They issue regular catalogues detailing more recently acquired volumes. Branch at:

📖 *43 Dover Street, W1S 4FF*
☎ *020 3763 3220*
✑ *www.peterharrington.co.uk*
🚃 *Green Park LU*
🕐 *Mon-Fri 10am-7pm, Sat 10am-6pm*

This second branch of Peter Harrington is located on one of London's most salubrious shopping streets near the Royal Academy. The shop boasts an elegant Victorian frontage, but the contemporary lighting and furniture make the place more like an upmarket boutique than a traditional fusty antiquarian bookshop. The stock is extensive and covers most subjects with a particularly good selection of modern first editions which recently included a signed, limited edition of Evelyn Waugh's 'Black Mischief' for £3750 and a copy of James Joyce's Ulysses in a fine binding from Harrington's own Chelsea Bindery (see page 263) for £1950. The staff are always on hand with advice and guidance and the atmosphere is welcoming, but this is definitely a store for the serious collector with few titles below the £100 mark. Harrington's also sell original artwork which is displayed amid the books on the ground floor as well as taking pride of place in the basement gallery which is worth exploring.

Peter Harrington, Dover Street

91 Fulham High Street S.W.6 736 4363 / 2448

"I'm really not in the book trade for the money ... I just love books and even prefer buying them to selling them."

Hurlingham Books

📖 *91 Fulham High Street, SW6 3JS*
☎ *020 7736 4363*
🖂 *www.hurlinghambooks.com*
🚌 *Putney Bridge LU*
🕐 *Ring for details of opening hours.*

Somewhat hidden away on the north side of Putney Bridge, this amazing shop requires a bit of effort to find, but is well worth it. Take the steep steps leading down to Willow Bank and walk around the corner to the junction with Ranelagh Gardens to reach this second-hand literary institution, which is run with eccentric charm by the always enthusiastic Ray Cole, who has been in the book trade for over forty years. There are so many books that they fill the windows and are piled so high on the bookshelves that ladders are provided to enabling visitors to search out the next addition to their library. Most general subjects are covered and there are some rare and antiquarian titles available to view on request. The selection of modern fiction is especially broad with many in the £3-£5 range.

Ray still loves his work, although by his own admission it is more a quixotic adventure than a sound financial enterprise:

"I'm really not in the book trade for the money ... I just love books and even prefer buying them to selling them. I also like the people you meet in this trade and the visitors to the shop."

A testament to Ray's bibliomania is the warehouse which is just around the corner from the shop and is said to contain over one million books. If time and staff are available book lovers can visit the warehouse for a more extensive browse or particular books can be brought to the shop in advance of a visit.

The shop keeps wonderfully erratic opening hours, so telephone before making a journey. If the store is closed when you arrive there's usually a bookshelf or two of books for sale outside operating on an honesty box system. Despite the delightful chaos, there is a printed catalogue in the shop to help customers find particular titles. Next door to the shop is The Eight Bells pub – good for a reviving drink and a pub lunch.

J

Jarndyce Bookshop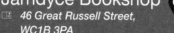

- 46 Great Russell Street, WC1B 3PA
- 020 7631 4220
- www.jarndyce.co.uk
- Holborn LU, Tottenham Court Road LU
- Mon-Fri 11am-5.30pm

Antiquarian bookshops always give the impression of being long established institutions and Jarndyce is no exception, being located in the former home of 19th-century illustrator Randolph Caldecott, and complete with a blue plaque. Inside, the walls are lined floor to ceiling with fine leather-bound editions, there's an open fire that is lit in the winter and a chair that is reputed to have belonged to the great WM Thackeray. However, Jarndyce was not founded by some venerable and long-deceased Victorian bookseller, but by the still vigorous Brian Lake who established the business in 1969 with a friend after studying at York University and has since been joined by his wife, Janet Nassau, and a small team including their son Ed. The company started from a modest office in Covent Garden and moved to this building in 1986.

Visitors are required to ring a bell to gain entrance, but this is only because Jarndyce is always a hive of activity, engaged in the serious task of preparing the next catalogue and despatching valuable tomes across the world. Once inside visitors are assured of a warm welcome and courteous help if required.

The wood-panelled offices upstairs, containing seventeenth and eighteenth-century books, nineteenth-century women's writing and the Romantics, are off limits to visitors as is the vast back room where piles of books await cataloguing and occasionally repair. Despite these limits there is plenty to see and staff are always willing to help if you are searching for a particular title.

The company's ever-evolving approach to bookselling (about a third of sales now come from their website) and the security of owning the premises, gives Jarndyce a sound commercial footing, but the company has seen a lot of change in the area with the closure of Unsworths, Ulysses and a branch of Quinto in recent years.

In recent years Jarndyce has begun exhibiting at the major American antiquarian book fairs as well as those in London, York and Edinburgh. Janet Nassau explains the thinking behind this latest development in the business:

"Attending the US fairs is a lot of logistical work, but we enjoy meeting book lovers and in recent years have made valuable contacts who are interested in our collections and catalogues."

As the name suggests, Jarndyce has a particular interest in Dickens, for whose bicentenary Simon Callow gave a reading at the premises. On a more frivolous note, Jarndyce have for many years published 'Bizarre Books', which catalogues all the weird and wonderful book titles such as 'How to Avoid Work', 'C is for Chafing' and the now infamous 'Scouting for Boys'. Jarndyce sell greetings cards of many of these covers and the window display of such titles is a souce of fascination to passers-by.

Jarndyce is always worth a visit and their catalogues are essential reading for those collecting literature of the seventeenth to nineteenth-centuries. Long may this superb bookshop continue to thrive.

Jarndyce

⣿⣿⣿ JUDD BOOKS ⣿⣿⣿

82 Marchmont Street
Between Russell Square Station and the British Library
11am to 7pm Monday-Saturday; 12-5pm Sunday

We have a large stock of used, bargain and review books on two floors. Art, Architecture, Film, Music, Literature; and downstairs History, Philosophy, Politics, Psychology, Economics.

Judd Books

- 🏠 *82 Marchmont Street, WC1N 1AG*
- ☎ *020 7387 5333*
- 🖊 *www.juddbooks.com*
- 🚌 *Russell Square LU*
- 🕐 *Mon-Sat 11am-7pm, Sun 12noon-6pm*

There is so much stock in this two storey gem (about ten minutes from the British Library) that step ladders are provided so customers can reach the upper shelves. The shop is full of second-hand and discounted new books in all subject areas but with particularly strong sections on art, economics, history, philosophy, Ireland, humanities, Eastern Europe, architecture, fiction, film, literary biography, photography, printing and publishing. The scope and number of volumes is vast and prices are competitive, with bargain tables outside, plus a 10% student discount. One of the most enticing bookshops in London.

K

Kirkdale Bookshop
see page 72.

Krypton Komics
see page 73.

L

Librairie La Page – French Bookseller
see page 74.

Lloyds of Kew

⌂ *9 Mortlake Terrace, Kew Richmond Surrey, TW9 3DT*
☎ *020 8948 2556*
✎ *www.lloydsofkewbooks.co.uk*
🚃 *Kew Gardens LU, Kew Bridge Rail*
🕐 *Tues-Sat 10am-5pm*

This unique bookshop was founded by the renowned dealer in botanical and horticultural books, Daniel Lloyd, over forty years ago. The shop still bears his name, but has changed ownership several times over the years and is now owned by Helen Edwards, who worked at Barnes Bookshop (see p.150) for many years but who found the opportunity to own her own second-hand bookshop impossible to resist:

"I was delighted to be able to step in and save this gem of a bookshop from the threat of closure."

Helen has broadened the shop's stock to include second-hand and antiquarian books on just about every subject, but with particular strengths in art, biography, travel writing, poetry, music and literature. The shop's proximity to Kew Gardens and the legacy of Mr Lloyd ensure a fine selection of botanical and gardening books.

Lloyds is still the epitome of a second-hand bookshop - lined floor to ceiling with wooden bookshelves and with an original Victorian shop front. One unusual feature is the "book tree" commissioned by former owner Ulrike Bulle and designed and constructed by Tim Vincent-Smith. The fabulous tree appears to have formed organically from its surroundings and sprouted into branches bearing books. The shop also stocks a range of beautiful gift wrapping and cards, making this a wonderful place to visit in the hunt for a literary present.

BOOKS ARE MY BAG™
#BAMB
LOVE BOOKS
LOVE BOOKSHOPS

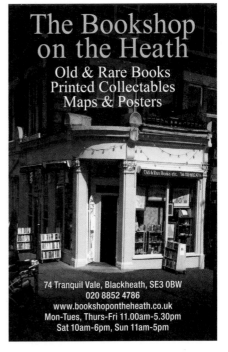

The Bookshop on the Heath
Old & Rare Books
Printed Collectables
Maps & Posters

74 Tranquil Vale, Blackheath, SE3 0BW
020 8852 4786
www.bookshopontheheath.co.uk
Mon-Tues, Thurs-Fri 11.00am-5.30pm
Sat 10am-6pm, Sun 11am-5pm

M

Maggs Bros Ltd

- 50 Berkeley Square, W1J 5BA
- ☎ 020 7493 7160
- ⬦ www.maggs.com
- 🚇 Green Park LU
- ◷ Mon-Fri 9.30am-5pm

Established in 1853, and with a royal warrant to boot, Maggs Bros is one of the premier rare and antiquarian booksellers in London with prices reflecting the superb quality of material. Operating out of a grand town house overlooking Berkeley Square, each department is run by highly knowledgeable, often multilingual, staff. A few of the specialisms are travel, Continental, modern and early British printed material, supplemented by an enormous range of autograph letters and manuscripts. Their beautifully produced catalogues are published frequently.

Maghreb Bookshop

see page 80.

Manor House Books / John Trotter Books

see page 81.

The Map House

- 54 Beauchamp Place, SW3 1NY
- ☎ 020 7589 4325
- ⬦ www.themaphouse.com
- 🚇 Knightsbridge LU
- ◷ Mon-Fri 10am-6pm, Sat 10.30am-5pm

Specialising in antique maps, atlases and globes, this shop has a good selection of books on cartography, both new and out-of-print. The Map House has revived its traditional roots as publisher Sifton Praed & Co, recently publishing 'The Mapping of Antarctica', with more books to follow.

Marchpane

- 16 Cecil Court, WC2N 4HE
- ☎ 020 7836 8661
- ⬦ www.marchpane.com
- 🚇 Leicester Square LU
- ◷ Mon-Sat 10.30am-6pm

A charming little two-storey shop selling children's and illustrated books from the eighteenth century up to the present day, especially Lewis Carroll titles and other classics of the genre – you'll always find 'Winnie-the-Pooh', 'The Wizard of Oz' and 'The Lion, the Witch and the Wardrobe' here. While the Harry Potter titles will appeal to customers with deep pockets, there's plenty here that makes a delightful and inexpensive present for that special child (or adult!). Visitors of a certain age will enjoy the two original Daleks that stand guard in the shop.

Marlborough Rare Books

- 1 St Clement's Court, EC4N 7HB
- ☎ 020 7337 2223
- ⬦ www.marlboroughbooks.com
- 🚇 Monument LU
- ◷ Mon-Fri 9.30am-5.30pm

This leading antiquarian bookseller has recently relocated from the hustle and bustle of Bond Street to a serene corner of the City of London, within the vestry of Wren's St Clement's Church. Marlborough continues to offer a small but quality stock concerning art, architecture, London, topography, decorative arts as well as illustrated books and fine bindings. Marlborough publish regular catalogues and also carry a stock of early optical toys, peepshows and panoramas.

JARNDYCE
THE NINETEENTH CENTURY BOOKSELLERS

Visit our shop opposite the British Museum
in the heart of Bloomsbury

46 Great Russell Street, London WC1B 3PA
Email: books@jarndyce.co.uk. Tel. 020 7631 4220

www.jarndyce.co.uk

MARLBOROUGH RARE BOOKS

Tel: 020 7337 2223

www. marlboroughbooks.com

PICKERING & CHATTO

Tel: 020 7337 2225

www. pickering-chatto.com

Rare and unusual books, manuscripts and ephemera

Catalogues issued

1 St Clement's Court
London, EC4N 7HB

P

Pages of Hackney

This great independent bookstore now has a second-hand basement offering a selection of used fiction and reference titles. See page 91.

Paul's Emporium

⌨ 386 York Way, N7 9LW
☎ 020 7607 3000
🚌 Kentish Town LU
🕐 Tues, Thurs & Fri 12noon-6pm,
Sat 10.30am-5pm

A general second-hand furniture shop that is worth a visit for the surprisingly extensive stock of second-hand art books towards the back of the shop. Prices aren't rock bottom but the range is good – and for bargain hunters there is a heavily laden £1 table of fiction and other subjects at the front.

Pickering & Chatto

⌨ 1 St Clement's Court, EC4N 7HB
☎ 020 7337 2225
🖰 www.pickering-chatto.com
🚌 Monument LU
🕐 Mon-Fri 9.30am-5.30pm
(and by appointment)

This top-class antiquarian dealer carries a general antiquarian stock but specialises in economics, science, medicine, women's studies, philosophy, social sciences, humanities, technology and engineering. The shop has recently moved along with Marlborough Rare Books (see p.152) to this tranquil spot within the grounds of St Clement's Church. Pickering & Chatto keep their customers informed with the publication of regular catalogues.

Pleasures of Past Times / David Drummond

⌨ 11 Cecil Court, WC2N 4EZ
☎ 020 7836 1142
🖰 www.cecilcourt.co.uk
🚌 Leicester Square LU
🕐 Tues-Sat 12noon-6pm

A store specialising in books and ephemera (including playbills) related to the performing arts, the Victorian era and social history. It is very strong on music hall, variety, conjuring and pop culture. They also stock a wide range of postcards.

Stephen Poole Fine Books

⌨ 10 Cecil Court, WC2N 4HE
☎ 020 7836 0999
🖰 www.cecilcourt.co.uk
🚌 Leicester Square LU
🕐 Mon-Fri 10am-6pm

Stephen Poole specialises in first editions of twentieth-century literary fiction including works in English translation and a fair number of signed copies. The store is strong on Granta Young British Novelists and on winners (and shortlisted authors) of the major literary awards. He also has useful holdings in first editions of twentieth-century poetry, crime fiction, printed literary letters and diaries and literary biography.

Henry Pordes

See full review on the page overleaf.

Potterton Books London

see p.95

Primrose Hill Books

see p.95

Arthur Probstain

see p.95

Henry Pordes

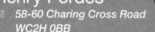

- 58-60 Charing Cross Road
  WC2H 0BB
- ☎ 020 7836 9031
- ✎ www.henrypordesbooks.com
- 🚇 Leicester Square LU
- 🕐 Mon-Sat 10am-7pm, Sun 1-6pm

Henry Pordes is a bookshop imbued with the history of the post-war London book trade. The eponymous Henry Pordes started trading in periodicals, antiquarian and remainder books as a young man in the East End and after several years in New Cavendish Street moved to Finchley Road in Hampstead. His daughter and her husband, Gino Della-Ragione, later joined the business and in October 1983, with incentives from the Greater London Council (GLC), Henry Pordes moved into this premises on Charing Cross Road in the heart of London's book trade.

Henry Pordes died in 1998 but the store that bears his name is still going strong and has recently invested in a new shop front. Within its doors there is still a slightly fusty feel, but that is part of the shop's appeal and while a modern design aesthetic would dictate walls being removed to create an open space, here there is a labyrinthine structure with several rooms dedicated to new remainder books, the front of store for antiquarian tomes and first editions, while towards the back and in the cramped basement there's an incredible array of reasonably priced paperback fiction.

Located in the heart of London, Pordes has an unusual assortment of customers. In the course of my visit a man enters the store declaring his musical talent while handing out handwritten leaflets pointing the curious to a Facebook page. A little later a homeless man comes in and asks about a book in the window, Gino politely deals with his enquiry but later explains that the man comes into the store every day. A serious looking student enquires about a hard to find esoteric text and Gino begins a long discussion about the rarity of such a book and its likely price. When the price becomes a point of negotiation Gino declares:

"I don't like losing sales or customers. We can always discuss the price ... If you're a student we can give you a discount!"

Alex has been working here since the mid 1980's and is explaining the history of Charing Cross Road to me when a woman enters the shop in search of a particular Smith Elder edition of 'Jane Eyre'. Gino immediately begins a hunt of the store and returns with a fine four volume set which is exactly what she is looking for and a price of £360 is agreed on the spot. It's great to witness a book lover finally united with the object of her desire:

"We've been searching for a long time for a nice set and this is by far the nicest we've encountered – I'm so excited!"

Such transactions are not unusual at Henry Pordes but Gino and his staff are acutely aware that times are tough on Charing Cross Road as high rents and rates have taken their toll.

However, despite the increasing rent and rates and the disruption of Cross Rail, the shop is still going strong and remains a great place to visit for anything from a £1 paperback to a rare and collectable tome for several hundred pounds. Henry Pordes would be proud that his legacy continues.

> *I don't like loosing sales or customers, we can always discuss the price... If you're a student we can give you a discount!"*

Henry Pordes

Q

Bernard Quaritch

🏛 *40 South Audley Street, W1K 2PR* ❸

☎ *020 7297 4888*

✎ *www.quaritch.com*

🚌 *Bond Street LU, Marble Arch LU*

🕐 *Mon-Fri 9am-6pm*
   (other times by appointment)

The grand entrance to Bernard Quaritch with its vast black lacquered door and brass name plate might seem daunting to the uninitiated but, having pressed the bell and gained admittance to the first floor reception, you are assured a warm welcome.

The main entrance leads to a high-ceilinged room with light wooden shelves displaying some of the books held by this revered name in London's antiquarian book world. Above the mantlepiece, a portrait of the eponymous Mr Quaritch looks down benevolently, no doubt satisfied that the business he established back in 1847 is still thriving.

Quaritch's vast stock extends into the staff offices but the first floor reception room is where most business is done. Staff will cheerfully fetch what visitors require. The company's main strengths are medieval manuscripts, English and Continental books, travel, the human sciences and early photography.

Alice Ford-Smith, formerly of the Wellcome Library and Dr Williams's Library, manages the firm's library and archive, alongside its publications and marketing activities. As she puts it:

"Bookselling at Bernard Quaritch is not just about selling books, manuscripts and photographs. We give advice to customers and provide valuations."

The offices might seem quiet by comparison with a typical shop, but a great deal of the company's business is transacted with a world-wide network of collectors and libraries, most of whom rarely cross the threshold but who communicate from afar and make their purchases on the strength of catalogues, detailed and accurate descriptions and photographs. The firm also attends the major book fairs, both at home and abroad, to meet customers face-to-face.

Mr Quaritch looks down benevolently, no doubt satisfied that the business he established back in 1847 is still thriving

The world of Bernard Quaritch is a fascinating one, but the prices do reflect the quality of their stock and the fact that many of their books are unique. A vellum bound copy of the 'Hitopad sa' that formerly belonged to William Morris can be yours for £400. A recent catalogue included a first edition of Karl Marx's 'Das Kapital' for £80,000.

Bernard Quaritch welcome enquiries. If you can't make it to their Mayfair offices, do drop them a line; they are always a significant presence at the ABA/PBFA Rare Books London event (see page 194).

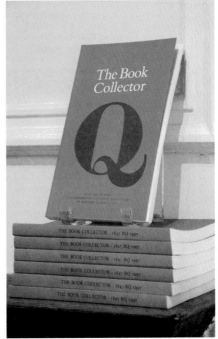

Bernard Quaritch

Quinto Bookshop

⌨ *72 Charing Cross Road,*
WC2H 0BB
☎ *020 7379 7669*
✍ *www.quintobookshop.co.uk*
🚇 *Leicester Square LU*
🕐 *Mon-Sat 9am-9pm, Sun 12noon-8pm*

Sharing an entrance with Francis Edwards (see p.141), this shop is everything a second-hand bookshop should be. The stock covers every imaginable subject (and some unimaginable ones as well) sold in a labyrinthine basement perfumed with the unmistakable aroma of old-books. There are weekly deliveries and the stock is changed totally at the beginning of every month. During the re-stock the shop closes on the Saturday afternoon, re-opening on the Tuesday at 2pm with queues often going around the block.

R

Ripping Yarns

⌨ *355 Archway Road, N6 4EJ*
☎ *020 8341 6111*
✍ *www.rippingyarns.co.uk*
🚇 *Highgate LU*
🕐 *Tues-Fri 12noon-5pm, Sat 10am-5pm,*
Sun 11am-4pm

Ignore the ghastly traffic rumbling outside (but not the bargain boxes) – the interior of this shop can turn up all sorts of delights. Children's books are one of the shop's strengths and include some rare and expensive old volumes. There is also an excellent and extensive range of general stock covering all subject areas, including quality fiction, politics, plays and a good selection of poetry.

Rye Books
see p.102.

S

Shapero Rare Books

⌨ *32 St George Street, W1S 2EA*
☎ *020 7493 0876*
✍ *www.shapero.com*
🚇 *Bond Street LU, Green Park LU,*
Oxford Circus LU
🕐 *Mon-Fri 9.30am-6.30pm, Sat 11am-5pm*

Specialising in travel, natural history, Baedeker guidebooks, colour plate books, cartography and modern first editions, this shop features high quality books and staff that are enthusiastic yet unobtrusive. Although there are some books under £50, notably many of the Baedeker guides, most stock is significantly higher in price. They issue regular catalogues.

Sims Reed
see p.108.

Skoob Books

⌨ *66 The Brunswick Centre,*
off Marchmont Street, WC1N 1AE
☎ *020 7278 8760*
✍ *www.skoob.com*
🚇 *Russell Square LU*
🕐 *Mon-Sat 10.30am-8pm,*
Sun 10.30am-6pm

Academic, general and specialist second-hand titles covering every imaginable subject area are to be found in this established bookseller. The atmospheric basement is a paradise for book lovers, jammed to the gills with piles, shelves and bookcases of books. There are plenty of chairs for browsers and there's even a piano in the heart of the music section should you feel the urge to tickle the ivories. Located in the heart of Bloomsbury, Skoob buy books from some of Britain's leading academics as well as books used as props from great films including The Imitation Game, Theory of Everything and Pride. If you're in search of a specific book, it may well be in Skoob's warehouse, which can be searched online and when found brought into the store for you to inspect. The year 2014 marked the 35th anniversary of this fabulous London institution, justly famous among bookworms the world over. The store is well worth a visit but The Brunswick Centre is difficult to navigate – Skoob can be found next to the rear entrance of Waitrose supermarket. An ethically minded outfit, Skoob Books is the first UK bookshop to be awarded Living Wage Employer accreditation.

Sokol Books

🏠 *239a Fulham Road, SW3 6HY*
☎ *020 7499 5571 / 020 7351 5119*
🖉 *www.sokol.co.uk*
🚌 *South Kensington LU*
🕓 *Tues-Sat 11am-7pm*

When so many antiquarian bookshops have given up their shops to become online book dealers, it is heartening to find a company that is moving in the opposite direction. Sokol Books have been trading in medieval and Renaissance manuscripts and early printed books (all pre-1640) for over thirty years and have now opened this small but charming shop on Fulham Road. Sokol produce regular catalogues and exhibit at the major antiquarian London book fairs.

Halfway between the British Library and the British Museum is London's biggest secondhand bookshop. We've supplied the local academic community for over 37 years with an excellent collection in all subjects as well as sparkling stock in fiction and non-fiction to suit all tastes.

The Bloomsbury shop (65,000 books) is for browsing but we also have over 110,000 in our online catalogue. Search at www.skoob.com.

London Living Wage Employer

Camden Business Awards 2015 Highly Commended

Skoob Books, 66 The Brunswick London, WC1N 1AE, 0207 278 8760
www.skoob.com enquiry@skoob.com

Sotheran's

Sotheran's

🏠 *2-5 Sackville Street,*
W1S 3DP

☎ *020 7439 6151*

🖋 *www.sotherans.co.uk*

🚇 *Piccadilly Circus LU*

🕐 *Mon-Fri 9.30am-6pm, Sat 10am-4pm*

Henry Sotheran founded his bookshop in York in 1761 and the business which still bears his name is now the oldest booksellers still trading in the world, having recently celebrated its 250th anniversary. The company long ago left York for the capital and Sotheran's now trades from an expansive double bayed premises just off Piccadilly and within walking distance of the Royal Academy. Vistors to the store are greeted with sombre lighting, dark oak shelves and display cases – an atmospheric interior entirely befitting the company that purchased the library of Laurence Sterne in 1768 and acquired Dicken's library a century later. The environment might be a little fusty, but the staff are welcoming and with Saturday opening times (unusual for an antiquarian bookshop) are used to dealing with casual browsers and willing to offer advice and remove some of the more precious titles from their display cabinets for careful examination when required.

The store's particular strengths are in modern first editions, literature, children's and illustrated books, natural history and travel but most subjects are covered in reasonable depth and they are not too proud to carry discounted and remainder titles, enabling even those on a budget to leave with a book from one of London's most venerable bookshops.

Those more interested in something for their wall rather than their bookshelf, should take time to explore the store's large basement where fine prints and illustrations are on display.

Sotheran's is always worth exploring when visiting Piccadilly, but if you can't make it to the centre of town their website is an excellent resource with regular updates concerning new stock and a newsletter to which you can subscribe.

T

Tenderbooks

📖 6 Cecil Court, WC2N 4HE
☎ 020 7379 9464
🖥 www.tenderbooks.co.uk
🚌 Leicester Square LU
🕐 Tues-Sat 11am-6pm

Set among the antiquarian bookshops of Cecil Court is Tenderbooks, a space for artist books. The shop hosts regular exhibitions, book launches, readings and events as well as offering a curated selection of unique contemporary art publications, handmade artists' books, magazines and collectable vintage books. Tenderbooks frequently commissions publications and limited editions often in conjunction with the exhibition programme at neighbouring gallery space Tenderpixel.

Tindley & Everett

📖 4 Cecil Court, WC2N 4HE
☎ 020 7240 2161
🖥 Leicester Square LU
🕐 Mon-Fri 10am-5.30pm, Sat 11am-5pm

This is a small shop but one that manages to hold an impressive stock of first editions of English and American late nineteenth and twentieth-century fiction and poetry. James Tindley runs his store with care but eccentricity, often discounting a book because he doesn't like it, rather than judging its market value. The basement of the store is easily missed, but well worth exploring by those interested in acquiring good condition first editions at a reasonable price.

Travis & Emery Music Bookshop

📖 17 Cecil Court, WC2N 4EZ
☎ 020 7240 2129
🖥 www.travis-and-emery.com
🚌 Leicester Square LU
🕐 Mon-Sat 10.15am-6.45pm,
   Sun 11.30am-4.30pm

A second-hand, antiquarian and out-of-print shop stuffed to the gills with music scores but well worth seeking out for its excellent selection of books. The book stock covers classical music, music history and theory but with small sections on jazz, popular music as well as theatre. They produce catalogues twice a year detailing a selection of the books and music on offer and also publish a selection of books on music.

Treadwell's

📖 33 Store Street, WC1E 7BS
☎ 020 7419 8507
🖥 www.treadwells-london.com
🚌 Gower Street LU
🕐 Mon-Fri 11am-7pm,
   Sat-Sun 12noon-7pm

Pagan religions and magic are the main subjects covered in this fascinating little store in the heart of Bloomsbury, with a mix of second-hand and out-of-print books, plus some new titles. However, the stock is very wide and there are also titles on myth, belief, history, travel, literature, poetry and philosophy. Browsers are genuinely welcome as proved by the wonderful sofa and the prominently displayed notice, 'Browsing is a dying art, keep it alive'. In addition to the books there are plenty of 'curiosities' including gift items. The shop hosts a packed programme of events related to their areas of interest.

Bernard Quaritch Ltd

Rare books & manuscripts since 1847

ART & ARCHITECTURE • CONTINENTAL • ENGLISH LITERATURE

FOREIGN LITERATURE • HUMAN SCIENCES • ISLAMIC

MEDIEVAL MANUSCRIPTS • MUSIC • PHOTOGRAPHY

SCIENCE • TRAVEL • ARCHIVES & VALUATIONS

40 South Audley Street, London W1K 2PR
020 7297 4888
rarebooks@quaritch.com
www.quaritch.com

Open 9am-6pm Monday to Friday, and by appointment

TRAVIS & EMERY
Music & Books on Music

Out of Print Music, New & Second-Hand Books on Music,
Antiquarian Music, Scores, Programmes, Libretti, Photos, Prints etc..

17 Cecil Court, London, WC2N 4EZ

Tel: 020 7240 2129 / Fax: 020 7497 0790

Open: Mon-Sat 10.15-18.45, Sunday 11.30-16.30

bll@travis-and-emery.com

Nearest tubes: Leicester Square or Charing Cross

(One minute from the ENO)

COME AND BROWSE

Turn the Page Bookshop

📖 *575 Garratt Lane, SW18 4ST*
☎ *020 8605 2290*
✍ *facebook.com/turnthepagebookshop*
🚃 *Earlsfield Rail*
🕐 *Mon-Fri 11.30am-6pm,*
   Sat 10am-7pm, Sun 11am-6pm

My Back Pages was a second-hand and antiquarian bookshop in Balham famous for its piles of books on every conceivable subject and the eccentric wit of its owner Doug Jeffers. The shop shut its doors for the last time in 2013, much to the consternation of south London's bookworms who had grown to rely on the place for their literary fix. Mr Jeffers was equally upset, having started from a book stall in Camden Market over 30 years ago, he at one stage owned five second-hand bookshops, but now found himself without a shop and with a warehouse full of second-hand books. As Doug puts it:

"I couldn't bring myself to get rid of the stock wholesale and I missed the business and the customers. I'm getting near retirement age, but I still love books and bookselling ... So with the help of my son Jake I've started again - 'like a phoenix from the ashes'..."

The shambling charm of My Back Pages has been preserved in this new bookshop with tens of thousands of books filling shelves and in piles spread through a labyrinthine net work of rooms leading from a main shop where Mr Jeffers has his desk amid further stacks of books waiting to be catalogued. The ground floor would be enough to detain any book lover for some time, but there are further surprises lurking below, with stairs identified by a printed sign with a quote from the author Carlos Ruiz Zafón:

'El Cementerio do los libros ovidados'
(The Cemetery of Forgotten Books)

The words are apt, for the cavernous basement is where many of the more academic titles are kept, covering subjects including medicine, languages, philosophy, politics, early English literature, music, poetry and a great deal more. The basement is a kind of literary dungeon where you could while away an afternoon and emerge into to the light with an armful of books to add to your own library.

> ❝ *So with the help of my son Jake I've started again - 'like a phoenix from the ashes' ...*❞

Turn the Page has something for everyone with new books scattered among the second-hand and antiquarian tomes, some reasonably priced first editions at the back of the store and bargain boxes outside with books for as little as 50p. Mr Jeffers is still a little crest-fallen about the loss of his old shop and a modern world where books are not treasured as in the past, but his face lights up when I express admiration for the shop. With his son involved in the business and a growing band of locals making regular visits to the shop, lets hope his bookselling talent if appreciated once more.

Garratt Lane is not short of cafés with Ben's Canteen, Mel's and the Earlsfield Deli surrounding the lone bookshop – offering a chance for book lovers to get refreshment while browsing the new additions to their collections.

V

Vintage Magazine Shop

⌨ 39/43 Brewer Street, W1R 3SD

☎ 020 7439 8525

✎ www.vinmag.com

🚌 Piccadilly Circus LU

🕐 Mon-Wed 10am-7pm, Thurs til 8pm,
Fri-Sat 10am-10pm, Sun 12noon-8pm
Basement – Mon-Thurs 10am-7pm,
Fri-Sat 10am-8pm, Sun 12noon-8pm

The ground floor of this Soho institution offers movie postcards, photographs, posters and other movie memorabilia. Collectors will be more drawn to the basement which is stocked to overflowing with more than 200,000 back issues of magazines of every genre. The stock covers just about every conceivable publication from 'Beano', 'Life', 'Vogue' and vintage copies of 'Playboy' to early copies of 1980s style mag 'The Face'. The stocks dates from as far back as the 1920's and there are enough gems here to occupy magazine enthusiasts for many hours.

W

Walden Books

⌨ 38 Harmood Street, NW1 8DP

☎ 020 7267 8146

✎ www.waldenbooks.co.uk

🚌 Chalk Farm LU, Camden Town LU

🕐 Thurs-Sun 10.30am-6.30pm

Hidden away off Chalk Farm Road, this shop is overflowing with second-hand bargains – they literally spill out onto shelves outside the shop. The emphasis is on literature (with plenty of poetry and plays), art, architecture, history, philosophy, antiques and collecting, but virtually every subject is covered. There is also a stock of first editions and antiquarian books for collectors. Book lovers will do well to search out this wonderful bookshop – a welcome escape from the bustle of Camden market. For those who can't make it to Camden, Walden Books are regular exhibitors at the Bloomsbury Book Fair (see page 192).

Waterstones

⌨ 82 Gower Street, WC1E 6EQ

☎ 020 7636 1577

✎ www.waterstones.com

🚌 Goodge Street LU

🕐 Mon-Fri 9.30am-8pm, Sat 9.30am-7pm,
Sun 12noon-6pm

The best academic bookshop in London, just around the corner from the University of London, has an extensive, well-organised second-hand department that encompasses the full range of academic subjects – the '-ology's' are well represented. They also stock new discounted titles and some antiquarian stock. There's a window-seat that's a magnet for browers and a coffee shop downstairs in the basement.

FOSTER BOOKS

Old & Rare Books Bought and Sold

183 Chiswick High Road London W4 2DR

020 8995 2768

Open: Mon-Sat 10.30am-5.30pm, most Sundays 11.00am-5pm

@fostersbookshop

www.fosterbooks.co.uk

Books from £1

Foster **the love of Books**

WALDEN BOOKS
-Established 1979-

38 Harmood Street, London NW1 8DP

Telephone: 020 7267 8146
Email: info@waldenbooks.co.uk
www.waldenbooks.co.uk
Open Thursday - Sunday 10.3-6.30
Books bought and sold

Literature and the Visual Arts, Philosophy, Psychology etc

Word on the Water - The London Book Barge

⌂ *Granary Square, King's Cross, N1C 4AA*

🚇 *King's Cross LU/Rail*

✎ *Facebook.com/wordonthewater*
@onthewater

🕐 *Daily 12noon-7.30pm*

This floating bookshop is the work of three people one of whom is an experienced bookseller and American literature specialist, the second of whom provided the boat while the third is an Oxford graduate called Paddy who runs the shop.

The venture began in May 2011 and since that time this ramshackle narrow boat, laden with quality second-hand books, has experienced more than its fair share of outrageous fortune. Paddy is more than happy to take a few minutes off from setting out his stock to explain:

"We traded in east London, but things never really took off ... Then we got a great mooring in Paddington Basin in November 2013 and things really took off, until we were evicted to make way for a floating café. This was a real blow and we started a campaign to persuade the Canal and River Trust to reverse their decision. We tried trading near the Olympic site but this didn't work. We eventually got a break and found this great mooring at the heart of Kings Cross which has given us a chance to survive and hopefully flourish."

The boat takes about 20 minutes to set up for trading with shelves put up on the exterior of the boat and signs put out to attract customers. The stock of second-hand books is very mixed with anything from an old Robert Ludlum novel to the collected works of Freud to be found on the shelves and a far more extensive stock available to browse in the boat's cosy interior, including a large children's section. Paddy is always on hand to give help and advice and will often hunt around before proudly emerging with the title the customer is seeking. The stock may be diverse but the pricing is kept simple with all paperbacks for £3 (two for £5) and hardbacks for just £5.

Another feature of this quirky little bookshop is the music that is constantly playing from two massive speakers on deck. The playlist is as eclectic as the book stock with anything from Dolly Parton to Gregorian Chant accompanying browsers. Paddy is convinced that music encourages sales but it's clear that he enjoys it too and occasionally darts inside to skip a track if he doesn't like what's playing.

With plans for more live jazz concerts, poetry slams and book launches, hopefully Word on the Water will become of permanent feature of this part of King's Cross. Paddy is active on social media (Twitter & Facebook) and this is the best way to find out about the shop's progress and future events.

"We're not making much money but we're making enough to survive and we love the job."

Word on the Water

World's End Bookshop

357 King's Road, SW3 5ES

020 7352 9376

www.worldsendbookshop.com

Sloane Square LU

Mon-Sat 10.30am-6.30pm,
Sun 11am-5pm

The World's End Bookshop has been
selling second-hand and antiquarian
books from this corner shop on the kink
in the King's Road for decades and is
something of a throwback to the days
when this area was considered a haunt
for bohemians, radicals and artists. The
store is packed floor to ceiling with books,
but the stock is well organised and the
helpful staff are on hand to help ferret
out a particular title. The World's End
Bookshop is particularly strong on art,
architecture, poetry, philosophy, counterculture and jazz and blues music, but just
about every subject and condition of book
can be found here, from a worn Penguin
paperback to antiquarian leather-bound
volumes and rare first editions. One of the
best bookshops in London, where a visit is
always a pleasure and a surprise.

Antiquarian Book Dealers

This section includes all those antiquarians who have turned their interest into a business and who trade from home or office as well as those few shops in London that are open by appointment only. If you are in search of a particular title or are developing your own library, these dealers can be invaluable contacts for not only are they often experts in their field with an interesting stock, they can also source books for clients as they roam the nether regions of the book world looking for rare and forgotten gems. Many of the book dealers listed exhibit at London's various Book Fairs (see p.189).

Allsworth Rare Books

⌖ PO Box 134, 235 Earls Court Road
W5 9FE
☎ 020 7377 0552
✐ www.allsworthbooks.com
☺ By appointment at
Central London premises

Voyages, travel, exploration and nineteenth-century photography.

Amwell Book Company

⌖ 53 Amwell Street, EC1R 1UR
☎ 020 7837 4891
✐ www.amwellbookcompany.co.uk
☺ By appointment

A second-hand, rare and out-of-print specialist in art, fashion, photography, architecture, design, children's and illustrated books and modern first editions including detective fiction. Their art, architecture and photography sections are especially strong. Stock can be viewed and ordered from their website or you can visit their Islington store by appointment.

Ash Rare Books

⌖ 43 Huron Road, SW17 8RE
☎ 020 8672 2263
✐ www.ashrare.com
☺ By appointment

A long-standing London book dealer specialising in literary first editions and modern poetry but with interests in a wide range of other subjects including library and publishing history, book collecting and London.

Aurelian Books

⌖ 31 Llanvanor Road, NW2 2AR
☎ 020 8455 9612
✐ www.aurelianbooks.com
☺ By appointment

A specialist in books about butterflies, moths and other insects, both British and overseas. Their oldest book dates back to 1634, but they also sell some new titles.

Detlev Auvermann Rare Books

⌖ Silk House, Flat B, 59 Gee Street
EC1V 3RS
☎ 020 3645 3140
☺ By appointment

This book dealer offers rare and collectable books concerning science, medicine, travel, early printing and continental literature.

Beaumont Travel Books

⌨ *33 Courthurst Road, SE3 8TN*

☎ *020 8853 0262*

✍ *www.abebooks.com/home/beaumont*

🕓 *By appointment*

A dealer in antiquarian and modern travel, exploration, anthropology, military, maritime and literature.

J & S L Bonham

⌨ *Flat 14, 84 Westbourne Terrace*
 W2 6QE

☎ *020 7402 7064*

✍ *www.bonhambooks.co.uk*

🕓 *By appointment*

Exploration, mountaineering and travel.

Books & Things

⌨ *PO Box 388, Stroud, GL6 1GG*

☎ *01453 750 774*

✍ *www.booksandthings.co.uk*

🕓 *Book fairs and mail order only*

Fine and decorative art, children's and illustrated books, modern first editions, photography, printing and literature.

Leo Cadogan Rare Books Ltd

⌨ *70b Freegrove Road, N7 9RQ*

☎ *020 7607 3190*

✍ *www.leocadogan.com*

🕓 *By appointment*

A specialist in books printed pre-1800 including law, commerce, professions, literature, political and intellectual history and literature.

Fiona Campbell

⌨ *158 Lambeth Road, SE1 7DF*

☎ *020 7928 1633*

✍ *fcampbell2@btinternet.com*

🕓 *By appointment*

Specialising in books about Italy and travel.

Cavendish Rare Books

⌨ *19 Chesthunte Road, N17 7PU*

☎ *020 8808 4595*

✍ *grigorbooks@aol.com*

🕓 *By appointment*

Voyages, travel and mountaineering including polar exploration and maritime history.

Collectable Books

⌨ *15 West Park, SE9 4RZ*

☎ *020 8851 8487*

✍ *www.collectablebooks.co.uk*

🕓 *By appointment*

A dealer in books published before 1800 including Bibles, music, cookery, classics, travel, topography, the arts, architecture and miniature books.

Elton Engineering Books

⌨ *32 Fairfax Road, W4 1EW*

☎ *020 8747 0967*

✍ *www.elton-engineeringbooks.co.uk*

🕓 *By appointment*

Civil, mechanical and structural engineering, railways, canals and telegraphy.

Fishburn Books

⌨ *43 Ridge Hill, NW11 8PR*

☎ *020 8455 9139*

✍ *www.fishburnbooks.com*

🕓 *By appointment*

Specialists in Judaica, Hebraica and books of Jewish interest. Fishburn also offer a range of Jewish ephemera.

Paul Foster Books

🖳 *9 Anstice Close, Chiswick, W4 2RJ*
☏ *020 8876 7424*
🖉 *www.paulfosterbooks.com*
🕓 *By appointment*

A large stock of rare and antiquarian books covering most subjects with an emphasis on nineteenth and twentieth-century first editions, history, children's and illustrated books and fine bindings.

Nicholas Goodyer

🖳 *8 Framfield Road, Highbury Fields*
   N5 1UU
☏ *020 7226 5682*
🖉 *www.nicholasgoodyer.com*
🕓 *By appointment*

Colour plate books and illustrated books on all subjects but especially natural history, architecture, fashion, costume and the applied arts. They also have some children's books and volumes on travel and typography.

Michael Graves-Johnston

🖳 *54 Stockwell Park Road, SW9 0DR*
☏ *020 7274 2069*
🖉 *www.graves-johnston.com*
🕓 *By appointment*

Subjects covered include Africa, Oceania, Native America, ethnography, travel, anthropology, archaeology and the ancient world.

Robin Greer

🖳 *The Old Chapel, Front Street, Chedzoy,*
   Somerset, TA7 8RE
☏ *01278 425 682*
🖉 *www.rarerobin.com*
🕓 *By appointment*

Formerly based in Fulham, Robin Greer continues to offer antiquarian children's and illustrated books and original drawings from his Somerset home.

Otto Haas

🖳 *49 Belsize Park Gardens, NW3 4JL*
☏ *07957 480 920*
🖉 *www.ottohaas-music.com*
🕓 *By appointment*

The longest established antiquarian firm in the world with a specialism in music, initially established in Berlin in 1866. They deal in autographs, manuscripts, printed music and music literature.

Hanshan Tang Books

🖳 *Unit 3, Ashburton Centre*
   276 Cortis Road, SW15 3AY
☏ *020 8788 4464*
🖉 *www.hanshan.com*
🕓 *By appointment*

A book dealer specialising in the art of East Asia, South East Asia and Central Asia.

Judith Hodgson

🖳 *11 Stanwick Road, W14 8TL*
☏ *020 7603 7414*
🖉 *judith.hodgson@btinternet.com*
🕓 *By appointment*

A dealer in antiquarian books about Spain, Portugal and Latin America.

Jonathan Kearns Rare Books & Curiosities

🖳 *3 Ewart Road, SE23 1AY*
☏ *07972 588 464*
🖉 *www.kearnsrarebooks.com*
🕓 *By appointment*

Jonathan Kearns describes his stock as a 'cabinet of curiosities' which can include anything from natural history to books about highwaymen. After many years in the book trade, Jonathan Kearns is a recent arrival to the world of book dealing and his website, blog and other social media are all worth exploring.

Edmund Pollinger

⌨ *27D Bramham Gardens, SW5 0JE*
☎ *020 7244 8498*
✍ *www.etpollinger.com*
🕑 *By appointment*

Mr Pollinger is a specialist in books concerning big game hunting, travel and exotic food and drink. Regular online catalogues are available.

John Price

⌨ *8 Cloudesley Square, N1 0HT*
☎ *020 7837 8008*
✍ *www.JohnPriceAntiquarianBooks.com*
🕑 *By appointment*

A specialist in books from the hand press era i.e pre-1820 with an emphasis on philosophy, literature and the performing arts plus books on music and musicians up to the end of the 19th century.

Paul Rassam

⌨ *12 Hill Close, Charlbury, Oxon, OX7 3SY*
☎ *01608 811 437*
✍ *paul@rassam.demon.co.uk*
🕑 *By appointment*

Late nineteenth and early twentieth-century literature, first editions, presentation copies and autograph letters. Catalogues can be sent on request.

Bertram Rota

⌨ *PO Box 7791, Kintbury, Berks, RG17 1DJ*
☎ *01488 608 181*
✍ *www.bertramrota.co.uk*
🕑 *By appointment*

Established in 1923, Bertram Rota were a respected name in the London book trade until their recent departure to leafy Berkshire. The company still specialises in first editions of English and American literature plus fine and applied arts (mostly architecture). London book lovers will now need to use their efficient online service, but are still assured a friendly and efficient service. The company also produces regular catalogues which can be sent on request.

Sophie Schneideman

⌨ *331 Portobello Road, W10 5SA*
☎ *020 8354 7365*
   07909 963 836
✍ *www.ssrbooks.com*
🕑 *By appointment*

Sophie Schneideman began her career at Maggs Bros (see page 152) before establishing her own gallery and rare book dealership in 2007. Her main area of interest is 'the art of the book' and this nebulous term encompasses fine bindings and printing, illustration, private presses and the prints and books of important illustrators and graphic artists. Parallel to these art-related themes, Sophie also maintains a significant collection of rare books relating to food and wine. Sophie's collection can be browsed online or at her gallery by appointment. Prices vary from £60 for a Golden Head Press edition of Edward Calvert engravings to over £60,000 for a very rare 1826 book of William Blake illustrations.

Susanne Schulz-Falster Rare Books

⌨ *4 Harrison's Lane, Woodstock, Oxon, OX20 1SS*
☎ *01993 811 100*
✍ *www.schulz-falster.com*
🕑 *Mail order*

Susanne has recently left London for leafy Oxfordshire, but still trades in Seventeenth and eighteenth-century books of the Enlightenment as well as rare books concerning economics, political history, social sciences, history of ideas and book history.

Benjamin Spademan

- *14 Masons Yard, SW1Y 6BU*
- *07768 076772*
- *benspademan@hotmail.com*
- *By appointment*

A dealer in English and Continental literature and travel.

Robert Temple

- *58 Ridge Road, N21 3EA*
- *020 8360 6117*
- *www.roberttemplerarebooks.co.uk*
- *By appointment*

A specialist in English and American Literary first editions both antiquarian and modern.

Tusculum Rare Books

- *20 Brechin Place, SW7 4QA*
- *0172 868 4880*
- *www.tusculum-rare-books.com*

By appointment

Specialists in Greek and Latin classics, history, philosophy, literature, fine bindings, private presses and modern book art.

W P Watson
Antiquarian Books

- *PO Box 29745, NW3 7ZW*
- *020 7431 0489*
- *books@watsonbooks.co.uk*

Appointment only

Science, medicine, natural history and illustrated books.

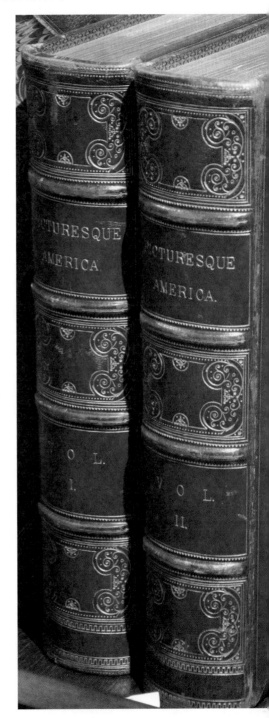

Alternative
Book Outlets

DEPTFORD DOCKYARD AND STORE-SHIPS.

Bloomsbury Auctions

Auctions

Most of the major London auction houses hold periodic book sales, and while many lots sell for thousands of pounds, other lots fetch much lower prices. Viewing days (detailed on the websites) are a great chance for ordinary book lovers to get close to extremely rare and valuable books and also to find out what volumes are currently in vogue with collectors. The sale catalogues can be a fascinating read in their own right and the auction house websites are lavishly illustrated and another source of scholarly information on the subject of fine books.

Bloomsbury Auctions

🏢 *Bloomsbury House,*
   24 Maddox Street,
   W1S 1PP
☎ *020 7495 9494*
✎ *www.bloomsburyauctions.com*
🚇 *Bond Street LU, Oxford Circus LU*

Bloomsbury Auctions is a specialist book and visual arts auction house which is now the only one of its kind in London. As such, the sales held at its relatively modest first floor offices near Oxford Circus are a major event in the antiquarian book world attracting prestigious bookshops and international collectors. Those attending in person will find themselves bidding against phone bids, online bidders and commission bids which are only declared once the bids amount has reached its limit in the room.

Bloomsbury's sales range from specialist auctions covering a particular theme or period, to the sale of a single collection (where the library of one person is sold). Bloomsbury still holds the world record price at auction for a first edition of a Harry Potter book (£17,000). A recent auction had nearly 200 lots covering Continental and English Literature and History, and Middle-Eastern Books and Manuscripts with some of the earliest examples of printed books (dating from the fifteenth century) going under the hammer. An obscure leather bound tome by the Bishop of Carthage dating from 1417 fetched £10,000 and the Epistles of Pope Pius II in moroccan leather binding and dating from 1473 was sold for £3,000.

Anyone interested in rare books, works of art and collectable letters, diaries and manuscripts should make the effort to attend one of the Bloomsbury's auctions. There will not be many lots that are within the reach of ordinary pockets, but the atmosphere is priceless. If you do visit with the intention of bidding it's important to remember that the winning bid is subject to VAT and the auctioneer's commission which adds nearly 29% to the hammer price. As with most auctions, in order to be able to participate, visitors need to register at the desk with proof of residence before receiving a card with a number (known as a paddle) with which they can bid, although the regulars here are always identified by their name. The website is a mine of information about future auctions and the latest sales catalogues can also be viewed here.

Bonhams

🖃 *101 New Bond Street,*
    W1S 1SR
☎ *020 7447 7447*
🖰 *www.bonhams.com*
🚇 *Bond Street, Oxford Circus LU*

and

🖃 *Montpelier Street, Knightsbridge,*
    SW7 1HH
☎ *020 7393 3900*
🚇 *Knightsbridge LU*

Bonhams holds regular auctions including specialist book and manuscripts events in its Knightsbridge saleroom. The books and manuscripts that go under the hammer here are of the highest quality and are sold to serious and wealthy collectors. A recent sale was largely dedicated to eighteenth and nineteenth-century books and manuscripts with prices starting at around £800 for an illustrated first edition book on Russian costume and ascending to many thousands for a rare book of photographs of the Elliot Marbles by one Captain L Tripe. In 2009 a cache of letters written by George Orwell fetched a record breaking £84,000 at auction here. Bonhams Magazine is a fascinating read that often includes articles of interest to book lovers and is available online.

Chiswick Auctions

🖃 *1 Colville Road, W3 8BL*
☎ *020 8992 4442*
🖰 *www.chiswickauctions.co.uk*
🚇 *South Acton Overground*

Chiswick Auctions hold sales of fine printed books and manuscripts five to six times a year, but lower value books are included in their weekly general sales. The fine book sales can include titles on natural history, literature, travel, science, modern first editions as well as children's books. The auction has also handled the sale of historically significant archives of letters and manuscripts as well as rare maps and atlases. Recent sales have included a copy of Montaigne's Essays dating from 1635 which went under the hammer for £2,600 and a presentation copy of a TS Elliot first edition which sold for £900. Chiswick Auctions is currently handling the sale of the vast and rare library of renowned bookseller, Hans Fellner, which has so far realised over £400,000. For more information about the next Chiswick Auction, consult their website where sales are announced 10-14 days before the auction, complete with sales catalogues to view online.

Dreweatts BLOOMSBURY AUCTIONS

Bloomsbury Auctions is seeking consignments in all subject areas, from Incunabula to Modern Firsts for our busy calendar of sales.

For a **free** auction valuation, please contact Rupert Powell:
rpowell@bloomsburyauctions.com | +44 (0) 20 7495 9494

www.dreweatts.com | www.bloomsburyauctions.com | www.mallettantiques.com

Christie's

🏛 *8 King Street, St James's,*
   SW1Y 6QT
☎ *020 7839 9060*
🖱 *www.christies.com*
🚇 *Green Park LU, Piccadilly LU*

and

🏛 *85 Old Brompton Road, SW7 3LD*
☎ *020 7930 6074*
🚇 *South Kensington LU*

This general auction house hosts regular book and manuscript sales and holds the world record prices for any book or manuscript (Leonardo da Vinci's Codex Hammer, which sold for US$30.8 million in 1994) and for any autograph letter (Francis Crick's 'Secret of Life' letter about the discovery of DNA, which sold for $6.1m in 2013). If that doesn't get you searching the attic or scouring the charity shops then nothing will. Free valuations for your finds are available at the South Kensington saleroom – see the website for details.

Sotheby's

🏛 *34-35 New Bond Street,*
   W1A 2AA
☎ *020 7293 5000*
🖱 *www.sothebys.com*
🚇 *Bond Street LU, Oxford Circus LU*

Sotheby's was founded by bookseller Samuel Baker in London in 1744 and his first auction was the sale of the library of Sir John Stanley. The auction house is now an international concern selling fine art, furniture and even vintage cars. Sotheby's has not forgotten its roots and still holds sales of rare books and collectors' libraries. Recent sales have included the work of comic book artists Will Eisner and Jean-Claude Gal and a further instalment of the sale of Franklin Brooke-Hitching's library of exploration and travel books. A Sotheby's auction will be of interest to bibliophiles with deep pockets, but the sales are fascinating theatre and for those with more limited means the Sotheby's online magazine is an interesting, and free, read.

chiswick auctions

viewings every
Sunday & Monday
bid in person or online

Established over 20 years

Buy & Sell Printed Books & Manuscripts

Sales throughout the year.
Entries always welcome, from single items to complete libraries.

1 Colville Road, London W3 8BL
020 8992 4442
chiswickauctions.co.uk

free valuations
Monday to Friday   10am – 6pm
Appointments not necessary

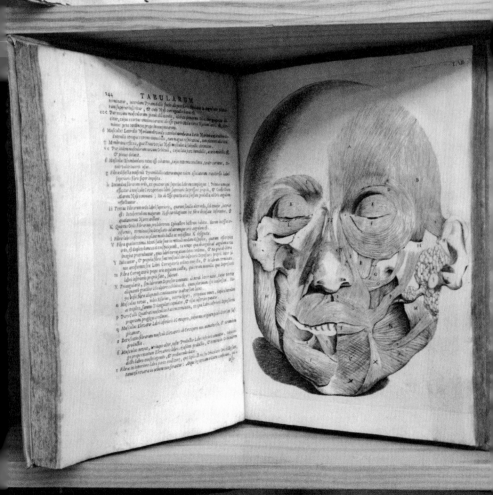

Book Fairs

London's general and specialist book fairs cater for every interest and budget. Many booksellers who otherwise operate a mail order service from their homes (often far from London) exhibit at these fairs, making them an excellent opportunity to browse normally unavailable stock and to make contact with booksellers who share your specialist interest. It's also worth looking out for flyers about upcoming book events in specialist bookshops and advertisements in the weekly London listings magazine 'Time Out' which also has web listings at (www.timeout.com/london/). Bear in mind too the regular London Photograph Fairs (www.photofair.co.uk) at Bloomsbury Holiday Inn (Coram Street) which include plenty of exhibitors with photography books. London Map Fairs (www.londonmapfairs.com) at the Royal Geographical Society also include reference books and atlases. Those interested in more contemporary comic art and graphic novels will enjoy London Comic Mart which regularly takes place at The Royal National Hotel (www.londoncomicmart.co.uk).

Amnesty International

- Human Rights Action Centre
  17-25 New Inn Yard, Shoreditch, EC2A 3EA
- 020 7033 1500
- www.amnesty.org.uk
- books@amnesty.org.uk
- Shoreditch High Street Overground

Amnesty holds regular book clearance sales at their Human Rights Centre in Shoreditch. The sales offer a mix of second-hand donated books and a smaller selection of new titles provided by publishers sympathetic to the the Amnesty cause. The books might be varied but the pricing is simple with everything sold for just £1, ensuring there are plenty of bargains for the eagle-eyed book lover. There are about four sales annually but the dates vary, so it's best to ask to be put on the mailing list for the latest information about future events.

Amnesty International

Annual Book Sale

- Church of the Ascension,
  Dartmouth Row, SE10 8AN
- www.amnestybg.wordpress.com
- Elverson Road DLR
- June & November

The Blackheath and Greenwich Group of Amnesty International holds an annual mega book sale in June. There are thousands of books on offer, both new and second-hand, with prices starting at 50p. Every November there is a smaller event. Get there early, the bargains get snapped up very fast. All money raised by the sales goes directly to Amnesty International.

The Antiquarian Booksellers' Association

🖃 *6 Bell Yard, WC2A 2JR*
☎ *020 7421 4681*
✎ *www.aba.org.uk*
🚉 *Chancery Lane LU*

Anyone seriously interested in collecting antiquarian or rare books will come across the ABA, which is the oldest professional organisation of its kind in the world having been founded in 1906. Many of the antiquarian bookshops and bookdealers listed in this book are members.

The ABA organises a large and illustrious international book fair every May at Olympia (www.olympiabookfair.com) as part of Rare Books London which runs at the same time as the PBFA event (see below). The ABA site hosts over 160 dealers and antiquarian bookshops exhibiting from across the world including major London names such as Sophie Schneideman, Bernard Quaritch and Thomas Heneage. As well as fabulous displays of rare books, the event also hosts a wide range of seminars and activities covering recondite aspects of the antiquarian book world to more practical advice about how to start book collecting. The ABA also holds a smaller autumn fair at Chelsea Town Hall (www.chelseabookfair.com) in November each year. Their website is an excellent source of information about other book events.

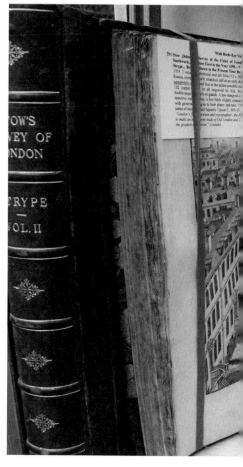

The ABA Book Fair, Olympia

The Bloomsbury Book Fair ❶

🖼 *Royal National Hotel, Bedford Way, WC1H 0DG*

☎ *01707 872 140*

✎ *www.bloomsburybookfair.com*

🚇 *Russell Square LU*

🕐 *Monthly*

♿ *Admission Fee: £2 until 12.30pm, free thereafter*

These days The Bloomsbury Book Fair is London's only monthly book event, attracting over 100 exhibitors from around the country. The atmosphere is hectic at the start of the day with a long queue of eager book lovers gathering before the doors open at 10am – all worried they might miss that much sought-after volume. Once the initial morning rush subsides, the fair assumes a more relaxed pace with regulars taking time to chat about their acquisitions, discuss some arcane aspect of book collecting or simply indulge in a bit of gossip. As the afternoon wears on, some of the book dealers who have travelled far and been up since dawn, even catch a quick nap.

There are plenty of rare and exquisite books on display here with on a recent visit a wonderful limited edition of 'Hansel and Gretel' by the Brothers Grimm, illustrated and signed by Kay Nielsen, for £2,500 and a perfect condition, first

US edition of 'Up the Junction' by Nell Dunn for just £65. It was also pleasing to see these books could be held and read by careful visitors and not kept shielded behind glass cabinets.

If you are uninitiated to the world of book collecting and wouldn't know a 'conjugated leaf' from a 'comb binding' you need not feel intimidated. There are plenty of books here that are intended for reading rather than collecting and lots of bargains with dealers such as Walden Books (see page 168) offering reasonable condition hardbacks for just £2 each. It's also a good idea to look around before you buy – I found a lavish English Heritage edition of 'Disappearing London' for £30, but Black Gull Books (see page 138) were selling the same for just £15 in the smaller back room.

As well as books, the fair also features maps and prints and other ephemera, with some dealers displaying their wares with great care, while others take a more haphazard approach, allowing visitors to sift through piles of prints spread across the table and floor. If you have a book that needs restoring to its former glory, Syston Bindery (see page 270) also have a stand here. They will give you a quote and return the book to you at the next fair and are trusted by many of the regular book dealers here.

Bloomsbury Book Fair is a great event for all bibliophiles and one made even more memorable because of its location in the Royal National Hotel which has carpet and fittings similar to those in the Outlook Hotel in Kubrick's '*The Shining*'. Fortunately visitors are a lot closer to civilisation here, with historic Bloomsbury and the attractions of the Brunswick Centre within walking distance offering a great way to round off a day's book browsing.

The Bloomsbury Book Fair

FASCINATING WALKING STICKS
A.E.Boothroyd

London Art Book Fair

🖳 *Whitechapel Gallery,*
80-82 Whitechapel High Street, E1 7QX
🖉 *www.whitechapelgallery.org*
🚌 *Aldgate LU*

The London Art Book Fair is an annual event that celebrates the best of international contemporary art publishing. Hosted by the Whitechapel Gallery, it showcases diverse publications from artist, galleries, colleges, arts publishing houses, rare book dealers and distributors.

The Fair takes over the Gallery for four days in September and attracts around 12,000 visitors. There are usually about 80 exhibitors from around the world and an extensive programme of related events. High profile artists that have participated in the event include AA Bronson, Jake and Dinos Chapman, Tracey Emin and Bridget Riley. For more information about the next Art Book Fair visit the Whitechapel Gallery website.

The Provincial Booksellers Fairs Association

🖳 *The Old Coach House,*
16 Melbourn Street,
Royston, Herts, SG8 7BZ
☎ *01763 248400*
🖉 *www.pbfa.org*

The PBFA has been running book fairs for over 40 years and currently organises over 50 book fairs each year across the country from Edinburgh to Bath. In London the major PBFA Book Fair takes place over three days in May and is now hosted in conjunction with the ABA (see p.190), but there are a further four smaller specialist bookfairs including the Travel & Exploration Fair held at the Royal Geographical Society in April and the December Christmas Book Fair. Take a look at the PBFA website for a full itinerary of events.

Rare Books London

🖳 *ILEC Suite, IBIS Hotel, Lillie Road,*
Earl's Court, SW6 1UD
🖉 *www.olympiabookfair.com or*
🖉 *www.pbfalondonbookfair.org*
🚌 *Kensington Olympia LU*

This major book fair includes over 300 of the world's most prestigious antiquarian book dealers. The event currently takes place at the IBIS Hotel (Earls Court) and is run by the PBFA in conjunction with the ABA fair at Olympia (see p.190). It is a great place to find rare books, photographs, manuscripts, ephemera, maps and prints with prices starting from just a few pounds and going up to many thousands for rare signed, first editions. Tickets are £15 on the door (including the ABA event) or you can register in advance for free at: www.olympiabookfair.com or www.pbfalondonfair.org

Room&Book: Art Book Fair

🖼 *Nash & Brandon Rooms
ICA, The Mall, SW1Y 5AH*
🖋 *www.roomandbook.com*
🕐 *Late May/ Early June*
🚌 *Charing Cross LU*

This annual three day art book fair is run by the good folk at Claire de Rouen Books (see p.100) and allows some of the best specialist art bookshops and dealers to engage with the public under one roof. The event includes anything from cutting edge fanzines to rare and collectable books and the list of participants is equally diverse with young upstarts such as Bookmarc (see p.28) and Anagram Books, rubbing shoulders with stalwarts of the book trade including Bernard Quaritch (see p.158) and Sims Reed (see p.108). Prices start from as little as £10 and entry to the event is free with day membership to the ICA.

Small Publishers Fair

🖼 *Conway Hall, Red Lion Square,
WC1R 4RL*
🖋 *www.smallpublishersfair.co.uk*
🕐 *First week in November*
💷 *Free entry*
🚌 *Holborn LU*

Every autumn Conway Hall hosts this popular fair celebrating independent publishing, book artists, writers and book design. There are over 60 independent publishers exhibiting and selling their wares at the fair, giving visitors the opportunity to meet authors and those in the independent book world and get their hands on some unique books that are difficult to find anywhere else. Entry to the fair is free of charge and with a busy programme of performances, readings and book launches, this is a unique event and a must for book lovers.

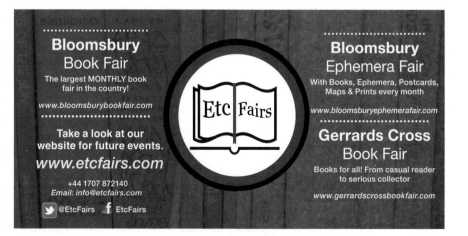

Bloomsbury
Book Fair

The largest MONTHLY book fair in the country!

www.bloomsburybookfair.com

Take a look at our website for future events.

www.etcfairs.com

+44 1707 872140
Email: info@etcfairs.com

🐦 @EtcFairs f EtcFairs

Etc Fairs

Bloomsbury
Ephemera Fair

With Books, Ephemera, Postcards, Maps & Prints every month

www.bloomsburyephemerafair.com

Gerrards Cross
Book Fair

Books for all! From casual reader to serious collector

www.gerrardscrossbookfair.com

Paper and Cup

Charity Shops

Charity shops can be a book lovers' paradise with their addictive combination of book bargains and the thrill of serendipity. Not all charity shops make an effort with their books and we have only reviewed stores that have a considerable book stock displayed and catalogued coherently. A further category of charity shop is the specialist bookshop and these offer an even wider selection of used and sometimes collectable books for the literary junkie to explore. Quite a few charities have specialist books stores, but none compare to Oxfam which now has 18 such outlets in London, which are given a special listing in this section. Those going on a trawl of London's charity shops for book bargains should plan their route and remember to take a sturdy rucksack or wheeled case, as you may come back with far more additions to your library than you expected.

Central

Age Concern UK

⌨ *53 Leather Lane, EC1N 7JJ*
☎ *020 7831 4928*
🚇 *Farringdon LU/Rail, Chancery Lane LU*
🕓 *Mon-Fri 10am-3.30pm*

This is a great charity shop with lots to sift through and always a good selection of well priced books.

Cancer Research UK

⌨ *24 Marylebone High Street,*
   W1U 4PQ
☎ *020 7487 4986*
🚇 *Baker Street LU, Bond Street LU*
🕓 *Mon-Sat 10am-6pm, Sun 11am-5pm*

This store has a good selection of books with paperback fiction for just £1.50 and a well stocked kid's section. Don't miss the Oxfam Bookshop just opposite.

Oxfam Bookshop

⌨ *12 Bloomsbury Street, WC1B 3QA*
☎ *020 7637 4610*
🚇 *Tottenham Court Road LU*
🕓 *Mon-Sat 10am-6pm,*
   Sun 12noon-5pm

See page 204 for more details.

Oxfam Bookshop

⌨ *91 Marylebone High Street, W1U 4RB*
☎ *020 7487 3570*
🚇 *Baker Street LU, Bond Street LU*
🕓 *Mon-Sat 10am-5.45pm, Sun 11am-5pm*

See page 204 for more details.

Oxfam

⌨ *52 Goodge Street, W1T 4LZ*
☎ *020 7636 7311*
🚇 *Goodge Street LU*
🕓 *Mon-Fri 10am-6pm, Sat 11am-5pm*

This is one of Oxfam's most central stores with a basement dedicated to a well organised selection of books with prices from around £2. On fine days the store has a discount shelf on the pavement to attract bargain hunting bookworms. If you're visiting, don't forget the YMCA Charity shop just a few minutes along Goodge Street towards Tottenham Court Road.

Salvation Army Charity Shop

- 9 Princes Street, W1R 7RB
- ☎ 020 7493 1909
- Oxford Circus LU
- ☼ Mon-Sat 10am-6pm

Renowned as a great place to find bargain designer clothes, but it also has a few good quality books at bargain prices.

YMCA

- 22 Goodge Street, W1T 2QE
- ☎ 020 7323 5073
- Goodge Street LU
- ☼ Mon-Fri 10am-6pm,
  Sat 11am-6pm, Sun 12am-4pm

This charity shop has a good selection of books on offer with prices starting from just 50p and going up to as much as £5.99 for a heavyweight art book. When visiting here, don't forget the Oxfam Shop just a few minutes along Goodge Street.

North

Animal Aid & Advice Bookshop

- 203 Blackstock Road, N5 9LL
- ☎ 020 7359 0294
- www.animalaidandadvice.org
- Finsbury Park LU/Rail
- ☼ Daily 10am-6pm

This charity shop is dedicated to books with a great selection of academic and language books and plenty of cheap paperback fiction.

British Heart Foundation

- 395 Green Lanes, N13 4JG
- ☎ 020 8886 8593
- Palmers Green Rail
- ☼ Mon-Sat 10am-6pm, Sun 11am-5pm

This charity shop is a bit far out for most people, but holds a good book stock with plenty of bargains.

British Heart Foundation

- 436 Holloway Road, N7 6QA
- ☎ 020 7697 9995
- Holloway Road LU
- ☼ Mon-Sat 10am-6pm, Sun 11am-5pm

A small but well stocked charity shop with a reasonable stock of books and a branch of Shelter next door.

British Red Cross Bookshop

- 385 Green Lanes,
  Palmers Green, N13 4XE
- ☎ 020 8886 8364
- www.redcross.org.uk
- Palmers Green Rail
- ☼ Mon-Sat 10am-6pm, Sun 11am-4pm

Established for over 20 years, this is the only specialist charity bookshop run by the Red Cross in London. The stock is extensive and well organised, making a visit here well worth the trek up to Palmers Green.

Cancer Research UK

- 69 Ballards Lane, N3 1XT
- ☎ 020 8349 4962
- www.cancerresearchuk.org
- Finchley Central LU
- ☼ Mon-Sat 9am-5pm, Sun 10am-4pm

A general shop but with a good selection of books, all at reasonable prices.

Mind

- 329 Archway, N6 5AA
- ☎ 020 8341 1188
- www.mind.org.uk
- Highgate LU
- ☼ Mon-Sat 10am-5.30pm, Sun 11am-4pm

This well organised charity shop has a comprehensive selection of art and history books, American fiction and children's books. This large shop is just opposite Highgate tube and next door to another good charity shop run by the RSPCA (see opposite page).

North London Hospice Shop

⌂ *44 Fortis Green Road, N10 3HN*
☎ *020 8444 8131*
✎ *www.northlondonhospice.org*
🚇 *Highgate LU*
🕑 *Mon-Sat 9.15am-5.15pm*

This small general charity shop is just a short hop away from the Muswell Hill Bookshop (see p.85). With a reasonable selection of books and prices starting at 75p, it is definitely worth a visit.

North London Hospice Shop

⌂ *839 High Road, N12 8PR*
☎ *020 8445 5148*
✎ *www.northlondonhospice.org*
🚇 *Woodside Park LU*
🕑 *Mon-Sat 9.15am-5.15pm*

This charity shop offers a good selection of books among its general stock.

North London Hospice Shop

⌂ *123 High Road, N2 8AD*
☎ *020 8883 6493*
✎ *www.northlondonhospice.org*
🚇 *Woodside Park LU*
🕑 *Mon-Sat 9.15am-5.15pm*

A good charity shop with a reasonable range of books among its stock.

Octavia Foundation

⌂ *179 Finchley Road, NW3 6IB*
☎ *020 7624 9053*
🚇 *Finchley LU*
🕑 *Mon-Sat 10am-6pm, Sun 12noon-5pm*

This branch of Octavia has a particularly good selection of second-hand books.

Oxfam

⌂ *246 West End Lane, NW6 1LG*
☎ *020 7435 8628*
🚇 *West Hampstead LU*
🕑 *Mon-Sat 10am-6pm, Sun 12.30pm-5pm*

This shop has an excellent book stock and is across the road from West End Books (see p.131). West End Lane is charity shop heaven with six charity shops along the strip offering a plethora of book bargains.

RSPCA

⌂ *335 Archway Road, N6 5AA*
☎ *020 8348 5725*
✎ *www.rspca.org.uk*
🚇 *Highgate LU*
🕑 *Mon-Sat 10am-5.30pm, Sun 11am-4pm*

A small general shop with a selection of books at excellent prices. Visit in conjunction with the Mind shop next door (see page opposite).

Second Chance

⌂ *7-9 St John's Way, N19 3TD*
☎ *020 7281 5449*
🚇 *Archway LU*
🕑 *Mon-Sat 10am-5pm*

This cavernous general charity shop is attached to the Archway Methodist Church and unlike some charity shops takes its book stock very seriously with a large dedicated area and two staff specialising in managing and pricing their literary donations. The store's efforts have been rewarded with a loyal following of book-worms who come to browse for literary bargains.

West

Oxfam

- 202B Kensington High Street, W8 7RG
- ☎ 020 7937 6683
- 🚌 High Street Kensington LU
- ☺ Mon-Sat 9.45am-5.45pm,
  Sun 12noon-5pm

A good selection of books line the wall of this light, airy shop in the heart of the smart Kensington High Street.

Oxfam

- 87 King Street, W6 9HW
- ☎ 020 8846 9276
- ☺ Mon-Fri 9.45am-5.45pm,
  Sat 9.45am-5pm, Sun 12noon-5pm
- 🚌 Hammersmith LU

Oxfam

- 144 Notting Hill, W11 3QG
- ☎ 020 7792 0037
- 🚌 Notting Hill Gate LU
- ☺ Mon-Sat 10am-6pm, Sun 11am-5pm

This Oxfam has a great selection of second-hand books and is worth a visit, particularly when combined with a trip to the nearby Portobello Road Market (see p.211).

Trinity Hospice Shop

- 20A Notting Hill Gate, W11 3JE
- ☎ 020 7792 2582
- 🚌 Notting Hill Gate LU
- ☺ Mon-Sat 10am-8pm, Sun 11am-5pm

A great charity shop, just a short walk from the underground station and easy to combine with a visit to Portobello Road Market. There is a good selection of books to rummage through and plenty of bargains.

South West

Boutique

- 19 Churton Street, SW1V 2LY
- ☎ 020 7233 8736
- 🚌 Victoria LU/Rail
- ☺ Mon-Sat 10am-6pm, Sun 12am-4pm

A general charity shop with an excellent selection of keenly priced books (paperbacks are mostly £2, hardbacks £4) with an especially good selection of fiction and arts books. Committed bargain hunters should look out for their 50p bargain boxes.

British Heart Foundation Books & Music

- 94 Streatham High Road, SW16 1BS
- ☎ 020 8664 7490
- 🚌 Streatham Hill Rail
- ☺ Mon-Sat 10am-6pm, Sun 11am-5pm

This large charity shop specialises in books as well as CDs and vinyl.
Among the book stock is a great selection of paperback fiction with prices starting from £2, but they also sell collectable first editions with some rare titles with price tags of several hundred pounds.

British Heart Foundation

- 62 St John Road, SW11 1PR
- ☎ 020 7978 4237
- 🚌 Clapham Junction LU/Rail
- ☺ Mon-Sat 10am-6pm, Sun 11am-5pm

British Red Cross

- 69-71 Old Church Street, SW3 5BS
- ☎ 0845 054 7101
- ✐ www.redcross.org.uk
- 🚌 Sloane Square LU
- ☺ Mon-Sat 10am-6pm

Just off King's Road, there are two Red Cross Shops here, very close together.

As befits literary Chelsea, there is a good quality, ever-changing stock of books across all subject areas. Combine a trip here with a pilgrimage to the great Chelsea bookshop, John Sandoe (see p.104).

Cancer Research UK

⌨ *127 Putney High Street, SW15 1SU*
☏ *020 8788 9305*
🚇 *Putney Rail, East Putney LU*
🕘 *Mon-Sat 9.30am-5.30pm,*
    Sun 11am-5pm

A general shop but with a good, well-priced selection of books. Check out the nearby Oxfam shop while you are here (see p.197).

FARA

⌨ *26 Gloucester Road, SW7 4RB*
☏ *020 7581 8219*
🚇 *Gloucester Road LU*
🕘 *Daily 10am-6pm*

This store occupies two floors with a large selection of books to be found in the basement. There is a good selection of paperback fiction with prices starting from £1.50 and they also have academic, reference and travel books.

Oxfam

⌨ *432 King's Road, SW10 0LR*
☏ *020 7351 6863*
🚇 *Sloane Square LU*
🕘 *Mon-Sat 9.30am-5.30pm,*
    Sun 12noon-5pm

Oxfam

⌨ *149 Putney High Street, SW15 1SU*
☏ *020 8789 3235*
🚇 *East Putney Rail, Putney Bridge LU*
🕘 *Mon-Sat 10am-6pm, Sun 12pm-4pm*

This shop has an excellent book selection and is just a few doors down from a Cancer Research UK shop which is also worth a visit (see above).

Oxfam

⌨ *15 Warwick Way, SW1V 1QT*
☏ *020 7821 1952*
🚇 *Victoria LU/Rail*
🕘 *Mon-Sat 10am-6pm*

This is a general shop, but the basement is dedicated to books and music. There are lots of charity shops in the area.

Trinity Hospice Shop

⌨ *16 Bute Street, SW7 3EX*
☏ *020 7589 2234*
🚇 *South Kensington LU*
🕘 *Mon-Sat 10am-6pm, Sun 11am-5pm*

In the French bookselling enclave close to the Institut Français, this shop has a ever-changing book stock at reasonable prices.

Trinity Hospice Shop

⌨ *124 Clapham High Street, SW4 7UH*
☏ *020 7498 7400*
🚇 *Clapham Common LU*
🕘 *Mon-Sat 10am-6pm, Sun 11am-5pm*

Trinity Hospice Shop

⌨ *785 Fulham Road, SW6 5HD*
☏ *020 7736 8211*
🚇 *Parsons Green LU*
🕘 *Mon-Sat 10am-5pm, Sun 11am-4pm*

There's a dedicated book area at the back of this general shop; it isn't huge but has a good quality range of books in most subjects. Combine this place with a visit to Nomad Books just opposite (see p.88).

Trinity Hospice Shop

⌨ *85 Wilton Road, SW1V 1DN*
☏ *020 7931 7191*
🚇 *Victoria LU/Rail*
🕘 *Mon-Sat 10am-6pm, Sun 11am-5pm*

At around £3 for hardbacks, prices are keen and there are lots of other charity shops in the area, including Boutique and Oxfam (Warwick Way).

South East

Bexley Cottage Hospice Shop

⌨ *163-5 High Street, SE9 1TW*
☎ *020 8850 6898*
🚌 *Eltham Rail*
🕐 *Mon-Sat 9.30am-5pm*

This shop doesn't look big from the outside but upstairs there is a book area with a good range of fiction and non-fiction, all at competitive prices.

British Heart Foundation

⌨ *10 Powis Street, SE18 6LF*
☎ *020 8316 0661*
🚌 *Woolwich Arsenal Rail*
🕐 *Mon-Sat 9am-5.30pm,*
   Sun 10.30am-4.30pm

An excellent range of books (plus music on CD and DVDs) make this place an oasis in the book-buying desert of Woolwich. The turnover is good and prices fair.

Cancer Research UK

⌨ *30 Westow Hill, SE19 1RX*
☎ *020 8766 6277*
🚌 *Crystal Palace Rail*
🕐 *Mon-Sat 9.30am-5.30pm,*
   Sat 9.30am-5pm, Sun 11am-5pm

A general shop, but with a good, well-organised range of books. If you are on a book-buying spree, Bookseller Crow on the Hill (see p.32) and Haynes Market (see p.210) are just around the corner.

Oxfam

⌨ *68 Tranquil Vale, SE3 0BN*
☎ *020 8852 6884*
🚌 *Blackheath Rail*
🕐 *Mon-Sat 10am-6pm, Sun 11am-4pm*

East

British Heart Foundation

⌨ *257 High Street, E17 7BH*
☎ *020 8521 9500*
🚌 *Walthamstow Central LU*
🕐 *Mon-Sat 10am-4.30pm*

In the heart of Walthamstow Market, close to the mall, there is an excellent range of books, mostly fiction but with solid non-fiction sections.

Hackney Paragon Trust

⌨ *227 Well Street, E17 7BH*
☎ *020 8521 9500*
🚌 *Homerton Rail*
🕐 *Mon-Sat 9.30am-5pm*

This vast charity shop might be a little bit out of the way for some, but their stock of second-hand books is considerable and the prices are very low. Worth a visit if you are in the area.

Helen Rollason Heal Cancer Charity

⌨ *136 George Lane, E18 1AY*
☎ *020 8989 9897*
✎ *www.helenrollason.co.uk*
🚌 *South Woodford LU*
🕐 *Mon-Sat 10am-4.30pm*

An abundance of books at bargain prices if you are prepared to rummage through the stock.

Oxfam

⌨ *514-518 Kingsland Road, E8 4AR*
☎ *020 7254 5318*
🚌 *Dalston Kingsland Rail/*
   Dalston Junction Overground
🕐 *Mon-Sat 10am-5pm, Sun 12pm-4pm*

This is a vast general shop (near the junction with Forest Road) that has a considerable book stock with paperback fiction starting from just 99p.

Oxfam

- 2-4 High Street, E17 7LD
- ☎ 020 8503 6334
- St James Street Rail
- ☯ Mon-Sat 10am-6pm, Sun 11am-4pm

This is one of London's largest charity shops with a well-stocked book section. The books are carefully displayed with areas dedicated to particular subjects such as history, philosophy and languages and a great selection of quality fiction. This store is worth the effort to visit, particularly when combined with a trip to Walthamstow Market.

Paper & Cup

- ✑ www.paperandcup.co.uk
- 18 Calvert Avenue, E2 7JP
- ☎ 020 7739 5358
- Shoreditch High Street Overground
- ☯ Mon-Fri 8am-6pm, Sat 9am-6pm, Sun 10am-5pm

- 83 St Paul's Way, E3 4AJ
- ☎ 020 7537 4427
- Mile End LU then Bus 277, D6 or D7
- ☯ Mon-Fri 8am-5pm, Sat 9am-5pm

These two east London coffee shops are run by the Spitalfields Crypt Trust (SCT) and serve an excellent range of café fare as well as a carefully selected range of second-hand books. All the stock is simply priced with paperbacks for £2 and hardbacks for £4.

Out of Town

FARA Books

- 34d Broad Street, Teddington, Middlesex, TW11 8RF
- ☎ 020 8977 6475
- Teddington Rail
- ☯ Daily 9.30am-5.30pm

This shop is a little out of the way for most Londoners, but as it is a specialist charity bookshop and open every day of the week making it worthy of inclusion here. Definitely worth a visit, particularly when combined with a trip to Ham House or the nearby Bushy and Richmond Parks.

Oxfam Bookshops

🖋 www.oxfam.org.uk

Oxfam is the largest retailer of second-hand books in Europe, selling more than 11 million books a year. They have over 100 specialist bookshops in the UK with Londoners lucky enough to have 18 of them to explore in the capital. Browsing in an Oxfam bookshop is a real pleasure with an extensive range of stock all displayed under the relevant category from Anthropology to Zoology, a good selection of quality fiction and usually a few collectable titles among the stock. Prices are reasonable, but don't expect any bargains to have slipped through the net as the staff here are knowledgeable and price their stock appropriately.

📖 166 Balham High Street, SW12 9BW
☎ 020 8772 6816
🚉 Balham Rail
🕓 Mon-Sat 10am-6pm, Sun 12noon-5pm

📖 12 Bloomsbury Street, WC1B 3QA **(3)**
☎ 020 7637 4610
🚉 Tottenham Court Road LU
🕓 Mon-Sat 10am-6pm, Sun 12noon-5pm

📖 1 The Green, W5 5DA
☎ 020 8567 2152
🚉 Ealing Broadway LU
🕓 Mon-Fri 10am-6pm,
    Sat 9.30am-5.30pm, Sun 12noon-5pm

📖 2 College Approach,
    Greenwich, SE1 9HY
☎ 020 8305 1656
🚉 Cutty Sark DLR
🕓 Mon-Sat 10am-6pm, Sun 12am-5pm

📖 9 Half Moon Lane, SE24 9JU
☎ 020 7978 8575
🚉 Herne Hill Rail
🕓 Mon-Sat 10am-6pm, Sun 11am-4pm

📖 45 Heath Street, NW3 6UA
☎ 020 7794 3060
🚉 Hampstead LU
🕓 Mon-Sat 10am-6pm, Sun 1pm-5pm

📖 47 Highgate High Street, N6 5JX
☎ 020 8347 6704
🚉 Highgate LU
🕓 Mon-Sat 9.30am-5.30pm,
    Sun 11am-4pm

📖 48 Upper Street, N1 0PN
☎ 020 7359 6020
🚉 Angel LU
🕓 Mon-Wed 10am-6pm,
    Thurs-Sat 10am-7pm, Sun 11am-5pm

📖 166 Kentish Town Road, NW5 2AG
☎ 020 7267 3560
🚉 Kentish Town LU
🕓 Mon-Thurs & Sat 10am-5pm,
    Fri 10am-6pm, Sun 12noon-5pm

📖 30 Old London Road
    Kingston-upon-Thames, KT2 6QF
☎ 020 8549 3559
🚉 Kingston Rail
🕓 Mon-Sat 9.30am-5pm, Sun 12am-3pm

📖 91 Marylebone High Street, W1U 4RB
☎ 020 7487 3570
🚉 Baker Street LU, Bond Street LU
🕓 Mon-Sat 10am-5.45pm, Sun 11am-5pm

📖 378 The Broadway,
    Muswell Hill, N10 0PN
☎ 020 8883 5171
🚉 Highgate LU
🕓 Mon-Sat 10am-6pm, Sun 11am-5pm

📖 22 Park Road, N8 8TD
☎ 020 8347 7942
🚉 Crouch Hill Rail
🕓 Mon-Sat 10am-6pm, Sun 11am-5pm

- 170 Portobello Road, W11 2EB
- ☎ 020 7727 2907
- 🚌 Ladbroke Grove LU
- 🕓 Mon-Thurs 10am-6pm,
  Fri & Sat 10am-6.30pm,
  Sun 12noon-4pm

- 61 St John's Wood High Street,
  NW8 7NL
- ☎ 020 7722 5969
- 🚌 St John's Wood LU
- 🕓 Mon-Sat 10am-6pm,
  Sun 12.30pm-4pm

- 34 Strutton Ground, SW1P 2HR
- ☎ 020 7233 3908
- 🚌 St James's Park LU
- 🕓 Mon-Thurs 9.30am-6pm,
  Fri 9.30am-5.30pm, Sat 11am-4pm

- 90 Turnham Green Terrace, W4 1QN
- ☎ 020 8995 6059
- 🚌 Turnham Green LU
- 🕓 Mon-Sat 10am-6pm,
  Sun 12noon-4pm

- 1 Clock House Parade, E11 2AG
- ☎ 020 8530 3413
- 🚌 Snaresbrook LU
- 🕓 Mon-Sat 10am-6pm, Sun 11am-4pm

Southbank Book Market

Markets

Alfie's Antiques Market

⌖ *13-25 Church Street, NW8 8DT*

☎ *020 7723 6066*

✍ *www.alfiesantiques.com*

🚌 *Edgware Road LU, Marylebone LU/Rail*

Alfie's is a large antiques market at the corner of Church Street and Ashridge Street. There's only one specialist book dealer within the market (see below) but several of the other stalls sell books.

East West Antiques and Books

⌖ *Stands SO54-6, SO67 next to the Rooftop Restaurant*

☎ *07708 863760*

🕐 *Tues-Sat 10am-4pm*

This stand carries a general second-hand and antiquarian stock with above average selections of children's books, natural history, typography and nineteenth-century literature plus postcards and ephemera.

Archway Market

⌖ *619 Holloway Road, N19 5SS Archway LU*

✍ *www.archwaymarket.org*

🕐 *Sat 10am-5pm, Thurs 12noon-6pm*

This great local market is home to Word on the Street, run by the eminent 'Pavement Professor' and his trusty dog, Star. The stall sells a great range of classic, cult, contemporary and kid's books from four tables at the market. The professor prides himself on being competitively priced with paperbacks for £1.50-£3 and hardbacks for £3-£5. The stall gradually evolves over the course of a market day, as more stock is put on display, so is best visited in the afternoon when the stall and professor are at their best. Word on the Street is part of the team that have created Word on the Water (see p.170).

The cycle themed café, The Spoke, is just a few minutes' walk down Holloway Road at number 710 and offers excellent coffee and burgers.

Book Wood Fair

⌖ *Netil Market, 23 Westgate Street, London Fields, E8 3RL*

🚌 *Bethnal Green LU (then bus 48 or 254), London Fields Rail*

✍ *facebook.com/bookwood*

🕐 *Last Sun of each month 11am-5pm*

This new book market takes place in a small courtyard off Broadway Market once a month and is run by the folks at Newham Bookshop (see p.88) and supported by photographic book traders NB Pictures (see p.208). Here you can expect to find a mix of stalls selling new and second-hand books and ephemera such as posters and old prints. It's early days for the market but the people involved are committed to making it work with book signings, the occasional freebie and an active social media campaign. Netil Market has a lot of permanent food outlets and quite a few of these are open during the book market, making it easy to browse, buy and graze on fine days.

Brick Lane Market

⌨ *Brick Lane, Cheshire Street and Sclater Street, E1 6QR*
🚌 *Aldgate LU, Liverpool Street LU/Rail*
🕓 *Sun 6am-1pm*

Brick Lane is a huge and chaotic market and plenty of the junk sellers have books among their stock. One of the regular specialist book stalls can be found on Brick Lane close to the main junction with Sclater and Cheshire Street, but they do not trade on rainy days. Combine a trip to the market with a visit to Brick Lane Bookshop (see p.36), Rough Trade (see p.100) and Columbia Road Flower Market (see p.210).

Broadway Market

⌨ *Broadway Market, E8 4PH*
🖎 *www.broadwaymarket.co.uk*
🚌 *London Fields LU/Rail*
🕓 *Sat 10am-4.30pm*

Broadway Market is one of London's best streets for bookshops with Broadway Bookshop (see p.40), Artwords (see p.16) and Donlon Books (see p.50) all within a few minutes of each other. On Saturdays the market is in full swing and these bookshops are joined by a regular market stall specialising in books:

NB Pictures

⌨ *Broadway Market, E8 4PH*
🖎 *neil@nbpictures.com*
🕓 *Sat 10am-4.30pm*

Neil has been a regular feature of Broadway Market for many years and occupies two stalls selling a selection of photographic books with some carefully selected contemporary titles the occasional used bargain. The stock is well displayed with some fantastic books featuring the work of renowned photographers from Robert Frank to Sabastiao Salgado. Careful browsing is welcome and Neil is always on hand to offer help and advice when needed.

Brunswick Centre Market

⌨ *11 O'Donnell Court, WC1N 1NY*
🚌 *Russell Square LU*
🕓 *Sat 11am-5pm*

On Saturdays, the posh shops of the Brunswick Centre are joined by a small food market. The nearby Skoob Books (see p.160) take the opportunity to run a book stall here on fine days and being Skoob, they do a very good job of it, with plenty of paperback fiction all at reasonable prices. If you can't find what you are looking for and have the time, their fabulous shop is not far away.

Camden Passage Market

⌨ *Pierrepont Row, Camden Passage, N1 8ED*
☎ *07775 513 384 (Nigel)*
🖎 *www.camdenpassageislington.co.uk*
🚌 *Angel LU*
🕓 *Thurs-Fri 7am-7pm*

Nigel Smeeton is now the only trader at this long-established book market which formerly extended along Camden Passage, but is now confined to the covered area on Pierrepont Row. The stock is largely concerned with factual books covering just about every subject from ornithology to history with particular strengths being collectable children's books and good condition cookbooks. As the only book trader Nigel has plenty of space to display his stock and there are always surprising things to be found here such as a selection of beautiful books published by the Folio Society and a good range of the old Observer pocket books. On Fridays Nigel is joined by a couple of antique dealers who further add to the appeal of this characterful corner of Islington.

Camden Passage Market

Camden Market

⌨ *Camden Lock and Stables,*
 off Camden High Street, NW1 8NH
✎ *www.camdenmarket.com/*
🚋 *Camden Town LU*
🕐 *Sat-Sun 10am-6pm*

Camden Market is packed with clothes stalls for the young and trendy, but there is also a clutch of shops catering for bibliophiles. Book outlets include Black Gull Books (see p.138) and Village Games (see p.122). Also in the area is the excellent Walden Books (see p.168).

Columbia Road Market

⌨ *Columbia Road, E2 7RG*
✎ *www.columbiaroad.info*
🚋 *Old Street LU/Rail*
🕐 *Sunday 10am-4pm*

This specialist plant and flower market has now spawned an array of shops along the road itself, some with a gardening theme. Above the Glitterati clothing and jewellery shop at 148 Columbia Road, there is a Sunday second-hand bookshop with two tiny rooms jammed to the ceiling. Stock includes an amazing array of paperback literature both classic and modern, plays and poetry and with some non-fiction and children's titles as well.

Greenwich Markets

⌨ *Greenwich Church Street, SE10 9HZ*
✎ *www.greenwichmarket.net*
🚋 *Cutty Sark DLR, Greenwich Rail/DLR*
🕐 *Wed 11am-6pm (food and homewares),*
 Thurs & Fri 10am-5.30pm (antiques and collectables),
 Sat-Sun & Bank Holidays 10am-5.30pm (food, arts and crafts)

The best place to look for books is the small market (Sat, Sun & Bank Hols 7am-5pm) opposite the post office, next to the cinema on Greenwich High Road, where a handful of good stalls can be found. The Collector's Market on Thursday and Friday also has some books. Combine a market trip with a visit to the excellent Halcyon Books (see p.144), Maritime Books (see p.82) and Greenwich Book Time (see p.58).

Hampstead Market

⌨ *Hampstead Community Centre,*
 78 Hampstead High Street, NW3 1RE
🚋 *Hampstead LU*
 Mon-Fri 10.30am-6pm and most Sundays.

There are usually some books for sale at this small community market every weekend although the regular bookseller who used to trade through the week has now left. The best time to visit the market is the second Sunday of each month when the market is largely focused on second-hand and collectable books. The first Sunday of the month is dedicated to the Hampstead Antiques and Collectors Fair where there are also usually some books featured. When visiting the market, don't forget the Oxfam Bookshop just around the corner on Heath Street (see p.204).

Haynes Lane Collectors Market

⌨ *off Westow Street, SE19 3AN*
🚋 *Crystal Palace / Gypsy Hill Rail*
🕐 *Fri 11am-5pm, Sat 11am-6pm,*
 Sun 11am-5pm

Rather tucked away, this market is definitely worth searching out for its somewhat shambolic book stall/shop selling a vast array of books. The subjects covered are extremely wide alongside plenty of general fiction. Be certain to check out Bookseller Crow on the Hill (see p.32) if you are in this part of London.

Northcross Road Market

🏛 *Northcross Road, SE22 9EV*

🚃 *East Dulwich Rail*

🕙 *Saturdays 9am-5pm*

This is lovely little local market (situated off Lordship Lane in Dulwich) is well worth a visit. Among the fresh food, bric-a-brac and second-hand furniture can be found an excellent book stall run by the people from Rye Books (see p.102). They manage to fit a good stock into their little van and include new and second-hand fiction as well as a good range of kid's books. Head up the market to the award-winning Blue Mountain Café (www.bluemo.co.uk) at Number 18 for refreshment.

Piccadilly Market

🏛 *St James's Churchyard,*
197 Piccadilly, W1J 9LL

🖥 *www.piccadilly-market.co.uk*

🚃 *Piccadilly Circus LU*

🕙 *Tues 10am-6pm*

This is a small open-air market and Tuesday is the day for antiques and collectables. The book selection isn't great but there are usually a few volumes among the jewellery and other interesting bits and pieces. Anyway, this is a fun place to visit if you are in the centre of London.

Portobello Road Market

🏛 *Portobello Road and Golborne Road, W11*

🖥 *www.portobelloroad.co.uk*

🚃 *Notting Hill Gate LU,*
Ladbroke Grove LU

🕙 *Sat 8am-5.30pm (although many*
dealers do start packing up in the
middle of the afternoon)

This huge market covers pretty much everything: antiques, clothes, vegetables, junk and of course books. The market extends north along Portobello Road from Lonsdale Road up to and including much of Golborne Road. Saturday is by far the busiest day when all the various parts of the market are open and the streets are awash with shoppers. For those seeking antiquarian and specialist books there are numerous antiques centres, many of which house specialist book dealers – some of which are listed below. For the best coffee in the area check out Coffee Plant at 180 Portobello Road and the Portuguese cafés on Golborne Road.

Ben Brierley Rare Books

🏛 *Outside 99 Portobello Road*
at Katrina Phillips.

☎ *07768 058632*

✉ *benbrb@gmail.com*

An enticing stall specialising in children's literature, illustrated and more general antiquarian books.

Demetzy Books

🏛 *Gallery 113, 113 Portobello Road*

✉ *demetzybooks@tiscali.co.uk*

A large general stock but with special strengths in cookery, travel, children's, illustrated and miniature books and also books about dogs.

Don Kelly

🏛 *Stand L16/20 Admiral Vernon Arcade,*
139-147 Portobello Road

☎ *020 7731 0482*

Downstairs in the Admiral Vernon Arcade, this stall features a fine selection of art reference books, art magazines and sale catalogues.

Charles Vernon-Hunt

🏛 *Harris Arcade, 161 Portobello Road*

☎ *020 8854 1588*

✉ *c.vernonhunt@btinternet.com*

This dealer offers a superb stock of art reference books (both new and out of print publications) and exhibition catalogues from around the world. He is especially strong on African, Indian, Islamic and Chinese art.

Southbank Book Market

  ▭ *Outside the BFI Southbank, SE1*
  ✑ *www.southbankcentre.co.uk*
  🚇 *Waterloo LU/Rail*
  ☉ *Daily 12noon-6pm (winter),*
     11am-7pm (summer)

This open-air book market on the south bank of the Thames has something that no branch of Waterstones can compete with – a sense of romance. Situated under the protection of Waterloo Bridge on a handsome tree lined pedestrian boulevard with a superb view of the Thames and the London skyline, it seems a long way from the hustle and bustle of Charing Cross Road (which is actually only about ten minutes' walk from here). This is where Hugh Grant's declaration of love in 'Four Weddings and a Funeral' was filmed and I know of at least one couple who have conducted a good deal of their courtship here.

Even if your interests are strictly literary, the market is worth a visit with its fantastic range of fiction, play texts and works concerning film and theatre (as befitting its location on the doorstep of the BFI Southbank and National Theatre), biographies and weighty art books. If you are seeking refreshment, there are plenty of restaurants, bars and cafés nearby. The literary appeal of this area has been enhanced by the arrival of a branch of Foyles (see p.55).

Spitalfields Market

  ▭ *West side of Commercial Street between*
     Folgate Street and Brushfield Street, E1
  ☎ *020 7247 8556*
  ✑ *www.oldspitalfieldsmarket.com*
  🚇 *Liverpool Street LU/Rail*
  ☉ *Mon-Wed General stalls;*
     Thurs Antiques (inc books & magazines);
     Fri (alternate weeks Record Fair or
     Produce Market), Sat (alternate arts
     and crafts, vintage, record fair, produce
     and African Market), Sun everything

Spitalfields is a thriving market located inbetween gleaming shops, restaurants and offices. The best day for books is the Thursday Antiques Market which offers a wide range of reference books covering most subjects, a reasonable choice of fiction plus lots of paper ephemera. Sunday also hosts a few book stalls but you'll need to root around amongst the crowds to find them. There's also a stall specialising in second-hand Penguin books (Tues-Thurs), a magnet for lovers of those old orange and green covers, all at great prices. On Sundays look out for the new discount book stall with a broad range of titles with paperbacks for £4 and hardbacks from £5.

Southbank Book Market

The British Library

Libraries

Canada Water Library

Public Libraries

There have been many library closures across London in recent years as councils attempt to manage increasingly tight budgets. One of the most notable of these was the demise of Kensal Rise Library which was opened by Mark Twain in 1900 and much loved by the local population who campaigned for it to be saved. Book Lovers naturally supports all those struggling to keep their local libraries open, but this chapter focuses on London's great public libraries that are worth making a special trip to visit. These incredible resources include the famous Swiss Cottage Library with its 1960s design and extensive psychology collection and also Peckham Library which remains the only library in the country to have won the Stirling Prize when it was opened in 2000. The section concludes with a feature about the ambitious rethinking of library services by Tower Hamlets Council with the creation of their Idea Stores. Visiting these busy and vibrant public spaces is evidence enough that libraries are still a vital part of the London's literary landscape.

Central

Barbican Library

⌖ *Level 2 The Barbican Centre*
Silk Street, EC2Y 8DS
☎ *020 7638 0569*
✎ *www.cityoflondon.gov.uk*
🚌 *Moorgate LU/Rail, Barbican LU*
🕐 *Mon & Wed 9.30am-5.30pm*
Tues & Thurs 9.30am-7.30pm
Fri 9.30am-2pm, Sat 9.30am-4pm

Occupying most of level two of the Barbican Centre, this library is the largest in the City of London with a vast selection of books, DVDs and CDs. The library has particular strengths in music, arts and children's books.

Charing Cross Library

⌖ *4-6 Charing Cross Road, WC2H 0HF*
☎ *020 7641 6200*
✎ *www.westminster.gov.uk/libraries*
🚌 *Leicester Square LU*
🕐 *Mon 9.30am-8pm, Tues 9.30-7pm*
Thurs-Fri 9.30am-7pm, Wed 10am-7pm,
Sat 10.30am-2pm, Sun 11am-5pm

This small library, just off Trafalgar Square, is one of London's most central libraries and contains London's largest collection of Chinese language books to cater for the residents and workers of Chinatown. The study areas have recently been upgraded, but all the reference material, papers and magazines are kept in the nearby Westminster Reference Library (see page 218).

City Business Library

⌖ *Guildhall, Aldermanbury, EC2V 7HH*
☎ *020 7332 1812*
✎ *www.cityoflondon.gov.uk*
🚌 *St Paul's LU, Bank LU*
🕐 *Mon-Fri 9.30am-5pm, Wed till 7.30pm*

In the heart of the City, this business library offers expert staff, a vast collection of business books, internet access and regular events and workshops.

Finsbury Library

⌨ *245 St John Street, EC1V 4NB*

☎ *020 7527 7960*

✑ *www.islington.gov.uk*

🚇 *Angel Islington LU*

🕒 *Mon, Thurs 9.30am-8pm*
Tues & Fri-Sat 9.30am-5pm

Finsbury Library was the first library in Britain to allow readers to choose their books from the shelves and still has some post-war optimism embodied in its fine 1950's modernist building. As well as having a good library, the building also holds the Local History Centre and Islington Museum.

Guildhall Library

⌨ *Aldermanbury, EC2V 7HH*

☎ *020 7332 1868*

✑ *www.cityoflondon.gov.uk*

🚇 *St Paul's LU, Bank LU*

🕒 *Mon-Fri 9.30am-5pm, Wed till 7.30pm,*
selected Sats 9.30am-5pm

This reference library specialises in the history of London and contains a collection of over 200,000 books on the subject, encompassing maritime history, food and wine, English law and an archive of parliamentary papers and statutes. The library is a vital resource for those interested London's history and contains renowned collections relating to some of the capital's great historical figures including Samuel Pepys, John Wilkes and Thomas More. The library has an extensive archive of London papers such as apprentice records, census documents and London trade directories, which are essential reference material for those studying their London family history.

Holborn Library

⌨ *32-38 Theobalds Road, WC1X 8PA*

☎ *020 7974 4444*

✑ *www.camden.gov.uk*

🚇 *Chancery Lane LU*

🕒 *Mon-Thurs 10am-7pm, Fri 10am-5pm,*
Sat 11am-5pm

This is one of London's most central libraries and offers a good collection of books, talking books, CDs and DVDs as well as newspapers and periodicals. The library also contains a dedicated children's library with regular groups and classes catering for kids from toddlers to teenage readers. The building is also home to the local study centre and archive for Camden.

Westminster Reference Library

⌨ *35 St Martin's Street, WC2H 7HP*

☎ *020 7641 6200 (press 2)*

✑ *www.westminster.gov.uk/libraries*

🚇 *Leicester Square LU*

🕒 *Mon-Fri 10am-8pm, Sat 10am-5pm*

This oasis of calm lies between Leicester Square and Charing Cross Road and offers extensive reference material with a particular emphasis on business, visual art and the performing arts.

North

Highgate Library

🏛 *Chester Road, N19 5DH*
☎ *020 7974 4444*
🖋 *www.camden.gov.uk*
🚌 *Archway LU*
🕓 *Tues-Wed 10am-5pm, Thurs 10am-7pm*
   Sat 10am-4pm

Due to council cut backs, this beautiful Edwardian library is now largely run by volunteers. Despite these changes the library remains a vital resource for the local community offering a reasonable selection of books, music and DVDs as well as periodicals and papers.

Islington Central Library

🏛 *2 Fieldway Crescent, N5 1PF*
☎ *020 7527 6900*
🖋 *www.islington.gov.uk*
🚌 *Highbury & Islington LU/Rail,*
   Holloway Road LU
🕓 *Mon, Wed-Thurs 9.30am-8pm*
   Tues, Fri-Sat 9.30am-5pm, Sun 1pm-5pm

This large library is an odd mix of a grand Edwardian building (which opened to the public in 1907) and an ugly 1970s extension which has nonetheless provided much needed space for this useful lending and reference library, including an extensive and comfortable study area.

St John's Wood Library

🏛 *20 Circus Road, NW8 6PD*
☎ *020 7641 6200*
🖋 *www.westminster.gov.uk/libraries*
🚌 *St John's Wood LU*
🕓 *Mon-Thurs 9.30am-7pm*
   (Wed 10am-7pm), Fri 9.30am-8pm,
   Sat 9.30am-5pm, Sun 11.30am-3pm

A well-stocked library offering a reasonable selection of books, CDs and DVDs as well as a children's library, study areas and services such as homework clubs and reading sessions for the under 5s.

Swiss Cottage Library

🏛 *88 Avenue Road, NW3 3HA*
☎ *020 7974 4444*
🖋 *www.camden.gov.uk/swisscottagelibrary*
🚌 *Swiss Cottage LU*
🕓 *Mon-Thurs 10am-8pm*
   Fri-Sat 10am-5pm, Sun 11am-4pm

This iconic building was designed by Sir Basil Spence and opened in 1964 – and it still manages to embody something of the optimism and idealism of the 60s. The library offers an excellent general stock but with particular strengths being children's books, philosophy and psychology. The library also offers extensive study areas, internet access and a café and gallery.

West

Kensington Central Library

⌖ Phillimore Walk, W8 7RX

☎ 020 7361 3010

✑ www.rbkc.gov.uk/libraries

🚇 High Steet Kensington LU

🕓 Mon-Tues, Thurs 9.30am-8pm,
Wed, Fri-Sat 9.30am-5pm

A large library close to Kensington High Street offering study areas and a wide selection of books for children and adults.

Mayfair Library

⌖ 25 South Audley Street, W1K 2PB

☎ 020 7641 6200

✑ www.westminster.gov.uk/libraries

🚇 Green Park LU, Hyde Park Corner LU

🕓 Mon-Fri 11am-7pm, Sat 10.30am-2pm

This attractive local library has a reasonable book selection and offers a rare public space amid the swanky shops of Mayfair.

Paddington Library

Adult:

⌖ Porchester Road, W2 5DU

Children:

⌖ Clifford Hall, Porchester Road, W2 5DU

☎ 020 7641 6200

🚇 Royal Oak LU

✑ www.westminster.gov.uk/libraries

🕓 Adult: Mon, Thurs-Fri 9.30am-10pm,
Tues 9.30am-9pm, Wed 10am-9pm,
Sat 9.30am-5pm, Sun 11am-5pm.

🕓 Children: Mon-Sat 9.30am-5.30pm
(closed for lunch 12noon-1pm)

The adult and children's libraries are in two separate buildings, but the facilities are first rate and in addition there are business and advice services, a reader's group, homework club and excellent study areas.

South West

Balham Library

⌖ 16 Ramsden Road, SW12 8QY

☎ 020 8673 1129

✑ www.better.org.uk

🚇 Balham Rail

🕓 Mon, Wed-Thurs 9am-8pm,
Fri 9am-5pm, Sat 10am-6pm

A local library in the heart of Balham with a reasonable offering of books for adults and children.

Battersea Library

⌖ 265 Lavender Hill, SW11 1JB

☎ 020 7223 2334

✑ www.better.org.uk

🚇 Clapham Junction Rail

🕓 Mon-Wed 9am-8pm, Fri 9am-6pm
Sat 9am-5pm, Sun 1pm-5pm

This is one of London's grandest public libraries with a large balconied central hall illuminated by a vast glass roof. The library holds particularly extensive collections of books on European history and also over 40,000 titles ong World War I and II. This is also the site of the Wandsworth Heritage Service which holds records and documents for the Borough of Wandsworth.

City of Westminster Archives Centre

⌖ 10 St Anne's Street, SW1P 2DE

☎ 020 7641 5180

🚇 St James's Park LU

✑ www.westminster.gov.uk/libraries

🕓 Tues-Thurs 10am-7pm, Fri-Sat 10am-5pm

This council-run archive extends over five floors and holds parish records, electoral registers, birth and death certificates for the City of Westminster as well as books on local history. The archive is an important resource for genealogists and local historians and also contains a local history bookshop.

Pimlico Library

- Lupus Street, SW1V 3EY
- ☎ 020 7641 6200
- 🚇 Pimlico LU
- ✎ www.westminster.gov.uk/libraries
- ◷ Mon-Fri 9.30am-8pm, Sat 9.30am-5pm, Sun 1.30pm-5pm

A great local library attached to the Pimlico Academy which also contributes to the library's funding. There is a particularly good stock of GCSE and A-level reference books as well as strong sections on literature, history and art.

Putney Library

- 5-7 Disraeli Road, SW15 2DR
- ☎ 020 8780 3085
- ✎ www.better.org.uk
- 🚉 Putney Rail
- ◷ Mon, Wed-Thurs 9am-8pm
  Fri-Sat 9am-5pm, Sun 1pm-5pm

A small but well organised library offering a reasonable choice of reading matter for adults and children, free internet access, study rooms as well as CDs and DVDs.

Tooting Library

- 75 Mitcham Road, SW17 9PD
- ☎ 020 8767 0543
- ✎ www.better.org.uk
- 🚇 Tooting Broadway LU
- ◷ Mon-Tues, Thurs 9am-7pm
  Fri-Sat 9am-5pm, Sun 1pm-5pm

This fine listed building has been entirely refurbished inside and offers a clean, spacious environment with a good general stock, computers, a teen library and comfy seating.

Victoria Library and Westminster Music Library

- 160 Buckingham Palace Road, SW1W 9UD
- ☎ 020 7641 6200
- ✎ www.westminster.gov.uk/libraries
- 🚇 Victoria LU
- ◷ Library: Mon 9.30am-8pm, Tues, Thurs-Fri 9.30am-7pm,
  Wed 10am-7pm, Sat 9.30am-5pm
- ◷ Music Library: Mon-Fri 11am-7pm, Sat 10am-5pm

This large red brick and Portland stone building in the heart of Victoria is one of the country's most important music libraries offering sheet music, periodicals, music software and even free use of a Yamaha digital piano. The main Victoria Library has an extensive general stock with particular strengths in biography and fiction.

Wandsworth Town Library

- 11 Garratt Lane, SW18 4AQ
- ☎ 020 8877 1742
- ✎ www.better.org.uk
- 🚉 Wandsworth Town Rail
- ◷ Tues-Thurs 9am-7pm, Fri-Sat 9am-5pm

A well-stocked library close to the centre of Wandsworth offering free internet access and study areas.

South East

Canada Water Library

⌖ 21 Surrey Quays Road, SE16 7AR
☎ 020 7525 2000
✎ www.southwark.gov.uk
🚌 Canada Water LU/Rail
🕐 Mon-Fri 9am-8pm, Sat 9am-5pm
Sun 12pm-4pm

This modern library looks something like a spaceship and its interior is equally stunning with wood clad walls, a wide spiral staircase and curved shelving. The library stock is extensive and includes books, CDs, DVDs and computer games. The library is always busy and offers excellent study areas, free Wi-Fi and a café on the ground floor.

John Harvard Library

⌖ 211 Borough High Street, SE1 1JA
☎ 020 7525 2000
✎ www.southwark.gov.uk
🚌 Borough LU, London Bridge LU/Rail
🕐 Mon-Fri 9am-7pm, Sat 9am-5pm,
Sun 12pm-4pm

This is one of Southwark's largest and best stocked libraries offering a range of services such as baby and toddler sessions, adult literacy classes and book groups.

Peckham Library

⌖ 122 Peckham Hill Street, SE15 5JR
☎ 020 7525 2000
✎ www.southwark.gov.uk
🚌 Peckham Rye Rail
🕐 Mon-Tues, Thurs-Fri 9am-8pm,
Fri 9am-8pm, Sat 10am-5pm
Sun 12pm-4pm

Peckham Library is the only British library to have won the Stirling Prize for architecture, back in 2000. The library has aged well and proved a popular resource for locals with a great selection of books, study areas, adult reading classes and lots of other services such as homework help sessions and free Wi-Fi.

East

Bethnal Green Library

🏠 *Cambridge Heath Road, E2 0HL*
☎ *020 7364 3492*
🖳 *www.ideastore.co.uk*
🚇 *Bethnal Green LU*
🕐 *Mon-Wed 10am-6pm, Thurs 10am-8pm, Fri 10am-6pm, Sat 9am-5pm*

This small local library is located in a Grade II listed building that has recently undergone a major refurbishment with improved Wi-Fi and study facilities and a much improved children's library.

Dalston CLR James Library

🏠 *Dalston Square, E8 3BQ*
☎ *020 8356 3000*
🖳 *www.hackney.gov.uk*
🚇 *Dalston Rail*
🕐 *Mon-Fri 9am-8pm, Sat 9am-5pm Sun 1pm-5pm*

This new library in the heart of Dalston opened in 2012 and proudly bears the name of its predecessor after a long campaign to preserve the memory of the renowned West Indian writer and academic after whom the library was named. The new building offers much improved facilities with free Wi-Fi, attractive study areas and a good offering of books for both adults and children with a self-service system making borrowing easy. The library is now the home for the Hackney Archives which is an invaluable resource for students of local history.

Hackney Central Library

Hackney Technology & Learning Centre
🏠 *1 Reading Lane, E8 1GQ*
☎ *020 8356 3000*
🖳 *www.hackney.gov.uk*
🚇 *Hackney Central Rail*
🕐 *Mon-Thurs 9am-8pm, Fri 9am-6pm Sat 9am-5pm*

This modern library has a great selection of books for adults and children as well as DVDs and CDs plus an extensive reference library offering books, magazines and newspapers. The library has a large study area with free Wi-Fi, which is very popular with the scholars of Hackney.

The Idea Stores
☞ www.ideastore.co.uk

Idea Store Whitechapel
▣ 321 Whitechapel Road, E1 1BU
☏ 020 7364 4332
🕐 Mon-Thurs 9am-9pm, Fri 9am-6pm
   Sat 9am-5pm, Sun 11am-5pm

Idea Store Bow
▣ 1 Gladstone Place
   Roman Road, E3 5ES
☏ 020 7364 4332
🕐 Mon-Thurs 9am-9pm, Fri 9am-6pm
   Sat 9am-5pm, Sun 10am-4pm

Idea Store Canary Wharf
▣ Churchill Place, E14 5RB
☏ 020 7364 4332
🕐 Mon-Thurs 9am-9pm, Fri 9am-6pm
   Sat 9am-5pm, Sun 12noon-6pm

Idea Store Chrisp Street
▣ 1 Vesey Path, East India Dock Road
   E14 6BT
☏ 020 7364 4332
🕐 Mon-Thurs 9am-9pm, Fri 9am-6pm
   Sat 9am-5pm, Sunday 10am-4pm

Idea Store Watney Market
▣ 260 Commercial Road, E1 2FB
☏ 020 7364 4332
🕐 Mon-Thurs 9am-9pm
   Fri 9am-6pm, Sat 9am-5pm

Back in 1998 the libraries of Tower Hamlets were in a sorry state. There was no shortage of libraries but most were located in run-down buildings in quiet back streets and very poorly used. Something needed to be done so the library team at the council had a rethink of the service and in 2002 the first of the Idea Stores was opened in Bow. Since then a further four have transformed library and adult education services throughout the borough.

The new stores combine modern, well-designed buildings, with a carefully chosen stock of mainstream fact and fiction books, and a wide range of adult learning classes and other public services. Sergio Dogliani was one of the key figures behind the new stores and he emphasises the importance of location:

"One of the strategies behind the Idea Stores is to make them accessible, not tucked away in a back street, but on the High Street for all to see and use."

This attempt to reconnect with the local population has also led to better customer service with guarantees that toddler classes, reading groups, after school clubs and all other services will be provided on time and schedule so that users can rely on the facilities. The overall approach is very different from the usual library and Sergio is proud that there are no notices asking people to be quiet in any of the Idea Stores:

"Libraries are not just about books, they are also a rare free public space for people to interact and that is very important."

This new approach to library services has proved a phenomenal success and the latest store in Watney Market even has a council One-Stop Shop on the ground floor, while all the Idea stores offer computer facilities and study areas, as well as a busy programme of adult learning classes – some even have cafés.

There are plans for more Idea Stores in the borough and Sergio and his team are always busy improving the service. There's certainly a real energy to Idea Stores and it's an incredible vote of confidence in the concept that the diverse population of Tower Hamlets have taken these new libraries to their heart.

The Idea Store

Specialist Libraries

The specialist libraries of London are as varied as they are numerous. Among the gems are those libraries run by institutions and dedicated to particular and often obscure subjects such as mountaineering, English Folk Dance and even the history of fans. As well as these unusual specialist libraries there are others that are unique for their atmosphere and history, such as the London Library, founded by Thomas Carlyle in 1841 and still providing a studious haven for its paying members, and the remarkable Bishopsgate Institute Library with its unrivaled collection of books about London and with free access to all. We have provided access information for all the libraries featured, but it is always a good idea to contact them first before making a special visit and many of the libraries have useful websites which are worth exploring.

Action on Hearing Loss

▣ *Library, Institute of Laryngology & Otology, Royal National Throat, Nose and Ear Hospital,*
330-332 Gray's Inn Road, WC1X 8EE
☎ *020 3456 5253*
✐ *www.actiononhearingloss.org.uk*
🚍 *King's Cross, St Pancras LU/Rail*
☉ *Mon-Tues 9am-7pm,*
Wed-Fri 9am-5.30pm

The largest library on deafness and hearing loss in Europe including books, magazines, journals, biographies and fiction with deaf characters for both adults and children.

Alpine Club

▣ *55/56 Charlotte Road, EC2A 3QF*
☎ *020 7613 0745*
✐ *www.alpine-club.org.uk*
🚍 *Old Street LU/Rail*
☉ *By appointment*

One of the largest collections of mountaineering literature in the world, including over 30,000 books from the sixteenth century onwards, newspaper cuttings dating from the nineteenth century, journals, pamphlets, guidebooks, letters and artefacts. The library also keeps the Himalayan Index, a database of all expeditions to Himalayan, Hindu Kush, Chinese and Karakoram peaks over 6000m and they hold more than 600 expedition reports for peaks around the world.

Alzheimer's Society

▣ *Dementia Knowledge Centre,*
Devon House,
58 St Katharine's Way, E1W 1LB
☎ *020 7423 3500*
✐ *www.alzheimers.org.uk*
🚍 *Tower Hill LU*
☉ *By appointment*

A specialist library containing literature on medical and social aspects of dementia and care including health and social care, housing and therapies as well as personal accounts of the condition.

Anti-Slavery International

▣ *Thomas Clarkson House,*
The Stableyard,
Broomgrove Road, SW9 9TL
☎ *020 7501 8920*
✐ *www.antislavery.org*
🚍 *Stockwell LU, Brixton LU/Rail*
☉ *By appointment*

Contemporary and historical material about slavery, its abolition and related issues. This includes material concerning human rights, a collection of eighteenth and nineteenth-century anti-slavery literature, and collections on modern forms of slavery including child, forced and bonded labour, forced marriage, trafficking and child prostitution.

Architectural Association

⌨ *36 Bedford Square, WC1B 3ES*
☎ *020 7887 4035*
✍ *www.aaschool.ac.uk*
🚌 *Tottenham Court Road LU*
🕐 *Access restricted to AA members*

This library contains more than 48,000 volumes on the history of architecture, architectural theory, contemporary architectural design, building types, interior design, landscape design and supplementary subjects. In addition, the library houses special collections on the Modern Movement, international exhibitions and the history of architectural education at the AA. The library subscribes to a range of online resources and databases and holds print editions of around 150 architectural, art and technical journals.

The Photo Library contains 500,000 images, among them important collections of photographs by FR Yerbury, Reyner Banham, Eric de Maré and Robin Evans. In addition they hold a vast photographic archive of AA student work dating from the 1920s, as well as architectural drawings, paintings and documents dating from the 1840s.

Belarusian Francis Skaryna

⌨ *37 Holden Road, N12 8HS*
☎ *020 8445 5358*
✍ *www.skaryna.org.uk*
🚌 *Woodside Park LU*
🕐 *By appointment*

The largest collection of Belarusian books and periodicals outside Belarus including Belarusian literature, literary history and criticism, ethnography, folklore, dictionaries and books on the Belarusian language. Most are in Belarusian but there are also publications about Belarus in English, Polish, Russian, German and French.

Bishopsgate Institute

⌨ *230 Bishopsgate, EC2M 4QH*
☎ *020 7392 9270*
✍ *www.bishopsgate.org.uk*
🚌 *Liverpool Street LU/Rail*
🕐 *Mon-Fri 10am-5.30pm, Wed till 8pm*

The Bishopsgate Institute has been an important place for adult learning and the dissemination of ideas since its opening in 1895. The Grade II listed building, designed by Charles Harrison Townsend, has recently undergone a major refurbishment, but the historic archive and library at the heart of the Institute remains largely unchanged with its elegant oak and glass book cabinets and a study area illuminated by a fine stained glass dome.

The appearance of fusty tradition is a little misleading, the old card index boxes at the main reception are simply for show and behind the counter librarians busy themselves at a computer system upon which the entire library's collection is catalogued, while free Wi-Fi is available to all users of the library. A further door leads to a modern balconied researchers' area and archive, where staff will help visitors find a particular item. The library holds a good general stock, but its photographic archive of over 150,000 images largely relating to London, is a unique and significant resource. The library also holds major collections of books and original documents relating to London history, Labour and Socialist History, Humanism, protest and LGBT history, as well as papers on key parliamentary figures.

Bishopsgate Institute Library operates an open access policy and is a wonderful amenity. When combined with the other courses, exhibitions and classes available within the Institute, it is a gem well worth seeking out.

Bishopsgate Institute Library

British Psychotherapy Foundation

⌑ 37 Mapesbury Road, NW2 4HJ

☎ 020 8452 9823

✎ www.britishpsychotherapyfoundation.org.uk

🚌 Kilburn LU

🕓 Restricted access

A specialist library with a large stock of books and journals plus some audiovisual material on psychoanalysis and psychoanalytic psychotherapy, Jungian analytic psychotherapy, child psychotherapy and related areas. Access to the library is restricted to members of the foundation and those training in the field of psychotherapy.

British College of Osteopathic Medicine

⌑ 6 Netherhall Gardens, NW3 5RR

☎ 020 7443 9910

✎ www.bcom.ac.uk

🚌 Finchley Road LU

🕓 By appointment

Historical and contemporary books and journals on naturopathy, osteopathy and related disciplines. The collection is especially strong on historical alternative medicine books.

BFI Reuben Library

⌑ BFI Southbank, Belvedere Road, SE1 8XT

☎ 020 7255 1444

✎ www.bfi.org.uk

🚌 Waterloo LU

🕓 Tues-Sat 10.30am-7pm

The BFI library has a long history, and for many years was something of a secret among the film students and media researchers who were its stalwart patrons. The library underwent a transformation in 2014, acquiring an additional name ('Reuben') and moving from the BFI's Stephen Street HQ to the main British Film Institute complex on the Southbank.

The new library remains the major national research collection specialising in British film and television, but has considerable international holdings. Established in 1934, the library's collection spans the history of the moving image and includes books, journals, press cuttings and digitalised materials. The new space has subtle lighting and individual study areas but the main transformation is in the library's ethos which means that the library is now open to all. The reader services librarian, Sarah Currant, explains:

"We actively want everybody, regardless of who they are, to have access to materials that are as well-thumbed as they are beautiful, well-known as they are arcane."

Visit the BFI's website or just call in during opening hours to find out more about this incredible library, as well as the BFI National Archive and Special Collections. BFI Southbank is a four-screen cinema venue, showing over 2,000 contemporary and classic films each year. View over 1,000 hours of free film and TV in the Mediatheque, or visit the BFI Shop, which boasts an incredible range of books, DVDs and gifts.

"We actively want everybody, regardless of who they are, to have access to materials that are as well-thumbed as they are beautiful, well-known as they are arcane."

BFI Reuben Library

The most spectacular aspect of the library is the six-storey glass tower which stands at its centre and contains the King's Library of over 65,000 volumes collected by King George III

The British Library

The British Library

- 96 Euston Road, NW1 2DB
- Switchboard: 0330 333 1144
  Customer Services: 01937 546 060
- www.bl.uk
- King's Cross, St Pancras LU/Rail
- Mon-Thurs 9.30am-8pm, Fri 9.30am-6pm
  Sat 9.30am-5pm, Sun 11am-5pm
  (times for the galleries, shop, reader
  registration, reading rooms and
  restaurants may vary)

The British Library came into existence as part of the British Museum and its famous circular reading room was where Karl Marx wrote many of his major works and included among its patrons Mahatma Gandhi, Virginia Woolf and Sir Arthur Conan Doyle. The gradual expansion of the library made it increasingly difficult for it to function within the British Museum and the two finally became separate entities in 1973. A long process began to design and build a new library on Euston Road. The resulting red brick edifice, designed by Sir Colin StJohn Wilson, finally opened in 1998 to mixed reviews, with one commentator describing the building's style as 'Sainsbury's vernacular'. The interior of the library has proved a greater success with a vast marble floored atrium greeting visitors, the recently redesigned British Library Bookshop (see page 38) to the left and two imposing flights of stairs leading to the various levels of this labyrinthine building.

The most spectacular aspect of the library is the six-storey glass tower which stands at its centre and contains the King's Library of over 65,000 volumes collected by King George III. The British Library is a surprising building with many levels and Reading Rooms only available to those engaged in research that requires access to this unique collection. Access is not restricted to postgraduate studies and the Library does make some effort to accommodate non-academics wishing to use the facilities.

General visitors to the British Library only see a small part of the building as much of it is given over to a vast automated storage system that holds over 170 million items, including over 14 million books and important holdings of maps, manuscripts, newspapers, sound recordings, historical manuscripts, play-scripts, patents and much more. All books published in the UK and Ireland are legally required to be placed within the collection and so a further 3 million items are added each year with many items stored at the British Library's second site in Boston Spa, West Yorkshire.

Some of the library's most historically important items are displayed in the 'Treasures of the British Library' exhibition. Entry is free of charge and the beautifully displayed gallery contains landmark books such as the Lindisfarne Gospels, Shakespeare's First Folio and the Diamond Sutra, The world's earliest dated printed book. Special exhibitions further showcase the library's rare and historic holdings, such as the recent 'Magna Carta: Law, Liberty, Legacy' to commemorate the 800th anniversary of the documents signing. Digitalised versions of some of the BL's treasures are also available to view on the website.

All London book lovers should take the opportunity to explore one of the world's great libraries which is on their doorstep. There are cafés within the building and outside in the vast stone courtyard, study areas open to all, an extensive events programme and a great bookshop (see page 38). Those that can't make it to the St Pancras or Boston Spa sites can find out more about the Library's holdings by browsing its very useful website.

British Medical Association

⌨ *BMA House, Tavistock Square, WC1H 9JP*
☎ *020 7383 6625*
✎ *www.bma.org.uk/library*
🚏 *Russell Square LU, Euston LU/Rail*
🕐 *By appointment*

One of the largest medical information services in the UK specialising in current clinical practice, medical ethics and health information. Access to the library is restricted to BMA members, but access to other visitors can be granted on a discretionary basis – contact them for more details.

British Museum

⌨ *Great Russell Street, WC1B 3DG*
☎ *020 7323 8000*
✎ *www.britishmuseum.org*
🚏 *Russell Square LU*
🕐 *By appointment*

Until the opening of the purpose-built British Library in St Pancras back in 1998, the British Museum had been the national repository of books and its famous reading room was renowned as the place where Karl Marx researched and wrote many of his works. The departure of such a vast book collection led to considerable restructuring within the museum and in 2000 the Paul Hamlyn Library opened, offering public access and use of the famous Reading Room designed by Sydney Smirke and completed in 1857. In recent years the museum has again undergone a further restructuring and the Paul Hamlyn library and reading rooms have been closed since 2011 while consultation as to their further use continues.

However, the museum's various curatorial and research departments have well established, specialized library collections. In most cases these can be accessed for research purposes but it is often necessary to make an appointment before visiting. For more details about the individual libraries, please visit the museum's website.

The largest of the museum's libraries, the Anthropology Library and Research Centre, and the Department of Prints and Drawings both offer public access. Their contact details are:

The Anthropology Library and Research Centre
(Department of Africa, Oceania & the Americas)

☎ *020 7323 8031*
✎ *anthropologylibrary@britishmuseum.org*
🕐 *Mon-Wed and Fri 10am-5pm*
Thurs 12noon-5pm

Material from the Hamlyn library can still be accessed via the Anthropology Library.

Prints & Drawings

✎ *prints@britishmuseum.org*
☎ *020 7323 8408*
🕐 *By appointment*

The British Museum Central Archive

☎ *020 7323 8224*
✎ *centralarchive@britishmuseum.org*
🕐 *By appointment*

The British Museum keeps a substantial archive relating to its own administration since its foundation in 1753 and this can be viewed by appointment.

British Olympic Association Archives

UEL Library Archives

⊞ *Docklands Campus*
   4-6 University Way, E16 2RD
☎ *020 8223 7676*
✎ *www.teamgb.com*
🚌 *Cyprus DLR*
☺ *By appointment*

The University of East London now holds the historical archive and book collection of the British Olympic Association (BOA). The collection contains material relating to the history and work of the Association from 1906-2009, and notably includes records concerning the organization of the 1908 and 1948 London Olympic Games. The collection is open to researchers, however some sections are still being cataloged.

The British Psychoanalytical Society

(incorporating The Institute of Psychoanalysis)

⊞ *Byron House, 112A Shirland Road,*
   W9 2BT
☎ *020 7563 5008*
✎ *www.psychoanalysis.org.uk*
🚌 *Maida Vale LU, Warwick Avenue LU,*
   Westbourne Park LU
☺ *Mon-Tues & Thurs 1pm-8pm*
   Wed 10.30am-5.30pm
   Fri 10.30am-5pm

A vast collection (almost 22,000 volumes) of psychoanalytic material dating from the mid eighteenth century to the present day. The library contains psychoanalytic works published in the UK, and abroad as well as donations from the private collections of leading psychoanalysts such as Ernest Jones, James Strachey and Donald Winnicott. The library catalogue can be viewed on line at: http://i10334uk.eos-intl.eu/I10334UK/OPAC/Index.aspx
The library does allow access to students that are not members of the society, but charges a £10 fee for a day pass.

British Rowing

⊞ *6 Lower Mall, W6 9DJ*
☎ *020 8237 6700*
✎ *www.britishrowing.org*
🚌 *Hammersmith LU*
☺ *By appointment*

This is the national governing body for rowing and it holds a considerable archive of historical and current material about the sport which can be viewed by appointment.

Campaign Against Arms Trade

⌧ *5-7 Wells Terrace, N4 3JU*
☎ *020 7281 0297*
✍ *www.caat.org.uk*
🚇 *Finsbury Park LU*
🕓 *By appointment*

The Campaign Against Arms Trade holds a considerable archive on the subject, especially as it relates to the UK. There's information on countries and companies that produce arms and a collection of sales brochures which make chilling reading. CAAT also publishes reports, fact sheets and a regular newsletter.

Centre for Armenian Information and Advice

⌧ *Hayashen Library,*
   105A Mill Hill Road, W3 8JF
☎ *020 8992 4621*
✍ *www.caia.org.uk*
🚇 *Acton Town LU*
🕓 *By appointment*

Material in English and Armenian about Armenia, its affairs, culture and history. There are also CDs, records and audiovisual materials and an archive of the bi-lingual quarterly newsletter, 'The Armenian Voice'.

Centre for Policy on Ageing

⌧ *Tavis House, 1-6 Tavistock Square*
   WC1H 9NA
☎ *020 7553 6500*
✍ *www.cpa.org.uk*
🚇 *Euston LU/Rail*
🕓 *By appointment*

The collection covers the social, behavioural, economic and, to a lesser extent, the medical aspects of older age. The library has more than 50,000 items including over 400 journals, making it the most comprehensive collection on this subject in the UK.

Chatham House

(The Royal Institute of International Affairs)
⌧ *10 St James's Square, SW1Y 4LE*
☎ *020 7957 5723*
✍ *www.chathamhouse.org*
🚇 *Green Park LU, Piccadilly Circus LU*
🕓 *By appointment*
   (restricted to post graduate research)

The Royal Institute of International Affairs is one of the foremost research organisations in the field. Their library at Chatham House contains around 70,000 books, 2,000 periodicals and 10 newspapers covering international relations and international aspects of economics, security and resource management. Their catalogue is available online.

Commonwealth Secretariat

⌧ *Knowledge Centre,*
   Marlborough House, Pall Mall,
   SW1Y 5HX
☎ *020 7747 6164*
✍ *www.thecommonwealth.org*
🚇 *Green Park LU*
🕓 *By appointment*

This library recently changed its name to 'Knowledge Centre' but continues to offer an excellent collection of 15,000 books, government publications, working papers and periodicals relating to the Commonwealth and its 53 member countries.

Confraternity of St James
(Stephen Badger Library of Pilgrimage)

🖃 *27 Blackfriars Road, SE1 8NY*
☎ *20 7928 9988*
🖉 *www.csj.org.uk*
🚇 *Southwark LU*
🕓 *By appointment*

This library contains material on the pilgrimage to the cathedral of St James of Compostela in Santiago, Spain. The collection includes personal accounts of pilgrimage, books on associated art, architecture, music and history as well as works on pilgrimage in general and the cult of St James. The library also houses the library of the Confraternity of Pilgrims to Rome.

Congregational Library

🖃 *14 Gordon Square, WC1H 0AR*
☎ *020 7387 3727*
🖉 *www.conglib.co.uk*
🚇 *Euston LU/Rail, Euston Square LU*
🕓 *By appointment*

Sharing premises with Dr Williams's Library (see p.259), this collection has been established since 1831 as the main library for the Congregational denomination and contains books, manuscripts and archives.

Conway Hall Ethical Society

🖃 *Conway Hall, 25 Red Lion Square WC1R 4RL*
☎ *020 7061 6747*
🖉 *www.conwayhall.org.uk*
🚇 *Holborn LU*
🕓 *Tues-Thurs 10am-5pm*

Conway Hall boasts the UK's largest Humanist research library which contains over 10,000 books, periodicals and pamphlets relating to philosophy, humanism, rationalism and ethics. It has particular strengths in the history of science and religion, cosmology, evolution and consciousness, the history of ideas and the history of ethical and Humanist

societies. The library's archive contains documents relating to the Conway Hall, the Humanist Society and the personal papers of several prominent nineteenth-century radicals including William Lovett and William Johnson Fox.

Crafts Council

🖃 *44a Pentonville Road, N1 9BY*
☎ *020 7806 2500*
🖉 *www.craftscouncil.org.uk*
🚇 *Angel LU*
🕓 *By appointment*

The Research Library offers more than 5,000 books, journals, exhibition catalogues and magazines on all major crafts and applied arts. The library is only available by appointment, but the collection is varied and a useful resource for those involved in crafts.

The Charles Dickens Museum
The Suzannet Research Library

🖃 *48 Doughty Street, WC1N 2LX*
☎ *020 7405 2127*
🖉 *www.dickensmuseum.com*
🚇 *Russell Square LU,*
   Chancery Lane LU, Holborn LU
🕓 *Mon-Fri 10.30am by appoinment*

The Charles Dicken's Museum contains the Suzannet Research Library which is a wonderful resource for anyone interested in Dickens and the Victorian era and contains a wealth of primary and secondary source material. Because of staff and space limitations, it is a service for researchers with specific interests or things to see, rather than casual browsers.

Egypt Exploration Society

- *3 Doughty Mews, WC1N 2PG*
- ☎ *020 7242 1880*
- *www.ees.ac.uk*
- *Russell SquareLU, HolbornLU, Chancery Lane LU*
- ☺ *Mon-Fri 10.30am-4.30pm*

This is one of the best resources on Egyptology in the world with over 20,000 books, journals and pamphlets. The website contains an extremely useful guide to bibliographic and research tools on the subject and the library is open to non-members.

Energy Institute

- *61 New Cavendish Street, W1G 7AR*
- ☎ *020 7467 7114*
- *www.energyinst.org*
- *Regent's Park LU, Oxford Circus LU*
- ☺ *Mon-Fri 9.15am-5pm (charge for non-members)*

The Energy Institute is a professional body for the energy industry with over 13,000 members. The library holds the most comprehensive collection of published materials on the oil and other energy industries in the UK including gas, renewables, wind, wave, solar, coal and nuclear. It includes books, pamphlets, periodicals, directories and conference proceedings dating from the mid-nineteenth century to the present day.

English Folk Dance And Song Society

(Vaughan Williams Memorial Library)
- *Cecil Sharp House, 2 Regent's Park Road, NW1 7AY*
- ☎ *020 7485 2206*
- *www.vwml.org*
- *Camden Town LU*
- ☺ *Tues-Fri 9.30am-5.30pm First & Third Sat 10am-4pm Closed in August Open to all with £3.50 charge for non-members*

This is a multimedia library and archive, covering the folk music, dance and folklore of Britain and other English-based cultures, such as North America and Ireland. There is coverage of social history, drama, musical instruments and biographies. The website allows visitors to access a vast archive of digitised manuscripts from 19 major song collections held by this and other libraries, as well a variety of other resources, including comprehensive indexes and catalogues.

The Evangelical Library

- *5-6 Gateway Mews, Ringway, N11 2UT*
- ☎ *020 8362 0868*
- *www.evangelical-library.org.uk*
- *Bounds Green LU*
- ☺ *Mon-Sat 10am-5pm*

Around 80,000 items of evangelical literature are held in this specialist library, covering the history and development of the movement from the early seventeenth-century Puritans through to modern times. There is an ongoing project to make significant texts available online.

Fan Museum

- *12 Crooms Hill, SE10 8ER*
- ☎ *020 8305 1441*
- *www.thefanmuseum.org.uk*
- *Greenwich Rail/DLR, Cutty Sark DLR*
- ☺ *By appointment*

A research facility and reference library covering everything related to the history of fans and associated subjects such as costume.

Feminist Library

🏛 *5 Westminster Bridge Road, SE1 7XW*
☎ *020 7261 0879*
🖉 *www.feministlibrary.co.uk*
🚌 *Waterloo LU/Rail, Elephant & Castle LU/*
   Rail, Lambeth North LU
🕓 *Tues and Thurs 6pm-9pm,*
   Wed 5pm-9pm, Sat 12noon-5pm

This library is run by volunteers and
concentrates on books and journals on the
Women's Liberation Movement, especially
materials from the late 1960s to the late
1990s, women's history and mental and
physical health. There is a large selection
of literature including poetry.

Freemasonry Library

🏛 *Freemasons' Hall,*
   60 Great Queen Street, WC2B 5AZ
☎ *020 7395 9257*
🖉 *www.freemasonry.london.museum*
🚌 *Covent Garden LU*
🕓 *By appointment*

A specialist reference library of books and
archives on the history and development
of Freemasonry both in the UK and
overseas and on subjects associated with
freemasonry and esoteric traditions.

Geffrye Museum

🏛 *Kingsland Road, E2 8EA*
☎ *020 7749 6049*
🖉 *www.geffrye-museum.org.uk*
🚌 *Hoxton Overground*
🕓 *Curatorial library by appointment*

There's a public access reading room
in the museum containing titles relating
to interior design and decoration,
architecture, social history, gardening and
garden history, applied arts and London
and there are books for children here as
well. The curatorial library is available to
researchers with specific requirements
and there's also an archive of mostly
trade catalogues from the late nineteenth-
century to the present day.

Geological Society

🏛 *Burlington House, Piccadilly, W1J 0BG*
☎ *020 7432 0999*
🖉 *www.geolsoc.org.uk*
🚌 *Green Park LU, Piccadilly Circus LU*
🕓 *By appointment*
   (see website for charges)

The Library of the Geological Society is
one of the world's major earth science
libraries containing over 300,000 books,
40,000 maps and over 600 journals
about earth sciences and palaeontology
collected since the founding of the
library in 1809. The library has a unique
collection of around 3,500 early books and
manuscripts concerning mineralogy and
palaeontology dating from the sixteenth
century. The Virtual Library (accessed via
the website) has a vast amount of online
information, for those unable to visit this
spectacular library in person.

German Historical Institute

🏛 *17 Bloomsbury Square, WC1A 2NJ*
☎ *020 7309 2050*
🖉 *www.ghil.ac.uk*
🚌 *Tottenham Court Road LU, Holborn LU*
🕓 *Mon-Wed & Fri 10am-5pm,*
   Thurs 10am-8pm

More than 80,000 books and 200 current
periodicals on German history from the
Middle Ages to the present, in German and
English. The focus is largely on modern
history with ample material on the World
Wars and post-1945 reconstruction and
unification.

Goethe-Institut

⌨ *50 Prince's Gate, Exhibition Road, SW7 2PH*

☎ *020 7596 4040*

✎ *www.goethe.de/london*

🚇 *South Kensington LU*

☺ *Mon-Thurs 1pm-7pm, Sat 1pm-5pm*

German and English material about Germany and German culture with an emphasis on literature, film and theatre, fine arts, photography and social studies but also including general reference works and dictionaries. The library also carries German newspapers, periodicals and journals, CDs and DVDs. There is a dedicated section of the library with resources especially useful to those teaching German.

Goldsmiths' Company

⌨ *Goldsmiths' Hall, Foster Lane, EC2V 6BN*

☎ *020 7606 7010*

✎ *www.thegoldsmiths.co.uk*

🚇 *St Paul's LU*

☺ *By appointment*

This library is dedicated to all things relating to the Goldsmiths' Company including jewellery, regalia, assaying and hallmarking and anything related to the precious metals of gold, silver and platinum. Housed within the grand edifice of Goldsmiths' Hall, the library holds over 8,000 books as well as 15,000 other source materials including periodicals, photographs, slides, films and videotapes. The Company's apprentice books and records can prove a useful resource for those researching their family history.

Highgate Literary and Scientific Institution

⌨ *11 South Grove, N6 6BS*

☎ *020 8340 3343*

✎ *www.hlsi.net*

🚇 *Archway LU, Highgate LU*

☺ *Tues-Fri 10am-5pm, Sat 10am-4pm Reference open to all, lending restricted to members*

Founded in 1839, this is one of the oldest institutions of its kind still in existence in London. They operate a general library with a bias towards biography, literature, history and fiction and also have a good children's library. There are many shelves dedicated to London with particular emphasis on Highgate and collections focusing on local authors Samuel Taylor Coleridge and John Betjeman.

Horniman Library

⌨ *Horniman Museum & Gardens, 100 London Road, SE23 3PQ*

☎ *020 8699 1872 ext 108*

✎ *www.horniman.ac.uk*

🚇 *Forest Hill Rail*

☺ *By appointment Mon & Tues*

A specialist library for ethnography, natural history and musical instruments. Its collection of nearly 30,000 books, journals and recordings relate closely to the museum's collection.

Huguenot Library

⌨ *The National Archive at Kew, TW9 4DU*

☎ *020 7679 2046*

✎ *www.huguenotsociety.org.uk*

🚇 *Kew Garden LU*

☺ *By appointment*

A small, independent reference library and archive. It contains material on the social history of Huguenot refugees in the UK and the broader history of the Huguenots across Europe.

Imperial War Museum

⊞ *Lambeth Road, SE1 6HZ*
☎ *020 7416 5000*
✏ *www.iwm.org.uk*
🚌 *Lambeth North LU*
🕓 *By appointment*

The museum specialises in all aspects of twentieth and twenty-first century warfare which have affected Britain and the Commonwealth countries. It has an almost unimaginable amount of research material which is held in separate departments but includes 270,000 printed items, 120 million feet of cine film, more than 10 million photographs, 15,000 collections of unpublished diaries, letters, memoirs and other papers, and 56,000 hours of sound archives. Log onto the website for further details about visiting the library.

INFORM

(Information Network Focus on Religious Movements)

⊞ *Lionel Robbins Building*
   London School of Economics,
   Sheffield Street, WC2A 2AE
☎ *020 7955 7654*
✏ *www.inform.ac*
🚌 *Holborn LU*
🕓 *By appointment*

Affiliated to and housed in the London School of Economics, this charity aims to provide up-to-date information on new and alternative religious movements. Their library contains academic books, journals and studies concerning over 4,000 religious groups worldwide as well as material from the religious groups themselves, former members and opponents, and media reports. The library's website is a useful resource for those interested in the subject.

INIVA – Institute of International Visual Arts

⊞ *The Stuart Hall Library,*
   Rivington Place, EC2A 3BA
☎ *020 7749 1255*
✏ *www.iniva.org*
🚌 *Old Street LU/Rail*
   Shoreditch High Street Overground
🕓 *Tues-Fri 10am-5pm*
   (closed for lunch 1-2pm)

INIVA is an arts and cultural studies institute with the focus on contemporary art from Africa, Asia, Latin America as well as British artists from many cultural backgrounds. The printed collection includes more than 4,000 exhibition catalogues, 1,000 monographs and more than 140 periodical titles. The library also has a collection of more than 4,500 slides of contemporary art and an online catalogue.

Institut Français (French Institute)

⊞ *La Médiathèque, 17 Queensberry Place,*
   SW7 2DT
   and Children's Library,
   32 Harrington Road, SW7 3ES
☎ *020 7871 3545*
✏ *www.institut-francais.org.uk*
🚌 *South Kensington LU*
🕓 *Tues-Sat 12pm-7pm, Thurs till 6pm*

Adult and children's French language libraries concerned with France and the works of French and French-speaking authors. As well as adult books, there are 13,000 children's titles, a comprehensive range of comic books, 3,400 films, 4,700 CDs and press-cuttings of French interest.

Institute for Indian Art and Culture

📖 *Megraj Library, Bharatiya Vidya Bhavan*
  4a Castletown Road, W14 9HE
☎ *020 7381 3086*
✎ *www.bhavan.net*
🚇 *West Kensington LU*
🕑 *By appointment*

The Bhavan Centre offers a busy programme of Indian culture including plays, concerts and exhibitions. The reference library here is also a useful resource for anyone interested in the culture, history and religions of India.

Institute of Alcohol Studies

📖 *Alliance House, 12 Caxton Street*
  SW1H 0QS
☎ *020 7222 4001*
✎ *www.ias.org.uk*
🚇 *St James's Park LU*
🕑 *By appointment*

A specialist reference library on all aspects of alcohol consumption. The library contains a collection relating to the Temperance Movement.

Instituto Cervantes

📖 *102 Eaton Square, SW1W 9AN*
☎ *020 7201 0757*
✎ *www.londres.cervantes.es*
🚇 *Sloane Square LU, Victoria LU/Rail*
🕑 *Tues-Wed 12.30pm-7pm*
  Thurs 12.30pm-6.30pm
  Fri 12.30pm-6pm, Sat 9.30-2pm

The Queen Sofia Library is dedicated to Spanish and Latin American books with an emphasis on history, art, philosophy, politics, economics and sociology and a selection of children's books. There are also materials for teachers and students of Spanish as a foreign language plus films, documentaries and music. Within the library's holdings is an archive of Spanish Civil war leaflets.

Islamic Cultural Centre

📖 *London Central Mosque,*
  146 Park Road, NW8 7RG
☎ *020 7725 2235*
✎ *www.iccuk.org*
🚇 *Baker Street LU, St John's Wood LU*
🕑 *By appointment*

Books and journals in English, Arabic and other languages on all aspects of Islam including theology, history, culture, the Arab/Muslim world and Muslim minorities in Europe.

Italian Cultural Institute Library

📖 *Biblioteca Eugenio Montale,*
  39 Belgrave Square, SW1X 8NX
☎ *020 7396 4425*
✎ *www.iiclondon.esteri.it*
🚇 *Hyde Park Corner LU*
🕑 *Mon-Thurs 12.30-7.30pm*

The library within the Italian Cultural Institute contains around 25,000 books as well as journals, newspapers, CDs and DVDs in Italian with an emphasis on the literature, history and culture of the country. There is also a children's section and a substantial collection of books about Italy in English.

Japanese Information and Cultural Centre

📖 *Embassy of Japan,*
  101-104 Piccadilly, W1J 7JT
☎ *020 7465 6541*
✎ *www.uk.emb-japan.go.jp*
🚇 *Piccadilly Circus LU, Green Park LU*
🕑 *Mon-Fri 9.30am-12.45pm, 2pm-5.30pm*
  (times may vary – check
  before your visit)

Japanese literature and information about Japanese education, history and culture, in both Japanese and English. There are more than 100 DVDs covering a wide range of subjects. Periodicals and Government papers are also available.

Kennel Club Library

⊞ *Clarges Street, Piccadilly,*
   W1J 8AB
☏ *020 7518 1009*
⊘ *www.thekennelclub.org.uk*
🚇 *Green Park LU*
🕔 *By appointment*

This is Europe's biggest dog library and contains books, journals, studbooks, canine ephemera, dog show catalogues, and DVD's – all you need to know about dogs in fact.

King's Fund Information Centre

⊞ *11-13 Cavendish Square,*
   W1G 0AN
☏ *020 7307 2568*
⊘ *www.kingsfund.org.uk/library*
🚇 *Oxford Circus LU*
🕔 *Mon-Fri 9.30am-5.30pm,*
   Thurs 11am-5.30pm

This is an independent charitable foundation whose goal is to understand how to improve the health system in England. The library is the only health and social care library in the UK open to the public.

Trinity Laban Library

⊞ *Creekside, SE8 3DZ*
☏ *020 8305 9333*
⊘ *www.trinitylaban.ac.uk*
🚇 *Cutty Sark DLR,*
   Deptford High Street Overground
🕔 *By appointment*

This is the largest collection on dance and associated subjects in the UK. There are books, journals and CDs plus various archive collections relating to the history of dance. The Laban Archive focuses on Rudolf Laban, one of the founders of European Modern Dance, the development of the institution that bears his name and the whole arena of contemporary dance.

Lambeth Palace Library

⊞ *Lambeth Palace, SE1 7JU*
☏ *020 7898 1400*
⊘ *www.lambethpalacelibrary.org*
🚇 *Westminster LU, Lambeth North LU*
🕔 *Tues-Fri 10am-5pm, Thurs till 7.30pm*

Lambeth Palace Library was founded in 1610 and is one of England's oldest public libraries with records that date back to the ninth century. It is the main library and record office for the Church of England. There is a vast collection of archives, books and manuscripts covering ecclesiastical history and genealogy. The Church Care Library is part of the collection dedicated to ecclesiastical architecture, art, design and liturgy and is to be found at:

⊞ *Church House, Great Smith Street,*
   SW1P 3AZ
☏ *020 7898 1884*
🕔 *Wed-Thurs 11am-4pm (by appointment)*

The Library for Iranian Studies

⊞ *The Woodlands Hall, Crown Street,*
   W3 8SA
☏ *020 8993 6384*
⊘ *www.iranianlibrary.org.uk*
🚇 *Acton Town LU*
🕔 *Tues-Sat 11am-5.30pm*

This library offers over 30,000 books and other publications on everything to do with Iran. Most of the holding is in Persian but there is a growing number of books in other languages and an increasing stock of books for younger readers.

The Linnean Society of London

📖 *Burlington House, Piccadilly, W1J 0BF*
☎ *020 7434 4479 ext 23*
✎ *www.linnean.org*
🚇 *Green Park LU, Piccadilly Circus LU*
🕐 *By appointment*

This specialist library contains over 90,000 volumes dating from 1483 to the present day on all aspects of biology but with an emphasis on plant and animal classification and including 300 current and 2,000 past journal titles. As the name would suggest, the library has one of the world's largest collections of books and archive material relating to Carl Linnaeus and his legacy. Charles Darwin was inspired and helped by the work of Linnaeus and there is a considerable collection relating to Darwin and Evolutionary Theory.

London's Buddhist Vihara

📖 *The Dharmapala Building,*
   The Avenue, W4 1UD
☎ *020 8995 9493*
✎ *www.londonbuddhistvihara.org*
🚇 *Turnham Green LU*
🕐 *By appointment*

This library contains more than 5,000 books and periodicals on all schools of Buddhism and related subjects.

London Contemporary Dance School

📖 *16 Flaxman Terrace, WC1H 9AT*
☎ *020 7121 1110*
✎ *www.lcds.ac.uk*
🚇 *Euston LU/Rail*
🕐 *By appointment*

This library of the London Contemporary Dance School contains books, periodicals, DVDs, CDs and CD-ROMs on all aspects of modern dance and particularly ballet. The library also covers subjects of relevance to modern dance including anatomy, art, cultural studies, gender studies, theatre, media, music, literature and film.

The London Library

📖 *14 St James's Square, SW1Y 4LG*
☎ *020 7930 7705*
✎ *www.londonlibrary.co.uk*
🚇 *Piccadilly Circus LU, Green Park LU*
🕐 *Mon-Wed 9.30am-8pm*
   Thurs-Sat 9.30am-5.30pm

Founded in 1841 by the philosopher and historian Thomas Carlyle as a subscription library, the London Library now has over one million volumes and is acquiring around 8,000 titles each year to ensure that it remains one of the largest independent lending libraries in the world. Its emphasis is on the humanities (particularly literature, biography and history) with good coverage on fine and applied art, architecture, philosophy, religion and travel. Library members appreciate the generous study areas and free Wi-Fi, making this the perfect place for tranquil study and work and with attentive staff on hand if you are seeking a particular book or journal.

The library has over 17 miles of shelving and in recent years has expanded to occupy several neighbouring buildings. Today's library with its labyrinthine structure is one that Mr Carlyle would find hard to recognise from the modest property he acquired over 170 years ago. Annual membership is open to all and costs £485, but with unlimited lending rights, access to over 750 academic journals and a postal loans service throughout Europe, this is great value for access to one of London's great libraries.

London Metropolitan Archives

- 🏢 *40 Northampton Road, EC1R 0HB*
- ☎ *020 7332 3820*
- ✐ *www.cityoflondon.gov.uk/lma*
- 🕑 *Mon 9.30am-4.45pm*
  Tues-Thurs 9.30am-7.30pm

The London Metropolitan Archives hold the records of the Greater London Council, City of London Corporation and London Authority Records Office. The collection includes documents, maps, books, photographs and films about the capital. As well as reference services the Metropolitan Archives also run a busy programme of talks, exhibitions and tours. Most visitors use the archives to find out about their family history and there are staff on hand to help novice genealogists in their research. The archive also contains a vast collection relating to the history of London with many original documents including the diary of seventeenth-century scientist Robert Hooke and a rare copy of the Magna Carta.

The London Society

- 🏢 *Mortimer Wheeler House,*
  46 Eagle Wharf Road, N1 7ED
- ☎ *020 7253 9400*
- ✐ *www.londonsociety.org.uk*
- 🚇 *Old Street LU/Rail*
- 🕑 *By appointment*

The library of the London Society is housed within its main offices at Mortimer Wheeler House and holds more than 3,500 books as well as maps and newspaper cuttings about the capital and its people. Access to the library is restricted to society members but individual membership is just £25 and includes a regular e-newsletter and two journals as well an active programme of talks and events.

London Transport Museum Library

⌨ *39 Wellington Street,*
   Covent Garden, WC2E 7BB
☎ *020 7565 7280*
✍ *www.ltmuseum.co.uk*
🚇 *Covent Garden LU*
🕐 *By appointment*

The Library holds more than 14,000 books, journals, pamphlets and reports about London's transport system. The collection is not just historical but also encompasses material relating to current and future plans for the capital's transport network. Details about access and making an appointment to use the library can be found on the website.

Marx Memorial Library

⌨ *37a Clerkenwell Green, EC1R 0DU*
☎ *020 7253 1485*
✍ *www.marx-memorial-library.org*
🚇 *Farringdon LU/Rail*
🕐 *Mon-Thurs 12pm-4pm*

This independent library is imbued with the history of London as a radical city. Lenin worked in the building while in exile and produced his journal ISKRA (The Spark) from a room that is now preserved and open to visitors.

The library itself was established on the fiftieth anniversary of Karl Marx's death in 1933 and remains as a museum and working library dedicated to the history and ideology of Marxism and Socialism. Among the attractions is a large socialist mural painted by Viscount Hastings in 1934 which can still be seen in the first-floor reading room.

The library is a useful resource and study area for those interested in the subject with books, newspapers and other archive material. The building also houses special collections on the Spanish Civil War and the history of the printers' unions. The library is available for reference purposes and hosts an educational programme including classes and one-off lectures. There are guided tours of the building and library which are a great introduction to this unique institution.

Marylebone Cricket Club

⌨ *Lord's Cricket Ground,*
   St John's Wood, NW8 8QN
☎ *020 7616 8559*
✍ *www.lords.org*
🚇 *St John's Wood LU*
🕐 *By appointment*

The world's largest and most comprehensive collection of publications about cricket with over 11,000 volumes ranging from rare books to the latest publications. The library holdings include a complete set of Wisden Cricketers' Almanack and the only known complete set of Britcher's Scores. Real cricket buffs will no doubt be interested in the MCC archive which includes the minutes and records of this august body dating back over 200 years. Other bat and ball games also feature, especially real tennis.

Model Railway Club

⌨ *Keen House, 4 Calshot Street, N1 9DA*
☎ *020 7837 2542*
✍ *www.themodelrailwayclub.org*
🚇 *King's Cross St Pancras LU/Rail*
🕐 *Thurs 7pm-9pm*

This library contains about 5,000 books and periodicals relating to railways and model railways including railways across the world and the development of railway modelling.

Museum of London

⌨ *150 London Wall, EC2Y 5HN*
☎ *020 7814 5588*
🖏 *www.museumoflondon.org.uk*
🚌 *Moorgate LU/Rail, Barbican LU,
   St Paul's LU, Bank LU*
☺ *By appointment*

The Museum of London is one of the capital's most popular tourist attractions, but its library is less conspicuous. The library holds a collection of books, journals and pamphlets relating to London and its history as well as books concerning to fashion, ceramics, museum studies and archaeology. The holding can only be viewed for research purposes by appointment.

Museum of London Archaeology

⌨ *London Archaeological Archive and
   Research Centre (LAARC),
   Mortimer Wheeler House,
   46 Eagle Wharf Road, N1 7ED*
☎ *020 7566 9317*
🖏 *www.mola.org.uk*
🚌 *Old St LU/Rail*
☺ *By appointment*

This archive holds records on around 5,000 excavations and archaeological projects that have taken place in Greater London over the last 100 years. It is a fascinating resource but one only available to researchers by appointment.

Museum of London Docklands

⌨ *Sainsbury Study Centre,
   No 1 Warehouse West India Quay,
   Hertsmere Road, E14 4AL*
☎ *020 7001 9844*
🖏 *www.museumoflondon.org.uk/docklands*
🚌 *Canary Wharf LU/DLR,
   West India Quay DLR*
☺ *Daily 10am-5.45pm (study centre)
   Archives by appointment*

This study centre and archive is located within the Museum of London Docklands. The archive is a vast collection covering the history of the Port of London from 1770 to the present day and includes a great deal about the demise of London's working docks and the regeneration of the Docklands as a commercial centre. The collection includes the surviving papers of plantation and slave owners Thomas and John Mills, giving a fascinating insight into the eighteenth-century slave trade. The Sainsbury Archive provides detailed information about the history of the supermarket from its humble origins on Drury Lane in 1869. The website is a useful resource and worth referring to before planning a visit.

National Art Library

- Victoria & Albert Museum, Cromwell Road, SW7 2RL
- ☎ 020 7942 2400
- ✎ www.vam.ac.uk/nal
- 🚇 South Kensington LU
- 🕐 Tues-Thurs & Sat 10am-5.30pm
  Fri 10am-6.30pm

The National Art Library at the V&A is the country's largest reference library for the fine and decorative arts and has the added appeal of remaining essentially unaltered since it was established during the reign of Queen Victoria with dark wood bookshelves, huge pendant lights and a surrounding first-floor mezzanine balcony. The library also serves as the curatorial department for book art at the museum and as such holds unique collections of early printed books, calligraphy and even contemporary graphic novels. A great deal of the library's collection is held in storage, so readers should order particular books in advance using the online catalogue. Considering the special nature of the library it is remarkably accessible to the general public and it also offers group visits and introductions to the library which can be booked on their website.

National Autistic Society

- 393 City Road, EC1V 1NG
- ✎ library@nas.org.uk
- ✎ www.nas.org.uk or www.autism.org.uk
- 🚇 Angel LU, King's Cross St Pancras LU/Rail, Euston LU/Rail
- 🕐 By appointment

This small library run by the Autistic Society holds a unique collection of books, journals and audio-visual material about autism. The society also maintains a research information database with references from journals, reports and books.

National Gallery

- Trafalgar Square, WC2N 5DN
- ☎ 020 7747 2542
- ✎ www.nationalgallery.org.uk
- 🚇 Charing Cross LU/Rail
- 🕐 By appointment

This library was established in 1870 from the private collection of 2,000 books belonging to the museum's first Director, Sir Charles Eastlake. Since its foundation the library has grown to over 75,000 volumes covering the history of European painting from the thirteenth century to the early twentieth century. The collection includes monographs, museum and gallery catalogues from around the world and a major collection of art books published before 1850. Access is restricted to academics and postgraduate students by appointment only, but the National Gallery's public records are available within the museum's study centre.

National Maritime Museum

- The Caird Library, Park Row, SE10 9NF
- ☎ 020 8312 6516
- ✎ www.rmg.co.uk/cairdlibrary
- 🚇 Cutty Sark DLR
- 🕐 Mon-Fri 10am-4.45pm
  Sat 10am-1pm and 2pm-4.45pm

The Caird Library in the National Maritime Museum is the largest maritime reference library in the world. Among the library's collection are original manuscripts, reference books, charts and maps dating from the fifteenth century. This library offers fascinating insights into the nation's past with maritime and naval records a useful resource for those searching their family history while merchant navy records throw light onto the history of empire and trade. The Caird Library is particularly notable for its original documents which include anything from Nelson's letters to a menu card from the Titanic. The library has an open access policy which is rare for such a unique and important collection.

National Art Library

National Portrait Gallery

🖻 *Heinz Archive and Library,*
   St Martin's Place, WC2H 0HE
☎ *020 7321 6617*
🖘 *www.npg.org.uk/research/archive*
🚌 *Charing Cross LU/Rail, Leicester Square LU*
🕓 *By appointment*

The Heinz Archive and Library is the primary centre for research into British portraiture, with material dating back to the earliest holdings of the National Portrait Gallery. The library includes 35,000 books, 70 periodicals, artists' and research papers and NPG records. One of the most popular features of the library are the 80,000 portraiture prints, collected from museums and galleries around the world. The Heinz Archive and Library is located behind the main gallery in Orange Street.

Natural History Museum

🖻 *Cromwell Road, SW7 5BD*
☎ *General and Zoology: 020 7942 5460*
   Botany: 020 7942 5685
   Earth Sciences: 020 7942 5476
   Entomology: 020 7942 5251
   Ornithology: 020 7942 6156
🖘 *www.nhm.ac.uk*
🚌 *South Kensington LU*
🕓 *By appointment*

The Natural History Museum library is one of the world's great collections of books, drawings and manuscripts relating to natural history. The library has grown over the years through the bequests of several major collections including those of nineteenth-century ornithologist Arthur Hay and letters and documents of naturalists donated by Charles Davies Sherborn. The library now holds over a million books (the oldest dating from 1489) and 14,000 periodicals on the biological and earth sciences, divided into several libraries which can be referred to by appointment only.

NSPCC

🖃 *Weston House, 42 Curtain Road, EC2A 3NH*
☎ *020 7825 2500*
✐ *www.nspcc.org.uk/inform*
🚌 *Liverpool Street LU/Rail*
🕓 *By appointment*

The most comprehensive UK reference library specialising in books, articles, reports and journals relating to child abuse and neglect. Themes covered include child protection, therapeutic techniques, social work with children and families, child welfare and positive parenting.

Museum of the Order of St John

🖃 *St John's Gate, St John's Lane, EC1M 4DA*
☎ *020 7324 4005*
✐ *www.museumstjohn.org.uk*
🚌 *Farringdon LU/Rail*
🕓 *By appointment*

The largest reference library outside Malta on the history of the Knights Hospitallers (the Order of the Hospital of St John of Jerusalem) and the history of the St John Ambulance. The small but fascinating museum, of which the library is a part, is also worth exploring for anyone interested in the subject.

The Poetry Library

Paul Mellon Centre for Studies in British Art

⌸ *15-16 Bedford Square, WC1B 3JA*
☎ *020 7580 0311*
✐ *www.paul-mellon-centre.ac.uk*
🚌 *Tottenham Court Road &*
   Goodge Street LU
🕓 *Mon-Fri 10am-5pm*

The Paul Mellon Centre has recently undergone a major refurbishment to accomodate its ever expanding collection of books on British art (painting, sculpture, drawing, garden history and architecture) from the mid-sixteenth century to the present. The archive's 20,000 books, 200 periodicals, 14,000 exhibition and auction catalogues and a photographic archive of more than 185,000 reference photographs, are all available for public reference. The centre also hosts a busy events programme and produces a regular online journal about British art.

The Poetry Library

⌸ *The Poetry Library, Level 5,*
   Royal Festival Hall, SE1 8XX
☎ *020 7921 0943/0664*
✐ *www.poetrylibrary.org.uk*
🚌 *Waterloo LU/Rail*
🕓 *Tues-Sun 11am-8pm*

It is reassuring to know that the most abstract and metaphysical branch of literature has a physical place it can call home, namely The Poetry Library. The library is tucked away on the 5th floor of the Royal Festival Hall, but is well worth seeking out, providing a rare place of calm and contemplation amid this busy cultural centre and offering free membership to all.

The library is not large, but its sliding shelf system enables it to hold the most comprehensive repository of modern poetry in Britain, with 200,000 items in a growing collection that includes almost all the poetry published in Britain since 1912. The extensive collection of poetry

magazines dates from the 1940's and includes publications from all over the English speaking world. There are plenty of desks where poets and lovers of poetry can while away the time under the penetrating gaze of Oloff de Wet's bust of Dylan Thomas which was brought out of storage and unveiled here on the 50th anniversary of the bard's death in 2003.

Dylan Thomas was famous for his live readings and recordings of these, among many others, can be heard in the audiovisual collection which supplements the library's printed material in a designated area complete with tape machines, headphones and television screens and great views across the South Bank. The library takes its responsibility to inculcate a love of poetry in the young very seriously and there is a considerable collection of poetry for children as well as a play area at the entrance with lots of games encouraging an interest in language. This is one of the most remarkable libraries in London and one that all lovers of poetry should take the opportunity to explore.

The Polish Library

⌸ *Polish Social and Cultural Centre,*
   238-246 King Street, W6 0RF
☎ *020 8741 0474*
✐ *www.posk.org*
🚌 *Ravenscourt Park LU*
🕓 *Mon & Wed 10am-8pm, Fri 10am-5pm,*
   Sat 10am-1pm

Established in 1942, this research library contains books in Polish and about Poland – it is one of the largest libraries of its kind outside Poland. It covers all subjects but has a particular strength in émigré social history and culture since 1945. The library also contains a lending collection for members of the cultural centre.

RAF Museum

⌨ *Department of Research and Information Services (DoRIS) Grahame Park Way, Hendon, NW9 5LL*

☎ *020 8358 4873*

✎ *www.rafmuseum.org*

🚇 *Colindale LU*

🕓 *Wed-Fri 10am-5pm*

The library has around 70,000 publications including books, technical manuals, journals, aviation ephemera and aeronautical maps, as well as commercially published magazines dating from 1909.

Religious Society of Friends (Quakers)

⌨ *Friends House, 173 Euston Road NW1 2BJ*

☎ *020 7663 1135*

✎ *www.quaker.org.uk*

🚇 *Euston LU/Rail*

🕓 *Tues-Fri 10am-5pm*

One of the largest and most important libraries about Quaker history, faith, thought and practice as well as issues of special interest to the Friends, such as peace, prison reform, humanitarian assistance and the anti-slavery movement. The library also administers an important archive of original documents and early books relating to the Quaker movement.

Royal Academy of Arts

⌨ *Burlington House, Piccadilly, W1J 0BD*

☎ *020 7300 5737*

✎ *www.royalacademy.org.uk*

🚇 *Green Park LU, Piccadilly Circus LU*

🕓 *Tue-Fri 10am-5pm by appointment*

The oldest fine arts library in the UK specialises in the history of British art and the Royal Academy, its exhibitions and members. There are around 30,000 monographs, catalogues and reference books. The holdings include a complete set of Summer Exhibition catalogues from 1769.

Royal Academy of Dance

⌨ *Philip Richardson Library, 36 Battersea Square, SW11 3RA*

☎ *020 7326 8010/8032*

✎ *www.rad.org.uk*

🚇 *Clapham Junction Rail*

🕓 *By appointment*

This library covers all aspects of dance and dance history with a particular emphasis on ballet. The collection includes books, journals and DVDs and there are viewing and listening facilities available. The archive's material includes rare books, photographs, costume designs and theatre programmes.

Royal Aeronautical Society

⌨ *4 Hamilton Place, W1J 7BQ*

☎ *020 7670 4362*

✎ *www.aerosociety.com*

🚇 *Green Park & Hyde Park Corner LU*

🕓 *Mon-Fri 9am-5pm*

The Royal Aeronautical Society was founded in 1866, long before the Wright brothers took to the air. Its library, established at the same time, has grown into one of the world's major aviation collections, The National Aerospace Library, which is located at the society's sumptuous headquarters on Hamilton Place.

Royal Artillery Museum

⌨ *The James Clavell Library, Firepower, The Royal Artillery Museum, Royal Arsenal (West), Warren Lane, Woolwich, SE18 6ST*

☎ *020 8312 7125*

✎ *www.firepower,org.uk/research*

🚇 *Woolwich Arsenal DLR / Rail*

🕓 *By appointment*

This library contains over 26,000 books on artillery history and holds a nearly complete set of Army Lists as well as the complete Minutes of the Proceedings of the Royal Artillery Institute. The library's archive contains over 7,000 original documents including regimental war diaries, personal papers and unit records with some documents dating from the sixteenth century. The library and archive is popular with genealogists tracing military ancestors as well as military historians and collectors.

Royal Asiatic Society

⌂ *14 Stephenson Way, NW1 2HD*
☎ *020 7388 4539*
✐ *www.royalasiaticsociety.org*
🚌 *Euston Square LU, Euston LU/Rail*
🕘 *By appointment*

More than 100,000 books, manuscripts, journals and art works relating to Asia including the Middle East and also Islamic North Africa and containing a particularly important archive relating to early British Orientalists. The archive and book collection are largely historic with books and archive material dating from the eighteenth to the early twentieth century, but there are also contemporary journals and a more limited range of academic books on the subject.

Royal Geographical Society

⌂ *1 Kensington Gore, SW7 2AR*
☎ *020 7591 3000*
✐ *www.rgs.org*
🚌 *South Kensington LU*
🕘 *Mon-Fri 10am-5pm*
(free to RGS members and accredited academics, £10 per day for other users)

The Society holds one of the most important geographical collections in the world. The collection includes more than 150,000 books (dating from as far back as 1830), 800 current journal titles, expedition reports (including David Livingstone's), maps and charts, atlases and a picture library holding more than 500,000 images from around the world. If all this encourages wanderlust, the RGS provides a great deal of information about planning expeditions.

Royal Horticultural Society

⌂ *Lindley Library, RHS, 80 Vincent Square, SW1P 2PE*
☎ *020 7821 3050*
✐ *www.rhs.org.uk*
🚌 *St James's Park LU, Pimlico LU, Victoria LU/Rail*
🕘 *Mon-Fri 10am-5pm*

The Lindley Library, within the Royal Horticultural Society, is one of the world's largest horticultural book collections. The library holds more than 50,000 books dating from the early sixteenth century and includes books on gardens, horticulture and garden history. The library also holds the RHS archives which include the country's largest collection of horticultural trade catalogues.

Royal Institute of British Architects (RIBA)

⌂ *66 Portland Place, W1B 1AD*
☎ *020 7307 3882*
✐ *www.architecture.com*
🚌 *Oxford Circus LU, Regent's Park LU, Great Portland Street LU*
🕘 *Tues 10am-8pm, Wed & Fri 10am-5pm, Sat 10am-1.30pm*

The RIBA Library is the largest and most comprehensive resource in the UK for information, books and journals on all aspects of architecture. The library is open to anyone interested in the subject (unlike the Architectural Association Library – see page 228) and offers generous study space, free Wi-Fi and a downstairs café. The drawings and archive collection are held at the V&A and can be studied in the RIBA Architecture Study Rooms at the museum (tel: 020 7307 3708).

Royal National Institute for the Blind

⊞ *Research Library*
   105 Judd Street, WC1H 9NE
☎ *020 7391 2052*
✐ *ww.rnib.org.uk*
🚌 *King's Cross LU/Rail*
🕓 *Mon-Fri 9am-4.30pm, Wed till 4pm*

Europe's most comprehensive and diverse collection of material covering all aspects of partial sight and blindness, including books, journals, videos, reports and Government papers. The library has computers with JAWS and Zoomtext software for general use by blind and partially sighted visitors.

The Royal Society

⊞ *6-9 Carlton House Terrace, SW1Y 5AG*
☎ *020 7451 2606*
✐ *www.royalsociety.org*
🚌 *Charing Cross LU/Rail,*
   Piccadilly Circus LU
🕓 *Mon-Fri 10am-5pm*
   (open to public with valid ID)

Founded in 1660, The Royal Society is the UK's national academy of science. Its library dates from that time although it has recently moved out of its original wood panelled room and now occupies a more modern space within the society's headquarters. The library contains over 70,000 titles covering the history of science from the 1470s to the present day. It is open to the public but is largely of interest to academics involved in the study of the history of science.

Royal Society for Asian Affairs

⊞ *25 Eccleston Place, SW1W 9NF*
☎ *020 7235 5122*
✐ *www.rsaa.org.uk*
🚌 *Victoria LU/Rail*
🕓 *By appointment*

This library holds more than 5,000 books on the Middle-East, Central Asia and the Indian subcontinent. The collection largely dates from the early twentieth century and covers history, geography, politics and travel. There is also an archive with maps, images and personal papers of many travellers and administrators dating from the mid-nineteenth century and a large photographic collection dating from the late nineteenth century to the present day.

St Bride Library

⊞ *Bride Lane, EC4Y 8EE*
☎ *020 7353 3331*
✐ *www.sbf.org.uk*
🚌 *Blackfriars LU/Rail*
🕓 *Closed for refurbishment*

St Bride Library opened in 1895 to provide technical and academic information to the flourishing print and publishing industry of Fleet Street. The industries for which the area was famous have long since departed but the St Bride Library remains, and is still one of the most important sources of information on printing, paper, binding, typography, calligraphy and just about anything else relating to printing and publishing. Since its foundation, the library has accumulated over 50,000 books including major book collections such as those of type founder and historian, Talbot Baines Reed and the technical print journalist, John Southward. In December 2014 the St Bride Library closed for a major refurbishment, but an ongoing programme of courses, exhibitions, events and talks ensures the library's presence remains active unitl it reopens (see p.278).

St Paul's Cathedral

🗓 EC4M 8AE

☎ 020 7246 8342

✎ www.stpauls.co.uk

🚌 St Paul's LU

🕒 By appointment

The library of St Paul's Cathedral lies behind the south-west tower in its original chamber designed by Christopher Wren. The library's historical collections centre on theology, church history and patristics, while books on Wren and the building of the cathedral form the focus of current acquisitions. The library includes the book collections of several major theologians including the eighteenth-century Bishop of London, Henry Compton. This is one of the last unspoilt libraries dating from the early eighteenth century, but access is restricted to those engaged in theological study. The archive of the Dean and Chapter of St Paul's is held in the Guildhall Library (see p.218).

Society for Co-operation in Russian and Soviet Studies

🗓 320 Brixton Road, SW9 6AB

☎ 020 7274 2282

✎ www.scrss.org.uk

🚌 Brixton LU/Rail

🕒 By appointment

This privately funded library contains more than 35,000 books, journals and pamphlets in English and Russian about Russia and the former Soviet Union.

Society of Genealogists

🗓 14 Charterhouse Buildings,
Goswell Road, EC1M 7BA

☎ 020 7251 8799

✎ www.sog.org.uk

🚌 Barbican LU, Farringdon LU/Rail

🕒 Tues-Wed & Sat 10am-6pm
Thurs 10am-8pm

This is the foremost library in the UK for anyone involved in genealogy. The collection includes professional and education records, family histories, census material and copies of Parish Registers. There is an Open Access area at the SOG with online resources and advice and a packed programme of events and courses.

South London Botanical Institute

🗓 323 Norwood Road, SE24 9AQ

☎ 020 8674 5787

✎ www.slbi.org.uk

🚌 Tulse Hill Rail, Herne Hill Rail

🕒 Thurs 10am-4pm, Sat 10am-2pm

This Institute exists to encourage the study of plants and its Norwood headquarters includes a herbarium, botanical garden and library. The library holds books, journals and slides on British and European floras as well as reference books and titles on botany, gardening history, botanical folklore and horticulture.

Rudolf Steiner House Library

🗓 Rudolf Steiner House,
35 Park Road, NW1 6XT

☎ 020 7724 8398

✎ www.rsh.anth.org.uk

🚌 Baker Street LU

🕒 Tues, Thurs & Sat 12pm-7pm
(closed 2-3pm)

This is the library of the Anthroposophical Society in Great Britain and contains material on all aspects of the work of Rudolf Steiner and anthroposophical thought. There is also an archive which contains some of Rudolf Steiner's original papers as well as a rare collection of anthroposophical journals.

The Swedenborg Society

⌨ *20-21 Bloomsbury Way, WC1A 2TH*
☎ *020 7405 7986*
✍ *www.swedenborg.org.uk*
🚌 *Holborn LU, Tottenham Court Road LU*
🕓 *By appointment*

The library of the Swedenborg Society contains books by and about the influential Christian mystic and thinker, Emanuel Swedenborg. The collection also includes a good deal of material about the influence of Swedenborg on subsequent generations and the Christian denominations informed by his writings (Swedenborgianism).

Tate Gallery

⌨ *Hyman Kreitman Reading Rooms, Tate Britain, Millbank, SW1P 4RG*
☎ *020 7887 8838*
✍ *www.tate.org.uk/research*
🚌 *Pimlico LU*
🕓 *Mon-Fri 11am-5pm*

The library material covers British art from 1500 and international art from 1900. The library includes more than 40,000 books, 2,000 journals and over 140,000 art exhibition catalogues. Use of the archive, artists' books and special collections are by prior appointment only.

Theosophical Society

⌨ *50 Gloucester Place, W1U 8EA*
☎ *020 7563 9816*
✍ *www.theosophical-society.org.uk*
🚌 *Baker Street LU*
🕓 *By appointment*

The Theosophy Society was founded in 1875 to promote the importance and unity of all religions. The library of its London headquarters contains books about theology, mysticism and other esoteric subjects which can be referred to by appointment.

Trades Union Congress Library Collections

⌨ *London Metropolitan University,*
✍ *www.londonmet.ac.uk/libraries/tuc*

This library was established in 1922 and is a major social science research library with material on the trade union movement, working conditions and industrial relations. There is also an important collection of pamphlets and ephemera and other original documents concerning these subjects within the library's archive. The library is at present in storage and due to move to a new site in Aldgate – check the website for further details.

Wallace Collection

⌨ *Hertford House, Manchester Square, W1U 3BN*
☎ *020 7563 9500*
✍ *www.wallacecollection.org*
🚌 *Bond Street LU*
🕓 *By appointment*

This reference library holds material on all areas of the famous art collection, encompassing European fine and decorative art up to the mid nineteenth century and the history of collecting. There are around 20,000 volumes including books, periodicals, exhibition catalogues and auction catalogues. The library also houses the De Walden collection of rare sixteenth to nineteenth-century fencing books and a significant collection of books about armour.

The Warburg Institute

▣ *University of London*
School of Advanced Study
Woburn Square, WC1H 0AB
☎ *020 7862 8949*
✎ *www.warburg.sas.ac.uk*
🚇 *Goodge Street LU, Russell Square LU*
🕓 *Access restricted to*
postgraduate students

This exceptional library is dedicated to European cultural history and is based on the collection of the German banking heir, Aby Warburg (1866-1929). The library offers a unique collection of over 350,000 books and over 350,000 images, but access is restricted to post graduate students, academics and researchers. Despite these restrictions, the Institute has embarked on an ambitious programme of digitisation, which means that a significant number of the library's books can be viewed and downloaded via the online catalogue.

The Warburg Institute

Wellcome Library

⊞ *Wellcome Collection*
   183 Euston Road, NW1 2BE
☎ *020 7611 8722*
✎ *www.wellcomelibrary.org*
🚇 *Euston LU/Rail, Euston Square LU*
🕓 *Mon-Fri 10am-6pm, Thurs 10am-8pm,*
   Sat 10am-4pm

The Wellcome Collection underwent a major redevelopment back in 2007 and its traditional Portland stone exterior now conceals a modern and bright interior of white walls, steel and glass. The Wellcome Library is less well known and a quieter part of the building, but is one of the world's major resources on the history of medicine and medical science with a holding of over 600,000 books and a large collection of medical journals. There is also an archive containing original manuscripts and documents. The library is a popular resource for medical students and those studying the history of medicine, but it also holds the records of practicing doctors which are of interest to genealogists with medical ancestors. The library offers comfortable study areas, free Wi-Fi and there is a café and restaurant in the building. If you can't make it to the library much of the collection is now available to view on their excellent website.

Westminster Abbey

⊞ *East Cloister, Westminster Abbey*
   SW1P 3PA
☎ *020 7654 4830*
✎ *www.westminster-abbey.org*
🚇 *Westminster LU*
🕓 *By appointment*

This ancient reference library is housed within the cloister of Westminster Abbey and is dedicated to books, manuscripts and archival material on the administration of Westminster Abbey and its history.

Wiener Library

For the Study of the Holocaust & Genocide
⊞ *29 Russell Square, WC1B 5DP*
☎ *020 7636 7247*
✎ *www.wienerlibrary.co.uk*
🚇 *Russell Square LU*
🕓 *Mon-Fri 10am-5pm, Tues till 7.30pm*

The Wiener Library was founded in 1933 by a Jewish refugee from Nazi Germany, to highlight the plight of the Jews. It has since become this country's largest Holocaust archive and includes refugee family papers, over 17,000 photographs and documents relating to the fates of over 1.7 million Jews. In 2007 the library moved to this spacious eighteenth century town house on Russell Square, allowing better storage and display of its collection of over one million items relating to the causes and legacy of the Holocaust. The library also concerns itself with the recent history of European Jewry and runs a busy programme of exhibitions and lectures on subjects relating to Jewish history, Israel, anti-Semitism and the Holocaust.

Dr Williams's Library

- 14 Gordon Square, WC1H 0AR
- 020 7387 3727
- www.dwlib.co.uk
- Euston Square LU, Euston LU/Rail
- Mon, Wed & Fri 10am-5pm
  Tues & Thurs 10am-6.30pm

Established in 1729 with a bequest from the will of nonconformist minister, Dr Daniel Williams, this library is dedicated to the history of English Protestant nonconformity. Since 1890 the library has been housed in a grand Victorian town house in the heart of Bloomsbury and now holds over 300,000 books dating from the earliest years of printing to modern times, as well as a considerable archive of original manuscripts and papers. The premises are shared with the Congregational Library (see p.259).

Kenneth Ritchie Wimbledon Library

- Wimbledon Lawn Tennis Museum,
  All England Lawn Tennis and Croquet
  Club, Church Road, SW19 5AE
- 020 8879 5609
- www.wimbledon.com/museum
- Southfields LU, Wimbledon LU/Rail
- Mon-Fri 10am-5pm by appointment

This library is housed within the Wimbledon Lawn Tennis Museum and contains material about lawn tennis including lawn tennis books, annuals, periodicals, programmes, newspaper cuttings and audiovisual material.

Women's Library

- LSE Library, 10 Portugal Street
  WC2A 2HD
- 020 7955 7229
- www.lse.ac.uk
- Holborn LU, Temple LU
- By appointment

This library specialises in the history and politics of women, including women's rights, suffrage, health, sexuality, education, employment, reproductive rights, the home and the family. There is some international material but the emphasis is on women in Britain. The library's holdings include books, pamphlets, periodicals, press cuttings, visual materials and archival collections. A significant part of the collection has been digitised and can now be viewed online.

Zoological Society of London Library

- Regent's Park, NW1 4RY
- 020 7449 6293
- www.zsl.org
- Baker Street LU, Regent's Park LU,
  Camden Town LU
- Mon-Fri 9.30am-5.30pm
  (photographic ID required)

Founded in 1826, The ZSL Library has amassed one of the world's major zoological collections. The library holds more than 200,000 books including rare sixteenth-century volumes as well as more recent publications on the subject. There is free Wi-Fi in the library, plenty of work areas and friendly staff on hand to provide help when needed. The library also holds a considerable archive of photographs and documents relating to the society and its history.

Book Art

London Centre for Book Arts (LCBA)

Bookbinders

Alinéa Bindery
🖳 *51 Westbourne Grove, W2 4UA*
☎ *020 7792 1030*
🖉 *www.alineabindery.com*
🕓 *Mon-Fri 9am-6pm, Sat 11am-2pm*
This little bindery undertakes all kinds
of work from dissertation binding to
restoration and repair. Take a look at the
website to see some of their fine leather
binding work. The company produces a
range of portfolios and boxes and will also
undertake bespoke designs. The bindery
shares premises with Edox Printers and
uses the printers to produce small print run
books with fine bindings.

Blissetts
🖳 *Roslin Road, Acton, W3 8DH*
☎ *020 8992 3965*
🖉 *www.blissetts.com*
🕓 *Mon-Thurs 7.30am-4pm,*
   Fri 7.30am-1pm
Founded by Frederick Blissett in 1920, the
company now employs over 50 people
in its large print works and bindery.
Blissetts is still owned and run by the
same family, but much else has changed
and the business now uses the latest
technology to produce photobooks, thesis
bindings and other short run publications.
The company has not forgotten its artisan
roots and offers a bespoke restoration
and hand-binding service which is trusted
by some of the world's leading libraries
and institutions.

bookobscure
🖳 *Unit 2a Co-op Centre,*
   11 Mowll Street, SW9 6BG
☎ *020 7582 2545*
🖉 *www.bookobscure.co.uk*
🕓 *By appointment*
This bookbinding and conservation studio
is run by book conservator and binder
Sayaka Fukuda. As well as conservation
work and fine bindings the studio also
specialises in bespoke boxes. Past clients
include the V&A and the Freud Museum.

Hannah Brown
🖳 *324 Kilburn Lane, W9 3EF*
☎ *07740 082 672*
🖉 *www.han-made.net*
Hannah Brown specialises in single
commissions, working in coloured
leathers, embroidery, woodwork and
gold tooling to transform family heirlooms
and private press books into rare and
collectable works of art. Her website is an
excellent resource which gives a good idea
of her work.

The Chelsea Bindery
🖳 *100 Fulham Road, SW3 6HS*
☎ *020 7591 0220*
🖉 *www.peterharrington.co.uk*
🕓 *Mon-Sat 10am-5pm,*
In a wonderful example of what
economists call 'vertical integration', the
antiquarian book dealer Peter Harrington
(see page 144) founded The Chelsea
Bindery in 2000. They offer a conservation
service, traditional leather bookbinding and
also make bespoke boxes.

Cockram Books

⌨ *Studio Five*
First Floor The Mews
46-52 Church Street, Barnes, SW13 0DQ
☎ *020 8563 2158*
✎ *www.markcockrambooks.co.uk*
☾ *By appointment*

Mark Cockram is one of the country's leading bookbinders and from his workshop come some startlingly beautiful contemporary books – his bookbinding is more of an art than a craft. He undertakes all kinds of binding commissions, sells his own work and also conducts regular bookbinding classes from his large studios in south west London.

Collis Bird & Withey Bookbinders

⌨ *1 Drayton Park, N5 1NU*
☎ *020 7607 1116*
✎ *www.collisbirdandwithey.co.uk*
☾ *Mon-Fri 8am-4pm*

Many large binderies have left London in recent years – selling their former sites to make way for luxury flats. Collis Bird & Withey have remained at the works they set up in the late 1970s, just off the Holloway Road and are now one of London's largest binderies. They offer a wide range of services from binding comic and magazine collections to fine leather book restoration. They undertake all kinds of corporate work but also welcome individual binding projects.

Delta Design Studio Ltd

⌨ *Studio 2, 14-16 Meredith Street,*
EC1R 0AB
☎ *020 7837 7557*
✎ *www.cathyrobert.com*
☾ *By appointment*

This creative bindery was founded by renowned binder Cathy Robert, who now woks as part of a team of three bookbinders. Delta Design will take on all kinds of projects from restoration work to bespoke boxes. They also produce a range of their own boxes and unique i-pad cases.

Grays Bookbinders

⌨ *Windsor House*
26 Willow Lane, Mitcham, Surrey
CR4 4NA
☎ *020 8640 1449*
✎ *www.graysbbb.co.uk*
☾ *Mon-Fri 9am-5pm*

Grays was founded in 1960 and specialises in printing and binding bespoke books, portfolios and presentation boxes. The company has many corporate clients but also welcomes individual enquiries and bespoke projects.

London Bookbinding Ltd

⌨ *Priory House, St John's Square,*
EC1M 4HD
☎ *020 7336 0880*
✎ *www.londonbookbinding.co.uk*
☾ *Mon-Fri 9am-6pm*

This printers and bindery has the look of a modern graphics bureau rather than a traditional bookbinder's workshop. The company offers all kinds of services from the printing and binding of theses to traditional leather bindings.

London Centre for Book Arts (LCBA)

London Centre for Book Arts (LCBA)

⌸ *Unit 18 Ground Floor*
  Britannia Works, Dace Road, E3 2NQ
☏ *020 8510 9810*
✑ *www.londonbookarts.org*
🕒 *Tues-Sat 10am-6pm*

This smart workshop in the heart of Hackney Wick (close to the Olympic Park) is dedicated to teaching and promoting all aspects of book art. Courses include a basic introduction to bookbinding and extend into more arcane subjects such as hand printing and foil blocking. Those who have already trained in a particular aspect of book art can access the facilities in several ways, from flexible passes which can be used whenever convenient to a full month's membership for £125. The LCBA is concerned with traditional book arts but the studio has a surprisingly modern feel, more akin to an architectural practice than a traditional bookbindery. It is a welcome addition to London's bookbinding community, bridging the gap between the old craft and the contemporary world with an active engagement in social media and a regular newsletter with information about the latest courses and exhibitions. The LCBA also runs letterpress courses and has an impressive collection of type and Adana presses.

Marba Bookbinding

⌸ *63 Jeddo Road, W12 9EE*
☏ *020 8743 4715*
✑ *marbabookbinding@gmail.com*
🕒 *By appointment*

Marba are an old school traditional bookbinders and does not have a website. They do all kinds of repair and rebinding and can also make fine bespoke boxes, but do not undertake restoration work.

J. Muir Bookbinders Ltd

⌸ *64-68 Blackheath Road, SE10 8DA*
☏ *020 8692 7565*
✑ *www.jmuirbookbindersltd.co.uk*
🕒 *Mon-Fri 9am-5pm*

J Muir are a Greenwich institution, having set up business here when Queen Victoria was on the throne. They are now a modern industrial bookbinders, but still have a small hand binding workshop where bespoke bindings and repair are undertaken.

London Centre for Book Arts (LCBA)

Rook's Books

Rook's Books

⌂ *9 Coopers Yard,*
Crystal Palace, SE19 1TN
☎ *020 8766 6398*
✎ *www.rooksbooks.com*
🕐 *By appointment*

Gavin Rookledge has been creating rare and unusual leather bound books since 1987 and his workshop is renowned for its skill in binding almost any object in any kind of leather from cow stomachs to chicken feet, although Gavin draws the line at forbidden exotic leathers. This is not just a nine to five business, in Gavin's case it has become something of an obsession with every aspect of his life and work carefully documented in leather bound diaries, most of which are bound in the remnants of a favoured pair of shoes or jacket. The shelves piled high with such volumes give a detailed account of the progress of Rook's Books, from a single workshop in this mews off Westow Hill, to the company's current premises occupying six workshops and a workforce of twelve full-time staff working on anything from the vellum-clad interior fixtures of a yacht, to the binding of 200 books for an architect responsible for a grand interior design.

Many of Rook's Books' clients are London's super rich and Gavin is obliged to keep their identity a secret and rarely meets the eventual recipient of his work, largely accepting commissions through an agent. If you should wish to commission a binding take the opportunity to make an appointment to visit Rook's Books' workshops – they are like a small museum devised by Heath Robinson, with an early twentieth-century clocking-in machine, a leather-clad car in the driveway complete with vast cow horns, and an old railway ticket shelving unit listing destinations long since closed.

Despite the application of ancient skills and the use of vast Victorian book presses and antique embossing tools, this workshop is also very much part of the modern world with Gavin using dictation software in his small office and flat screen televisions distributed throughout the complex of buildings. With a large commission having just arrived and plans to takeover yet another unit in the mews, Rook's Books is currently thriving, and it's comforting to know that the future of this special enclave of Crystal Palace is secure.

Syston Bindery

▫ *Unit 5A, St Marks' Work*
   Foundry Lane, Leicester, LE1 3WU
☎ *0116 2539 552*
✎ *www.systonbindery.co.uk*

This family run bindery has acquired an excellent reputation for restoration work since it was established in 1962. The workshop is based in Leicester, but every month they have a stand at the Bloomsbury Book Fair (see page 192) where detailed quotes are provided and books taken away for return the following month. Syston Bindery are trusted by many of the book dealers that attend the fair and their past clients include Leicester City Library and Henry Pordes Books (see page 156).

Shepherds

▫ *76 Rochester Row, SW1P 1JU*
☎ *020 7233 5298*
✎ *www.bookbinding.co.uk*
🕓 *By appointment*

This established bookbinders offers a restoration service, bespoke fine bindings and beautiful gift and storage boxes. Alison is the main contact at the Rochester Row bindery but you can also visit their Mayfair shop where many of their fine books and stationery are on display and for sale.

Branches at:
▫ *46 Curzon Street, W1J 7UH*
☎ *020 7495 8580*
🕓 *Mon-Fri 10am-6pm, Sat 10.30am-5pm*

▫ *30 Gillingham Street, SW1V 1HU*
☎ *020 7233 9999*
🕓 *Mon-Fri 10am-6pm, Sat 10am-5pm*

St Bride Foundation

see p.278.

Paolo Taddeo – Books & Design

▫ *The Glass Door,*
   10 Manor Road, N16 5SA
☎ *07884 083 848*
✎ *www.paolotaddeo.co.uk*
🕓 *By appointment*

Paolo Taddeo has over 20 years book binding, typography and graphic design experience and now specialises in fine bookbinding, box making, gilding and leather design from his studio in north London. Take a look at his website to see some of Paolo's exquisite bindings.

The Wyvern Bindery

56-58 Clerkenwell Road, EC1M 5PX

020 7490 7899

www.wyvernbindery.com

Mon-Fri 9am-5pm

The Wyern Bindery is run with ebullient charm by Mark Winstanley, who founded the company with two colleagues (Hannah More and Rosie Gray) in 1990. They moved to this shop on Clerkenwell Road a few years later and have continued to thrive despite many changes in the industry and the area, as Mark explains:

"We used to do a lot of magazine and legal document binding for all the big legal practices in the area, but the internet reduced that kind of work. This was also an area with lots of photographers and we were employed to make their portfolios... We still do this kind of work, but it is not the mainstay of our business, as it was in our early years."

The business has adapted and now has eight full-time staff using traditional bookbinding skills in all kinds of ways including making bespoke boxes, film set props, unique photo albums and a great deal of work for architectural practices, keen to present their cutting edge projects in traditional bindings. They also do a fair amount of dissertation binding and, as if on cue, a student pops in to collect her cloth bound and gold embossed Phd thesis.

There are always jobs that are particularly memorable and Mark is eager to show the three volumes of the eighteenth-century 'Vitruvius Britannicus' whose tatty leather bands and faded labels Wyvern are replacing with loving care. Likewise, the vast accounts ledgers of Savile Row's oldest tailors, Henry Poole & Co., recording the sartorial extravagance of kings are being rebound in green felt with due reverence by Mark and his team.

In recent years the bindery has shrunk a little, owing to a re-structuring of the building, but there is still considerable space and the change has only added to the shop's cluttered charm. There are quite a few antique book presses scattered among the work stations, many of which were made in long since closed Clerkenwell workshops. Hopefully this little oasis of craftsmanship will remain for many years to come.

BURN THE INTERNET

courage [kur-ij]

boldness, braveness

fearlessness
determination
spunk
recklessness

f an ancient sag
knows me.
erates my ways.

ickiest tongue,
lse control:
le? Am I wrong
u have a soul?

a monkey,
onkey yet.
a little family.
g knows it.

Letterpress

A Two Pipe Problem

⌷ *Unit 041 C-D, Leyton Industrial Village, Argall Avenue, E10 7QP*

☎ *020 8988 1241*

✍ *www.atwopipeproblem.com*

The clever folk at A Two Pipe Problem have a great website which allows punters to order traditional letterpress prints with their own message from just £30 and the bespoke poster arrives within 10 days. They also sell their own range of weird and comic prints in a variety of letterpress styles. Take a look at their website for more details.

Hand & Eye

⌷ *6 Pinchin Street, E1 1SA*

☎ *020 7488 9800*

✍ *www.handandeye.co.uk*

This letterpress workshop is run by Phil Abel and Nick Gill and specialises in printing cards, posters, stationery and even books, using traditional monotype machines. Unlike some of the small hand press courses and workshops, Hand & Eye work on large mechanical Heidelberg machines and operate like an old school print workshop of the kind that was common 60 years ago but with digital printing has become a rare and specialist activity. To find out more about Hand & Eye take a look at their website which contains short films about their work.

Harrington & Squires Ltd

see p.275

I.M. Imprimit

⌷ *219a Victoria Park Road, E9 7HD*

✍ *www.imimprimit.com*

This print workshop was started in 1969 by artist Ian Mortimer with a single Albion machine, initially to print his own woodcuts and wood-engravings. Over the years Ian has acquired foundry type, a collection of wood poster types and several more machines to transform this one man venture into a thriving business offering artist's prints, limited edition books, stationery and posters. Take a look at the website for more information.

London Centre for Book Arts (LCBA)

see p.266

New North Press

⌷ *45 Coronet Street, N1 6HD*

☎ *020 7729 3161*

✍ *www.new-north-press.co.uk*

This small team of enthusiasts has been keeping the craft of letterpress alive for nearly 30 years with both commissioned work and the teaching of regular workshops in typography, hand-setting and printing. They undertake all kinds of commissions from wedding invitations to limited edition books.

St Bride Foundation

see p.278

The Typography Workshop

✍ *www.thetypographyworkshop.com*

Alan Kitching has been working and teaching traditional letterpress printing techniques for over 50 years and now hosts regular themed talks on the subject from his Kennington workshop complete with a slide show and exhibits of original work from his substantial archive.

Harrington & Squires Ltd

The Corridor, 136a Fortess Road, NW5 2HP

☎ *020 7267 1500*

✎ *www.harringtonandsquires.co.uk*

🕐 *Mon-Fri 10am-6pm*

Harrington & Squires is the brain child of two graphic design graduates, Chrissie Charlton of Hornsey College of Art and Vicky Fullick of St Martin's School of Art and later the London College of Communication. They started their careers during the 'hands on' design sensibility of the 70s and 80s and, during the more sterile world of desk top publishing in the 90s, wanted to return to the tactile environment of traditional letterpress printing.

They started the business in the corner of Chrissie's design practice studio in 2002 and in 2004 stumbled upon a recently closed art gallery which is without doubt one of the narrowest shop fronts in London. The three galley-like floors are probably too narrow for a conventional shop, but suited their requirements for a workshop and small retail space perfectly.

Part of Chrissie and Vicky's time is spent teaching one day letterpress printing workshops for up to two students at a time with lunch thrown in. The classes show how to use the famous Adana letterpress printing machines – designing the text, filling what is called the 'metal chase area' with the selected type and blocks and then choosing the inks and setting up the press for the printing of cards, poems and in some cases small pamphlets. There is something unique about the look and feel of things printed on a letterpress. As Chrissie explains:

"Letterpress produces a unique impression on the paper called a 'bite' and people really like that texture to the finished product."

Vicky and Chrissie also dedicate a good deal of time designing and printing all kinds of cards, letterheads, business cards and invitations for clients. This might sound like the work of a standard printer, but Vicky makes clear:

"We're not jobbing printers as we usually don't print other people's designs and the work is very different from digital or litho printing. Our customers understand they are getting something unique."

Vicky and Chrissie often do the initial design digitally, bearing in mind that it is then set in metal using the type they have in stock. Once the digital proofs are approved by the client, the painstaking work of hand setting, locking up in the metal chase and preparing the press is undertaken. The actual operation of these hand-driven, old machines, is slow but very satisfying with each piece of paper placed in the press by hand for each impression taken.

The final part of the Harrington & Squires jigsaw is the production of their own unique cards, fridge magnets and calendars that are sold from their small shop as well as online and through quite a few retail outlets. This side of the business has really benefitted from being on a busy shopping street with a regular contingent of locals popping in to commission cards and other work.

The original Bob Harrington and Horace Squires, who were renowned type compositors and teachers at Hornsey College of Art, would no doubt doff their caps in the direction of Vicky and Chrissie as they keep these valued skills alive. For those interested in their work or taking a class, their website is an excellent first point of call.

"Letterpress produces a unique impression on the paper called a 'bite' and people really like that texture to the finished product."

Harrington & Squires

St Bride Foundation

St Bride Foundation

14 Bride Lane, Fleet Street, EC4Y 8EQ
020 7353 3332
www.sbf.org.uk/workshops

The St Bride Foundation was established over a century ago to provide a cultural and social centre for the print trade that once dominated nearby Fleet Street. The newspapers have now all left the area but the St Bride Foundation has remained as a place of education for the traditional skills of letterpress printing, wood engraving (relief printing), lino printing and bookbinding.

Mick Clayton is the tutor for the letterpress course here and one of the old school print men, who can remember Fleet Street in its bibulous heyday and still wears his NUJ badge with pride.

The print workshop is a living museum with working examples of many early hand presses from a 2014 reconstruction of an early sixteenth-century press based upon an Albrecht Durer wood print, to a large steel Heidelberg machine dating from the early twentieth-century. These vast machines are too large for domestic use, but Adana hand presses are scattered around the place and are a popular way for students to begin learning the skills involved in letterpress printing.

The old print works of Fleet Street have gone, but there are still people interested in traditional print skills with many students coming from a modern design background but keen to get their hands dirty. Classes range from one day intensive instruction to evening courses over several months and because the engraving and bookbinding courses are all within the same building there is the opportunity to learn several disciplines. To find out more about St Bride and its courses take a look at their website.

Morris Gallery

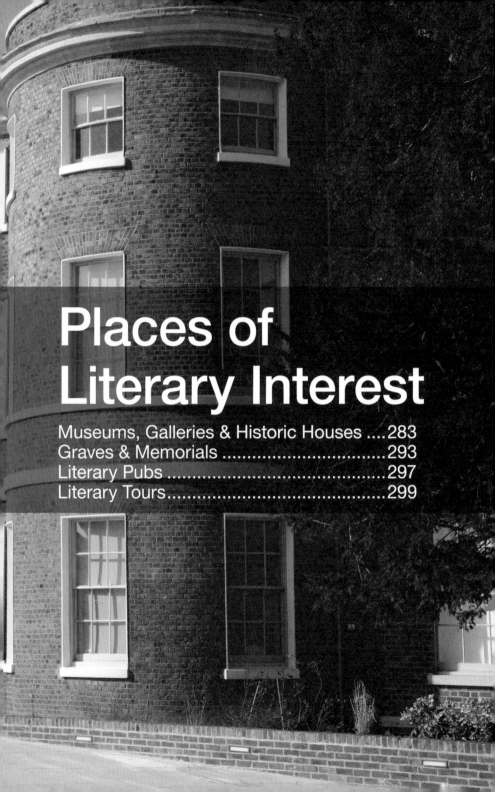

Places of
Literary Interest

Keats Portrait at Keats House

Museums, Galleries & Historic Houses

The places listed below are a good way for book lovers to get a more intimate knowledge of their literary heroes and heroines. Those who don't see the point in such shrines and prefer to explore the works should read Julian Barnes' 'Flaubert's Parrot', a wonderful account of walking in the footsteps of a great writer.

The British Library

⌨ *96 Euston Road, NW1 2DB*
☎ *020 7412 7332*
✎ *www.bl.uk/whatson*
🚌 *Euston LU,*
King's Cross St Pancras LU/Rail
🕐 *Mon-Fri 9.30am-6pm*
(Tues until 8pm), Sat 9.30am-5pm,
Sun & Bank Holidays 11am-5pm
🎫 *Admission free (admission charges for*
some temporary exhibitions)

This is the undoubted highlight for any book lover in London – a place to savour and visit time and again. As well as holding the 14 million books (on 625 kilometres of shelving) which make up the national library of Britain (see p.232 for details about reading rights), there are exhibition galleries for visitors to explore. The real delight is The Sir John Ritblat Gallery: Treasures of the British Library, which displays some incredible texts, manuscripts, maps and musical scores. Here you can view the likes of the Lindisfarne Gospels, a First Folio of Shakespeare and Leonardo da Vinci's notebooks plus many sacred texts. Some of the most remarkable books can be examined in digital versions using the Turning the Pages system on screens located in the Gallery and also on the library's website.

The Folio Society Gallery, near the entrance hall, features book-related exhibitions while stamps from the Philatelic Collection are located in racks near the café. The Centre for Conservation has a small but fascinating display and the Digital Space offers a changing programme of materials from the library's digital holdings, including the sound archive.

A visit to the café or to the restaurant is a grand experience, located as they are beside the stunning King's Library, the collection of around 65,000 books amassed by King George III. The stack of sumptuous leatherbound volumes stretches upwards, housed in a six storey, seventeen-metre high glass tower situated at the centre of the library.

Tours of the library allow access to areas not normally open to the public. Booking is advisable, either at the Information Desk or by ringing the event line on 01937 546 546. The British Library also hosts an extensive array of events of interest to anyone interested in books (see p.303).

Carlyle's House

⌖ *24 Cheyne Row, SW3 5HL*
☏ *020 7352 7087*
✐ *www.nationaltrust.org.uk*
🚌 *Sloane Square LU*
   South Kensington LU
🕑 *Wed-Sun & Bank Hols 11am-4.30pm*
   (March to October). Check website for
   details / dates.
⊛ *£5.10 (adults), £2.60 (children),*
   £12.80 (family)

Although he is no longer a well-known figure, the Victorian historian, critic and essayist Thomas Carlyle (1795-1881) was hugely influential and famous in his own lifetime. He lived at this house from 1834 until his death. Most revered for works such as 'The French Revolution' and 'Frederick the Great', Carlyle was also a founder of The London Library (see p.244). He and his wife Jane were visited at this house by many of the great names of the day including Dickens, Tennyson, Chopin, Browning, George Eliot, Darwin, Thackeray, John Stuart Mill and John Ruskin. The house still contains its original furniture as well as Carlyle's books and belongings. However, don't get too carried away imagining domestic tranquillity – the Carlyles had a notoriously volatile relationship. A statue of Carlyle stands in nearby Cheyne Walk.

Charles Dickens Museum

⌖ *48 Doughty Street, WC1N 2LX*
☏ *020 7405 2127*
✐ *www.dickensmuseum.com*
🚌 *Russell Square LU*
🕑 *Mon-Sat 10am-5pm, Sun 11am-5pm*
⊛ *£8 (adults), £6 (concessions), £4*
(children), £15 (family ticket)

Charles Dickens (1812-1870) lived in this late-Georgian terrace between 1837 and 1839. During his time here he wrote parts of 'The Pickwick Papers' and 'Barnaby Rudge' and all of 'Nicholas Nickleby' and 'Oliver Twist'. Dickens lived at around fifteen London addresses but this is the only house which survives. Laid out over four floors, some of the rooms are furnished as they would have been in his time while others hold displays including family portraits, an extensive family tree, letters, papers, memorabilia and first editions of Dickens' books.

Freud Museum

⌖ *20 Maresfield Gardens, NW3 5SX*
☏ *020 7435 2002*
✐ *www.freud.org.uk*
🚌 *Finchley Road LU*
🕑 *Wed-Sun 12noon-5pm*
⊛ *£7 (adults), £4.00 (concessions),*
   free (children under 12 years).
   An audioguide is available for £2.

In 1938 Sigmund Freud fled from Nazi Vienna with enough belongings to recreate a replica of his Austrian home in London, including his famous couch which is the centrepiece of the museum. When Freud arrived in London he was already sick with cancer and he died here in 1939 but Anna, Freud's daughter (herself a psychoanalyst), lived on in the house until her death in 1982. The house remains as it was in Freud's time and it contains many of the ancient Egyptian, Greek, Roman and Oriental antiquities that he avidly collected. He admitted that his passion for collecting such items was second only to his passion for cigars! There is a portrait of the man himself painted by Salvador Dali and video footage from the Freud family home movies is also on show.

Charles Dickens Museum

Carlyle's House

Freud Museum

Dr Johnson's House

- 🖼 *17 Gough Square, EC4A 3DE*
- ☎ *020 7353 3745*
- 🖉 *www.drjohnsonshouse.org*
- 🚌 *Chancery Lane LU, Temple LU, Holborn LU*
- 🕐 *Mon-Sat 11am-5.30pm (May-Sept), Mon-Sat 11am-5pm (Oct-April)*
- ♿ *£4.50 (adults), £3.50 (concessions), £1.50 (children), family ticket £10*

Dr Samuel Johnson (1709-1784) is famous as the compiler of the first dictionary of the English language and for his many sayings – carefully recorded by his biographer, James Boswell. He moved to this house, built around 1700, with the advance that he got for his dictionary and it was during his time here (1748-1759) that he and his six scribes, standing at high desks in the attic, compiled the enormous work (containing over 40,000 definitions and over one hundred thousand quotations), which was published in 1755. The house has been restored to its original condition and furnished with carefully chosen eighteenth-century pieces, including Johnson memorabilia such as a brick that is supposed to have come from the Great Wall of China and portraits of Johnson and his associates. The house is also the venue for regular lectures related to the life and times of Dr Johnson and his time – see the website for details.

Keats House

- 🖼 *10 Keats Grove, NW3 3RR*
- ☎ *020 7332 3868*
- 🖉 *www.cityoflondon.gov/keats*
- 🚌 *Belsize Park LU, Hampstead LU*
- 🕐 *Tues-Sun 1pm-5pm (May-Oct), Fri-Sun 1pm-5pm (Nov-April)*
- ♿ *£5.50 (adults), £3.50 (concessions), free (children 17 and under)*

The Romantic poet (1795-1821) John Keats lived in this Regency house from 1818 to 1820 and is said to have written his famous 'Ode to a Nightingale' under a plum tree in the garden. The Brawne family lived next door and Keats fell in love with and became engaged to Fanny Brawne, the daughter of the house. Sadly, they never got married as Keats died from TB at the age of just twenty five. The house contains many mementos of their love, including her garnet engagement ring and his love letters. There is a portrait of Keats in the National Portrait Gallery (see below). Keats is buried in the Protestant Cemetery in Rome; there is no name on the tombstone only the lines 'Here lies one whose name was writ in water'. Fanny Brawne wore her engagement ring until she died in 1865 despite marriage to Louis Lindon and the birth of three children. She is buried in Brompton Cemetery. The Keats House Poetry Appreciation Group meets every Friday.

National Portrait Gallery

- St Martin's Place, WC2H 0HE
- ☎ 020 7306 0055
- ✎ www.npg.org.uk
- 🚌 Charing Cross LU/Rail,
  Leicester Square LU
- 🕑 Daily 10am-6pm (Thurs & Fri until 9pm)
- ♿ Admission free (admission charges for some temporary exhibitions)

The National Portrait Gallery is a wonderful institution and an excellent place where book lovers can discover what their literary heroes actually looked like. It's fascinating to see images of favourite writers for perhaps the first time and to try to square their picture with what may be in your mind's eye. Remember this is a collection of national portraits so don't expect to see any writers from outside Britain.

Visitors should note that displays do change and portraits may not be on regular display. Either ring the Gallery or access the database via the website if you intend travelling here to see a particular portrait.

An audio guide is available to take around the gallery with you and provides more detailed information about the exhibits. It includes the Writers Gallery Trail, a guide to ten of the literary highlights in the NPG. The IT Gallery on the Mezzanine Floor features the Portrait Explorer, a database of tens of thousands of the portraits owned by the Gallery which helpfully indicates where they are on display and provides high-quality illustrations for many of them. The service can also be accessed via the website.

The oldest portraits are on the second floor and so for a chronological visit, start from the top and work your way down. We've listed the rooms where you'll find most writers:

Room 2 The Elizabethan Age:
Amidst several famous paintings of Queen Elizabeth I and her courtiers there's one of Sir Walter Raleigh, a writer and poet as well as an explorer.

Room 4 Shakespeare and his Circle:
It's here you'll find the famous portrait of William Shakespeare attributed to John Taylor (the painter's identity has never been fully established). Also to be found here are polymath Francis Bacon, playwright Ben Johnson, poet John Donne and literary patron, poet and translator Mary Sidney.

Room 6 Science and the Arts in the 17th Century:
Here you'll find paintings of poets John Milton, Andrew Marvell, George Herbert, Anne Finch and Aphra Behn and philosopher John Locke. There's also a small engraving of John Donne, poet and orator.

Room 7 Charles II The Restoration of the Monarchy: This room features John Dryden, Samuel Butler and Samuel Pepys. Nell Gwyn, one of King Charles II's many mistresses, is also in this room.

Room 8 Later Stuarts: John Locke features here as does scientist Isaac Newton.

Room 9 The Kit-Cat Club: This was a group of influential Whigs who helped bring William III to the throne. This room includes William Congreve, Sir John Vanbrugh, the essayist and poet Joseph Addison, physician and poet Sir Samuel Garth and Sir Richard Steele, dramatist and essayist.

Room 10 The Arts in the Early 18th Century: Hanging here are Jonathan Swift, Alexander Pope, Samuel Richardson, Horace Walpole and Tobias Smollett. Architects Christopher Wren and Nicholas Hawksmoor are also represented.

National Portrait Gallery

Room 11 Britain in the Early 18th Century:
The religious writer Elizabeth Burnet can be found alongside poets Alexander Pope, William Somerville, Stephen Duck, William Mason and Sir Richard Steele.

Room 12 The Arts in the Later 18th Century:
Book lovers should look out for portraits of Laurence Sterne, Samuel Johnson, Alexander Pope and Fanny Burney.

Room 17 Royalty, Celebrity and Scandal:
More scandal than literature here but take a look at Lady Hamilton and Horatio Nelson, whose love affair has inspired many literary works.

Room 18 Art, Invention and Thought. The Romantics:
Literary portraits include those of John Clare, Robert Burns, John Keats, Samuel Taylor Coleridge, Mary Shelley, William Wordsworth, Percy Bysshe Shelley, Robert Southey, Mary Wollstonecraft and Walter Scott. One of the most famous pictures here is of George Gordon, Lord Byron (1788-1824) painted by Thomas Phillips in 1835. There's also the small portrait of Jane Austen by her sister Cassandra.

Room 19 Art, Invention and Thought. Making the Modern World:
Explorer Mungo Park, cartographer and navigator Matthew Flinders and the collector, scholar and British diplomat Sir Thomas Raffles all figure here as does prison reformer Elizabeth Fry.

Room 20 The Road to Reform:
Edmund Burke, William Cobbett, Sydney Smith and playwright and reformer Hannah More, plus busts of Walter Scott and Felicia Dorothea Hemans, poet and playwright.

Room 24 Early Victorian Arts:
This room contains the famous oil painting of all three Brontë sisters and a separate portrait of Emily Brontë. Other likenesses include Charles Dickens, Charles Kingsley, Robert Browning and Elizabeth Barrett Browning.

Room 26 Portraits by G F Watts:
Algernon Charles Swinburne, John Stuart Mill, Thomas Carlyle, William Morris and Matthew Arnold.

Room 28 Late Victorian Arts:
Robert Louis Stevenson (a painting and a bronze head), Thomas Hardy and Sir William Schwenck Gilbert.

Room 29 The Turn of the Century:
Henry James, Max Beerbohm and a bust of Joseph Conrad as well as critic and author Edmund Gosse.

Room 30 The First World War:
Emmeline Pankhurst, suffragette and Radcliffe Hall, novelist.

Room 31 The Armistice to the New Elizabethans:
This room has paintings, sculptures and photographs, including likenesses of Aldous Huxley, Kingsley Amis, Jerome K Jerome, Edith Sitwell, Osbert Sitwell, Aleister Crowley, Noël Coward, Lytton Strachey, Bertrand Russell, EM Forster, Beatrix Potter, James Joyce, HG Wells, Laurie Lee, TS Eliot, Dylan Thomas, Dorothy L Sayers, Virginia Woolf and John Betjeman.

Room 32 Balcony Gallery Artists and Sitters. Britain 1960-90:
Iris Murdoch is the most illustrious literary figure on display. However, Bryan Organ's portrait of Diana, Princess of Wales from 1981 is also here, next to his matching one of Prince Charles.

Britain Since 1990:
This floor seems especially prone to changes and always warrants a bit of exploration. Writers on this floor usually include Derek Walcott, David Hare, Doris Lessing, AS Byatt, Seamus Heaney, Salman Rushdie and Germaine Greer.

Shakespeare's Globe Theatre

- 🖃 *21 New Globe Walk, SE1 9DT*
- ☎ *020 7902 1400*
- ✑ *www.shakespearesglobe.com*
- 🚌 *Cannon Street LU/Rail, Southwark LU,*
  London Bridge LU/Rail,
  Blackfriars LU/Rail
- 🕓 *October to April: Daily 9am-5pm.*
  April to October:
  Mon- Sat 9am-12.30pm
  NB Precise dates vary annually,
  check on the website.
- 💷 *£13.50 (adults), £11.00 (concessions),*
  £8.00 (children), £36 (family)

This theatre is a reconstruction of the Globe Theatre in which Shakespeare was an actor and shareholder, and where many of his greatest plays were first performed (including 'Hamlet', 'Othello', 'King Lear' and 'Macbeth'). The Globe opened in 1599, and was one of four theatres on Bankside – known in those days as an area of rough and bawdy entertainment. At that time, London had a population of around one hundred thousand and an estimated forty thousand people went each week to one of the Bankside theatres. The original site of The Globe was in Park Street (about two hundred metres away), but this was the closest piece of land available for the project. The original Globe burned down on 29th June 1613 – a fire started by a stray spark from a cannon fired in a performance. By that time Shakespeare had retired to Stratford-upon-Avon a rich man. The theatre was rebuilt the next year but eventually shut down under Oliver Cromwell's puritan government.

American actor Sam Wanamaker was the moving force behind the current Globe, a remarkable building constructed of green (unseasoned) oak and topped by a thatch roof (the first in London since 1666). Partly open to the elements, the theatre only stages performances from April to October but a visit to the exhibition and a tour of the theatre is worthwhile at any time of the year. In addition to the inside of the theatre, you'll see excellent displays about Elizabethan theatre, Shakespeare and his life, costumes, music and special effects and learn about the reconstruction of the theatre. Every afternoon from Tuesday to Sunday, during the summer, visitors can also see live dressing demonstrations to learn how Elizabethan actors transformed themselves into their characters. During matinée performances the tour cannot visit the inside of the Globe Theatre so instead, goes to the archaeological site of the Rose Theatre, which was the first theatre on Bankside and the home of many of Shakespeare's first productions (*see www. rosetheatre.org.uk*).

The Sherlock Holmes Museum

🏠 *221b Baker Street, NW1 6XE*
☎ *020 224 3688*
🖳 *www.sherlock-holmes.co.uk*
🚌 *Baker Street LU*
🕐 *Daily 9.30am-6pm*
💷 *£15 (adults), £10 (children)*

This is a reconstruction in a building with no known connection to Holmes or to his inventor, Sir Arthur Conan Doyle. It is intended to show how Holmes and Watson could have lived in the nineteenth century had they not been creations of Conan Doyle's overactive imagination. According to his creator, Holmes lived at this address from 1881-1904. It's an interesting idea for Sherlock Holmes fans, but builds fiction on top of fiction.

William Morris Gallery

🏠 *Lloyd Park, Forest Road, E17 4PP*
☎ *020 8496 4390*
🖳 *www.wmgallery.org.uk*
🚌 *Walthamstow Central LU*
🕐 *Wed-Sun 10am-5pm*
💷 *Admission free*

Designer, craftsman, writer and Socialist, William Morris (1834-1896), lived in this house as a young man, from 1848-1856. It is now a celebration of his life, work and influence and that of some of his contemporaries such as Edward Burne-Jones, Philip Webb, Dante Gabriel Rossetti and Ford Madox Ford, and features paintings, drawings, fabrics, rugs, carpets, wallpaper, stained glass and tiles. As well as being a pivotal prescence in the Arts and Crafts Movement and a friend of the Pre-Raphaelites, Morris was also involved in the Socialist League and published several political works. For book lovers, the items of most interest relate to the Kelmscott Press – the beautiful Kelmscott edition of Chaucer (published in 1896), is on display here.

Those with an interest in William Morris may also want to visit Kelmscott House, 26 Upper Mall, W6 9TA (Tel: 020 8741, www.morrissociety.org), the headquarters of the William Morris Society which was Morris's home from 1878 to 1896.

Brompton Cemetery

Graves & Memorials

London has been the home of many writers and publishers and has featured in innumerable literary works. Chaucer's pilgrims departed from the Tabard Inn in Southwark, Shakespeare's plays were first performed in the theatres of Bankside, Dickens' novels were steeped in both the author's love of and contempt for the Victorian capital in which he lived. More recently, the Bloomsbury Group were so bound up with London life that they were named after the small area of the capital in which they lived and worked.

London has also been home to great literary figures from abroad. The list of those expat writers to have become familiar with London's streets is illustrious; Dostoevsky, James Joyce, Emile Zola, TS Eliot, Voltaire, Tolstoy, Henry James and Ezra Pound. London has also provided a backdrop for works by modern writers such as Angela Carter, Martin Amis, Peter Ackroyd, Penelope Lively, Anita Brookner, Iain Sinclair and Michael Moorcock. In addition to the printed works, the physical landmarks of literary London take several forms, not least the graves and memorials to some of the most famous writers in the canon.

To check the whereabouts of the grave of a particular person the website *www.findagrave. com* is useful although it is not restricted to London sites or literary figures.

Brompton Cemetery

🖃 *South Gate off Fulham Road,*
   North Gate off Old Brompton Road,
   SW10 9UG
☎ *020 7352 1201*
✐ *www.theroyalparks.org.uk*
🚇 *West Brompton LU*
🕐 *Summer 8am-8pm, Winter 8am-4pm*

Although not as illustrious as the other big London cemeteries, there are more than 200,000 souls buried here. Among the graves are those of Fanny Brawne (Keats' fiancée) and Emmeline Pankhurst, the suffragette. There are regular free guided tours of the cemetery and the annual Open Day, held every summer, is a great chance to see areas of the cemetery, such as the catacombs, usually closed to the public. For more details about tours refer to the website.

Golders Green Crematorium

🖃 *62 Hoop Lane, NW11 7NL*
☎ *020 8455 2374*
🚇 *Golders Green LU*
🕐 *8am-7pm (April-Oct),*
   8am-6pm (Nov-Mar)

Many famous figures have been cremated here and commemorated with plaques – although finding any particular one isn't easy. The literary figures include TS Eliot, Enid Blyton, Rudyard Kipling, George Bernard Shaw, Bram Stoker, Kingsley Amis, Joe Orton and Sigmund Freud.

Highgate Cemetery

🏛 *Swain's Lane, N6 6PJ*
☎ *020 8340 1834*
🖋 *www.highgatecemetery.org*
🚇 *Archway LU*

In the nineteenth century, as a means of coping with the terribly overcrowded city churchyards, a number of cemeteries were opened in what were in those days the green areas outside London. Highgate Cemetery was established in 1839 and with its attractive layout, stone carvings, catacombs and Egyptian obelisks soon became an extremely popular burial place. As a result, the West Cemetery was soon full and the newer, East Cemetery opened in 1854. The cemetery is now considered to contain some of the finest Victorian funerary architecture still in existence.

East Cemetery

🏛 *Mon-Fri 10am, Sat & Sun 11am*
🕐 *(last admission 4.30pm 1st April to 31st October, last admission 3.30pm 1st November-31st March)*
🏷 *Entry £4, Optional map £1, guided tours first Sat of each month (£8.00)*

The most famous grave in the East Cemetery is that of Karl Marx (1818-1883). Nearby is the grave of George Eliot (1819-1880), who lived openly with her lover, George Lewes for many years (a state of affairs that outraged the society of the time) – he is buried close by. William Foyle, the founder of the eponymous bookshop, journalist Paul Foot and the author of 'The Hitchhiker's Guide to the Galaxy', Douglas Adams, are also here.

West Cemetery

Access only on guided tours (booking recommended)
🕐 *Guided tours: Mon-Fri at 1.45pm (except Dec, Jan, Feb); Sat & Sun hourly from 11am-3pm*
🏷 *£12, £6 for children, children under 8 not permitted*

Mrs Henry Wood, author of 'East Lynne', Christina Rossetti, the poet (1830-1894) and Radclyffe Hall and her lover Mabel Batten are all buried here. The Charles Dickens' family tomb containing the author's wife and daughter are here but Dickens is buried in Westminster Abbey, against his wishes and at the insistance of Queen Victoria. See the website for further information and some excellent photographs of the cemetery.

Kensal Green Cemetery

🏛 *Harrow Road, W10 4RA*
☎ *020 8969 0152*
🖋 *www.kensalgreen.co.uk*
🖋 *www.kensalgreencemetery.com*
🚇 *Kensal Green LU*
🏷 *Admission free; The Friends of Kensal Green offer tours at 2pm every Sunday from March to October and the first and third Sundays of each month from November to February*

Opened in 1832, this was the first of the large Victorian cemeteries and it soon gained in popularity. Thackeray, James Leigh Hunt, Anthony Trollope, Thomas Hood, Wilkie Collins and Terence Rattigan are all buried here. Personalities slightly removed from literary fame include Lord Byron's wife, Oscar Wilde's mother, Charles Dickens' in-laws and the original WH Smith. There is an annual summer Open Day (see the website for details).

St Paul's Cathedral

- St Paul's Churchyard, EC4M 8AD
- ☎ 020 7236 4128
- www.stpauls.co.uk
- St Paul's LU
- ⏱ Mon-Sat 8.30am-4pm
  last admission 4pm)
- £18 (adults), £16 (seniors & students),
  £8 (children), £44 (family)

There are far fewer memorials to literary figures here than in Westminster Abbey, but the list is still impressive and includes John Donne (1572-1631), Dean of St Paul's and preacher and poet, the philosopher Francis Bacon, Walter de la Mere and Dr Johnson. There is also a commemorative bust to the writer and adventurer TE Lawrence in the crypt. An audio tour (£4) and guided tour (£3) are available.

John Donne

Westminster Abbey

- 20 Dean's Yard London, SW1P 3PA
- ☎ 020 7222 5152
- www.westminster-abbey.org
- Westminster LU
- ⏱ Mon, Tues, Thurs, Fri 9.30am-4.30pm
  (last admission 3.30pm);
  Wed 9.30am-7pm (last admission 6pm);
  Sat 9.30am-2.30pm (last admission
  1.30pm)
- £20 (adults), £17 (concessions), £40-£45
  (family); a free audio guide is included in
  the price of the ticket; Verger led tours
  (£5) are also available

Poets' Corner in the South Transept contains a huge number of memorials to literary figures. The first two poets to be buried there were Geoffrey Chaucer (1400) and Edmund Spenser (1599). Other graves include those of John Dryden, Samuel Johnson, Robert Browning, Tennyson, Dickens and Thomas Hardy (his heart was buried in Dorset). Some statues are simply memorials to major figures who were buried or cremated elsewhere, for example, Shakespeare, Milton, Keats, Byron, Rudyard Kipling, the Bronte sisters, T.S Eliot, Jane Austen, John Betjeman and Oscar Wilde. This part of the abbey also contains the graves of other artistic figures, including the composer Handel, and David Garrick, the eighteenth-century actor. Apparently the overcrowding is now so severe that no further burials will be possible – the actor Laurence Olivier (who died in 1989) was the last to get a plot here.

Literary Pubs

The Anchor

⌂ *34 Park Street, Bankside, SE1 9EF*
☎ *020 7407 1577*
🚇 *London Bridge LU/Rail, Southwark LU*

With fine views across the river to St Paul's Cathedral, this pub is a short walk from Shakespeare's Globe and was frequented by Dr Johnson and Samuel Pepys – it was one of the places from where Pepys watched the Great Fire of London. On a less highbrow note, parts of the first 'Mission Impossible' film were shot here.

The Dove

⌂ *19 Upper Mall, W6 9TA*
☎ *020 8748 9474*
✎ *www.dovehammersmith.co.uk*
🚇 *Ravenscourt Park LU*

This is a pretty, seventeenth century riverside pub, with an impressive list of literary patrons including William Morris, Graham Greene and Ernest Hemingway. AP Herbert wrote, 'The Water Gypsies' featuring a pub called the Pigeon, which is generally believed to be the Dove. By the way, its panelled snug is listed as one of the smallest in Britain.

Fitzroy Tavern

⌂ *16a Charlotte Street, W1 2NA*
☎ *020 7580 3714*
🚇 *Tottenham Court Road LU,*
    Goodge Street LU

Between the 1920s and the 1950s this area, between Soho and Bloomsbury, was named Fitzrovia by the group of artists, sculptors, composers, critics, poets and writers who met in the area. The Fitzroy Tavern became the main Bohemian meeting place of the time. Patrons included Lawrence Durrell, Dylan Thomas (who first met his wife, Caitlin, here), Louis MacNiece and George Orwell.

The Flask

⌂ *77 Highgate West Hill, N6 6BU*
☎ *020 8348 7346*
✎ *www.theflaskhighgate.com*
🚇 *Archway LU*

It is said that Dick Turpin hid from his pursuers here. On a more literary note, TS Eliot and John Betjeman drank here.

The George Inn

⌂ *75-77 Borough High Street, SE1 1NH*
☎ *020 7407 2056*
✎ *www.george-southwark.co.uk*
🚇 *London Bridge LU/Rail*

This pub dates back at least to 1542 when Shakespeare was a regular – there's even a rumour that he acted from the back of a cart in the courtyard here in the days before the Globe Theatre was built. Borough High Street was at that time the only road out of London to the south and at its height The George dealt with 80 coaches a week. It remained busy and famous into Charles Dickens' time and is mentioned in 'Little Dorrit'. Following the Victorian's redevelopment of the capital, this pub is now the sole surviving example of London's old galleried coaching inns, the current building dates from 1676.

The Grapes

⌂ *76 Narrow Street, E14 8BP*
☎ *020 7987 4396*
✎ *www.thegrapes.co.uk*
🚇 *Limehouse DLR, West Ferry DLR*

Established in 1583, although this building dates from 1720. Charles Dickens knew the pub as a child when he entertained customers here by singing, but also in later years as a customer. Dickens possibly fictionalised the pub in 'Our Mutual Friend', although some argue that it was The Prospect of Whitby (see below) that has that honour. The renowned actor Ian McKellan is the leaseholder of the pub.

Museum Tavern

⌨ *49 Great Russell Street, WC1B 3BA*
☎ *020 7242 8987*
🚇 *Tottenham Court Road LU, Holborn LU*

Located just opposite the entrance to the British Museum – Karl Marx was a regular and JB Priestley and Sir Arthur Conan Doyle are reputed to have drunk here.

Prospect of Whitby

⌨ *57 Wapping Wall, E1W 3SH*
☎ *020 7481 1095*
🚇 *Wapping LU*

This pub was originally called The Devils Tavern (after the villainous characters who frequented it). It dates back to the sixteenth century when Samuel Pepys was a patron. It has a gruesome history and was reputedly the site of public executions.

Spaniards Inn

⌨ *Spaniard's Road, NW3 7JJ*
☎ *020 8731 8406*
✎ *www.thespaniardshampstead.co.uk*
🚇 *Golders Green LU, Hampstead LU*

A four hundred year-old pub, located near Kenwood House and Hampstead Heath. Shelley, Keats and Byron all drank here as did Charles DIckens, who used it as the setting for Mrs Bardell's tea party in 'The Pickwick Papers'.

Trafalgar Tavern

⌨ *Park Row, SE10 9NW*
☎ *020 8858 2909*
✎ *www.trafalgartavern.co.uk*
🚇 *Cutty Sark DLR, Maze Hill Rail*

Built in 1837 (the year that Queen Victoria came to the throne) beside the river at Greenwich and mentioned in 'Our Mutual Friend', this pub was supposedly a favourite drinking spot of Charles Dickens. At that time the pubs in Greenwich were famous for thier whitebait dinners and Dickens, Wilkie Collins, Macaulay and Thackeray all ate here. Whitebait is still on the menu.

Ye Olde Cheshire Cheese

⌨ *Wine Office Court, 145 Fleet Street, EC4A 2BU*
☎ *020 7353 6170*
🚇 *Blackfriars LU/Rail, Temple LU*

This is the oldest remaining pub on Fleet Street. The cellar dates back to the guesthouse of a thirteenth-century monastery that originally occupied the site. The current building dates from the mid-seventeenth century, when the pub was rebuilt after the Great Fire. Many literary greats have drunk here: Dr Johnson, Thackeray, Sir Arthur Conan Doyle, Dickens, Yeats and Mark Twain among them.

Ye Olde Cock Tavern

⌨ *22 Fleet Street, EC4Y 1AA*
☎ *020 7353 8570*
🚇 *Blackfriars LU/Rail, Temple LU*

TS Eliot was a regular here in the 1920s, following in the footsteps of Pepys, Dickens and Tennyson. Pepys makes mention of travelling to the tavern by boat and dining on beer and lobster. The pub is just opposite Temple Church, which was one of the locations in Dan Brown's 'The Da Vinci Code'.

Ye Olde Mitre Tavern

⌨ *1 Ely Court, off Ely Place, EC1N 6SJ*
☎ *020 7405 4751* ·
✎ *www.yeoldmitreholborn.co.uk*
🚇 *Chancery Lane LU*

Hidden away in an alleyway between numbers 8 and 9 Hatton Garden, this is one of the most historic pubs in London. It is said that Queen Elizabeth I danced in the original Mitre which was built in 1546. The current building dates from 1772 and was a haunt of Dr Johnson, who lived nearby on Gough Square.

Literary Tours

A guided walk is a great way to explore aspects of the city in more detail and many of these walks have a literary theme. Participating in a walk is simply a matter of turning up at the specified time and place and paying the guide, but it's advisable to ring beforehand to check and some companies do recommend booking. Below are listed some of the walks which have literary associations:

City Sidewalks

☎ 020 8449 4736
🖳 www.citysidewalks.co.uk

This company offers a wider range of walks across London which need to be booked privately and always involve a qualified City of London guide. There are several walks with a literary theme, such as 'The London of Dickens and Shakespeare'.

London Walking Tours

☎ 020 8530 8443
www.londonwalking.co.uk

Most of the walks offered by this company are conducted by published author and renowned London expert, Richard Jones. The company's website is a useful resource with information about booking and the schedule of walks for the coming week.

London Walks

☎ 020 7624 3978
🖳 www.walks.com

This is one of the larger companies offering a busy programme of walks with a literary theme. Walks include a tour of Literary Bloomsbury and also the London sites associated with Harry Potter.

Muggle Tours

☎ 07914 151 041
🖳 www.muggletours.co.uk

This company specialise in tours of Harry Potter film locations, as well as places that inspired JK Rowling when writing the books. Harry Potter fans are never in short supply, so advance booking is advised.

Hay Festival

Appendix

Literary Venues

Reading and enjoying books is considered by many to be a solitary pastime, but this need'nt be the case and the capital plays host to public readings, signings and book events virtually every day of the week. Literary events vary from local poetry meetings, where you might be expected to read your own verse, to a major book reading where you will be lucky to get a seat. For information about what is on offer, the Timeout website www.timeout.com/london has a section devoted to literary events and the websites www.poetrylondon.co.uk and www.poetrylibrary.org.uk also have listings. As well as many of London's bookshops there are other venues hosting regular literary events, some of which are listed below:

The Sun & 13 Cantons

- *21 Great Pulteney Street, Soho, W1F 9NG*
- ☏ *020 7734 0934*
- ✍ *www.ambitmagazine.co.uk*
- 🚇 *Piccadilly Circus LU, Oxford Circus LU*

Ambit Magazine hosts quarterly events at this pub in Soho.

Bishopsgate Institute

- *230 Bishopsgate, EC2M 4QH*
- ☏ *020 7392 9200*
- ✍ *www.bishopsgate.org.uk*
- 🚇 *Liverpool Street LU/Rail*

This cultural institution, founded in 1895, offers a busy programme of talks, walks, debates, discussions and other literary events (see p.228).

The British Library

- *96 Euston Road, NW1 2DB*
- ☏ *020 7412 7332*
- ✍ *www.bl.uk/whatson*
- 🚇 *EustonLU/Rail, King's Cross St Pancras LU/Rail*

The British Library runs a vibrant programme of talks and lectures.

Cafe Oto

- *18-22 Ashwin Street, E8 3DL*
- ☏ *020 7923 1231*
- ✍ *www.cafeoto.co.uk*
- 🚇 *Dalston Kingsland Overground*

This trendy venue features poetry, literature and live performance alongside a packed music programme.

Kings Place

- *90 York Way, N1 9AG*
- ☏ *020 7520 1490*
- ✍ *www.kingsplace.co.uk*
- 🚇 *King's Cross St Pancras LU/ Rail*

Kings Place is a fantastic arts centre and gallery offering regular spoken word events alongside music and visual arts. Events can include anything from Judy Blume talking about her latest novel to Richard Dawkins discussing his life in science.

Poetry Society

- *22 Betterton Street, WC2H 9BX*
- ☏ *020 7420 9880*
- ✍ *www.poetrysociety.org.uk*
- 🚇 *Covent Garden LU*

The Poetry Society is engaged in many activities promoting poetry throughout Britain. The Poetry Café (Mon-Fri 11am-11pm, Sat 7pm-11pm) is a great place for poetry lovers to meet, eat, relax and browse poetry magazines or pick up fliers for competitions and events all over London. Take a look at their website for more information.

Royal Society of Literature

⌨ *Somerset House, Strand, WC2R 1LA*
☏ *020 7845 4679*
✎ *www.rsliterature.org*
🚇 *Temple LU*

The Royal Society of Literature might sound rather grand, but membership is open to all and offers the chance to attend lectures, discussions and readings. Past events have features renowned writers such as Andrew Motion, Peter Carey and Harriet Walter.

Southbank Centre

⌨ *Belvedere Road, SE1 8XX*
☏ *020 7960 4200*
✎ *www.southbankcentre.co.uk*
🚇 *Waterloo LU/Rail*

The Southbank Centre hosts plenty of events and the Book Club meets monthly, but you must book in advance. This is also the location of the Poetry Library (see 251) and hosts the London Literature Festival, Poetry International and Imagine, a festival of children's literature (see p.306).

Torriano Meeting House

⌨ *99 Torriano Avenue, NW5 2RX*
☏ *020 7267 2751*
✎ *www.torriano.org*
🚇 *Kentish Town LU*

This community arts centre has been hosting Sunday poetry readings for many years as well as other literary performances and workshops.

Troubadour Coffee House

⌨ *263-7 Old Brompton Road, SW5 9JA*
☏ *020 7370 1434*
✎ *www.troubadour.co.uk*
🚇 *Earl's Court LU*

This legendary café first opened its doors in 1954 and has acquired a reputation for live music and a place in the affections of Jimmy Page and Van Morrison, who have both preformed here in recent years. The poetry evenings take place every Monday during term time and there are also occasional poetry workshops.

Book Slam

⌨ *First Floor. 51 Hoxton Square, N1 9PB*
✎ *www.bookslam.com*
🚇 *Old Street LU*

Book Slam host regular literary club nights which feature top writers such as Hanif Kureishi, Dave Eggers and Nick Hornby combined with live music and DJs. These unique events take place at venues across London – take a look at the website for more details.

Festivals

London plays host to an array of annual arts festivals, some of which are dedicated to literature while others feature literary events among a wider programme of music, theatre, dance, art and other events. For a countrywide list of UK Literary Festivals look at www.britishcouncil.org for a month by month listing. Two other useful sources of information are www.artsfestivals.co.uk and www.literaryfestivals.co.uk.

London Festivals

Asia House Bagri Foundation Literature Festival

- 63 New Cavendish Street, W1G 7LP
- 020 7307 5454
- www.asiahouse.org

The only festival in the UK dedicated to Asian writing and writing about Asia. It takes place in May at Asia House in central London.

Archway with Words

- @archwayword
- www.archwaywithwords.com

This festival of words and ideas has put Archway on the literary map. The festival takes place every autumn with recent participants including Will Self, Stella Duffy and newcomers such as Louise Millar.

Battersea Literature Festival

- www.literaryfestivals.co.uk
- 020 7627 3182

An annual September bonanza of literary readings, workshops and talks centred around the Clapham Junction area. Past events have included Richard Curtis talking about comic writing and James Daunt discussing the future of bookshops.

City of London Festival

- 020 7583 3585
- www.colf.org

Founded back in 1962, the City of London Festival brings a packed progamme of art and entertainment to the workers, residents and visitors to London's Square Mile. The festival extends over three weeks from June to July and includes live music, walks, talks, tours and films with both free and ticketed events.

Chiswick Book Festival

- www.chiswickbookfestival.net

This local literary festival has been running since 2009 and is supported by the local Waterstones branch and other independents, as well as Chiswick Library. Past festivals have included well-known literary names such as historian Antonia Fraser, children's author Jacqueline Wilson and poet Andrew Motion.

Dulwich Festival

- www.dulwichfestival.co.uk

A community arts festival held every May, which encompasses literary events as well as theatre, film, music and art. Past events have included historian Dr David Starkey talking about Magna Carta and Guardian columnist Zoe Williams discussing inequality.

Greenwich Book Festival

☎ 020 8331 7688

✍ www.greenwichbookfest.com

This recent arrival on London's festival scene takes place over a weekend every May in the magnificent grounds of the Old Royal Naval College. The event is hosted by the University of Greenwich and in its inaugural year of 2015 attracted well known names such as Jessie Burton, Viv Albertine and Tracy Thorn.

Imagine: Children's Festival

☎ 020 7960 4200

✍ www.southbankcentre.co.uk

This annual festival offers a fortnight of readings, storytelling, poetry and workshops for 5 to 11-year-olds. The event takes place every February and has become an established and popular feature of the Southbank Centre calander.

Kilburn Literary Festival

✍ www.kilburnliteraryfestival.co.uk

This festival was founded in 2014 with a week of workshops, competitions and readings.

Kingston Connections Festival of Stories

☎ 020 8174 0090

✍ www.rosetheatrekingston.com

This celebration of the spoken word extends over a week in June and is run in conjunction with Kingston University. The festival involves theatre, live performance, workshops and talks with plenty of free events.

Jewish Book Week

☎ 020 7446 8771

✍ www.jewishbookweek.com

This is a major festival of Jewish writing attracting interest and participants from around the world. It takes place annually in early March across the country with many events in London. Jewish Book Week can include anything from a performance of the work of Gershwin to Jonathan Sperber discussing Karl Marx with the Guardian's Jonathan Freedland.

Lambeth Readers and Writers Festival

☎ 020 7926 1000

✍ www.lambeth.gov.uk/events

A month of literary events in May including workshops, readings and talks hosted at libraries across Lambeth.

London Literature Festival

☎ 020 7960 4200

✍ www.southbankcentre.co.uk

This festival takes place in the iconic Southbank Centre every October and attracts novelists, poets and performers from across the globe.

London Short Story Festival

✍ www.lssf.co.uk

This festival dedicated to bite-size literature was founded in 2014 and is hosted by Waterstone's flagship store on Piccadilly. The event has proved a great success and now attracts over sixty writers including famous names such as Ben Okri and Toby Litt.

Peckham Literary Festival

✍ *www.reviewbookshop.co.uk*
☎ *020 7639 7400*

This November festival is run by the good
folk at Review bookshop (see page 97)
and offers a host of free events with local
authors and poets – a surprising number of
which live in and around Peckham.

Penge Festival

☎ *020 3565 4125*
✍ *www.pengepartners.co.uk*

Penge might not inspire the literary
imagination in the same way as
Hampstead or Bloomsbury, but its spring
festival does include literary walks, poetry
reading and other events and the area can
claim Walter de la Mare as its most famous
literary son.

Poetry International

☎ *020 7960 4200*
✍ *www.southbankcentre.co.uk*

This three-day-long festival in July is the
biggest poetry festival in the UK attracting
poets from across the globe. Readings,
workshops, debates and lectures are all
part of the heady mix.

Richmond Upon Thames Literature Festival

🖽 *Orleans House Gallery, Riverside,*
   Twickenham, TW1 3DJ
☎ *020 8831 6000*
✍ *www.richmondliterature.com*

Leafy Richmond has been hosting this
popular literary festival every November
for over 20 years with past participants
including broadcaster Peter Snow and
children's author Jacqueline Wilson.

Spitalfields Music

☎ *020 7377 1362*
✍ *www.spitalfieldsmusic.org.uk*

This bi-annual festival (winter and summer)
is largely dedicated to music but includes
a selection of walks and talks of literary
interest.

Streatham Festival

✍ *www.streathamfestival.com*

A local festival that takes place every July
with all kinds of arts events at locations
throughout the borough. As well as
music, theatre and preformance there are
also a few local authors giving readings,
talks and running workshops.

Stoke Newington Literary Festival

✍ *www.stokenewingtonliteraryfestival.com*
☎ *020 7609 1800*

This literary festival is a relative newcomer
but the borough has a long literary
history dating back to Daniel Defoe and
with many notable local authors this
celebration of literature and ideas has
gone from strength to strength. The
festival takes place over a weekend in
June with past participants including Will
Self and Iain Sinclair.

Wimbledon BookFest

✍ *www.wimbledonbookfest.org*
☎ *020 8947 3495*

This long-established literary festival
takes place in SW18 every October and
always attracts a high calibre list of literary
participants.

Outside London

The following festivals are all easily accessible from London and can be visited on an excursion from the city.

Brighton Festival

☎ *01273 709709*

✑ *www.brightonfestival.org*

Brighton is often called 'London-on-Sea' and its three week festival in May offers a range of events that would make any capital city proud. The festival covers all arts but literature figures strongly and past events have included big literary names such as Ali Smith and Carol Anne Duffy.

Broadstairs Dickens Festival

☎ *01843 861 827*

✑ *www.broadstairsdickensfestival.co.uk*

A general arts festival inspired by the works of Dickens and including readings, talks, events, guided walks and all manner of other entertainments. It runs in the third week of June every year.

Charleston Festival

✑ *www.charleston.org.uk*

☎ *01373 811 626*

A May literary festival, which usually coincides with the Brighton Festival. Charleston is a brilliant setting, seven miles east of Lewes, it was the country meeting place for the Bloomsbury Group. The festival regularly attracts well-known authors such as David Lodge and historian Andrew Roberts.

In the autumn Charleston hosts 'Small Wonder' – a festival dedicated to short stories with readings, workshops and discussions featuring well-known writers.

Essex Book Festival

☎ *01206 872 618*

✑ *www.essexbookfestival.org.uk*

This month-long festival takes place throughout the county in March and attracts an impressive array of literary names with past participants including Jessie Burton and Jon Ronson.

Essex Poetry Festival

✑ *adrian@essex-poetry-festival.co.uk*

✑ *www.essex-poetry-festival.co.uk*

In October Chelmsford plays host to a wide range of poetry events including readings, open mic sessions, competitions and workshops.

Guildford Book Festival

☎ *01483 444 334*

✑ *www.guildfordbookfestival.co.uk*

This is an annual October festival offering a busy week of readings, performances and talks across Guildford. The event is very well run and attracts some major literary names. Take a look at their website for further information.

Hay Festival

see page opposite

Henley Literary Festival

✑ *www.henleyliteraryfestival.co.uk*

☎ *01491 843 404*

This three day literary festival takes place in the autumn and offers a wide range of literary events featuring many famous household names from Maureen Lipman to Kirsty Wark.

Hay Festival

The Drill Hall, 25 Lion Street
Hay-on-Wye, HR3 5AD
Box Office: 01497 822 629
www.hayfestival.com

Over the last 40 years the small market town of Hay-on-Wye on the Welsh borders has acquired a reputation as a book lover's paradise. The reason for this bookish enclave can be largely attributed to the efforts of Richard Booth who proclaimed himself 'King of Hay' back in 1977 when as a publicity stunt he declared Hay-on-Wye an 'independent kingdom'. Mr Booth sold his bookshop and left the village over ten years ago, but his legacy lives on and Hay-on Wye currently boasts over 20 second-hand and antiquarian bookshops amid a population of less than 2,000 people. Perhaps Booth's greatest achievement was the foundation of the Hay Festival which

has become in the words of Bill Clinton when he visited in 2001 "The Woodstock of the mind".

Like penitents in medieval times, for ten days towards the end of May, the literary world goes on pilgrimage to Hay-on-Wye. Visitors can choose from a vast menu of readings, talks, performances and discussions from a stellar cast that has included historian Simon Shama, writer and comedian Stephen Fry and Nobel prize-winning author VS Naipaul, and even the Dutchess of Cornwall has been involved. The event has come a long way since its humble beginnings and many of the key performances and lectures are now broadcast on BBC television and Radio 4. Nothing beats visiting in person however and the festival's website has all the information you will need regarding travel, accommodation and booking tickets.

Hay Festival

FOYLES FOR BOOKS

FOYLES

Changing Britain

GENERAL ELECTION

MIND THE GAP

PUSH

Foyles, Southbank

INDEX

T

U

V

W

Y

Z

Maggs Bros Ltd

AREA INDEX

Central

EC1

EC2

EC3

EC4

SE1

SW1

W1

North

South East

South West

West

East

Persephone Books

91 Fulham High
THE BROTHERHOOD
PICASSO
KINGSLEY AMIS
IN HARM'S WAY
JACKIE CHAN

SUBJECT INDEX

Art

Asia

Astrology

Audio Books

New Age/Esoteric

Photography

Poetry

Politics/Philosophy

Psychology/Psychotherapy

Science

Image Credits

Cover Image © Eric Nathan; p.81 © Maison Assouline; p.119 © Luke Hayes; p.196 & p.203 © James Bellorini; p.231 © BFI / Morton; p.282 © Keats House; p.285 © Charles Dickens Museum; p.285 © Freud Museum; p.285 © Carlysle House; p.288 © National Portrait Gallery; p.290 © Shakespeare's Globe Theatre; p.300 & p.309 © Hay Festival.

PLATE I.

'COLD SALMON SOUFFLÉ.'

About us:

Metro is a small independent publishing company with a reputation for producing well-researched and beautifully-designed guides on many aspects of London life.

In fields of interest as diverse as shopping, bargain hunting, architecture, the arts, and food, our guide books contain special tips you won't find anywhere else.

How to order:

The following titles are available to buy from our website (P&P free)

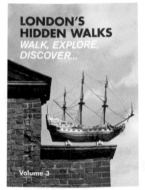

LONDON'S MONUMENTS
FROM BOUDICCA AND BYRON TO GUY THE GORILLA

LONDON'S CITY CHURCHES
SEE THE SCORCH MARKS OF THE GREAT FIRE, OR VISIT AN ALTAR BY HENRY MOORE

LONDON'S CEMETERIES
SPEND THE DAY WITH KARL MARX, ENID BLYTON, KEITH MOON AND MANY MORE

LONDON ARCHITECTURE
MARIANNE BUTLER (foreword by Maxwell Hutchinson)

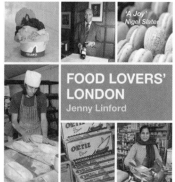

'A Joy'
Nigel Slater

FOOD LOVERS' LONDON
Jenny Linford

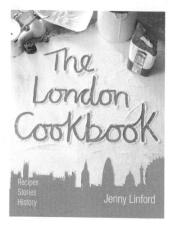

The London Cookbook

Recipes
Stories
History

Jenny Linford

Museums & Galleries of London
Abigail Willis